"I cannot say enough about how *Nine Marks of a Healthy Church* was used to shape my personal understanding of the biblical church and the local church I was planting when I first read the second edition of the book. Amidst so many controversial ideas and methods presented to church planters by church-planting best sellers, *Nine Marks of a Healthy Church* simply brought me back to Scripture, centered my heart on what a biblical church must be and do, and also relieved me from the perspective that I had to shape the congregation before me Sunday after Sunday. Don't misunderstand me; I knew all these marks before, but they were not appropriately connected and applied. In practice, the use of these nine marks were tainted with foreign ideas and a lack of intentionality that prevented them from bearing the right fruits. I am glad for Dever's reshaping of the content to consider two other marks that are also neglected in the contemporary church: prayer and missions. The book still has nine marks. If you are wondering how, you will have to read it! Do not hesitate!"

Mauro Meister, President, Andrew Jumper Graduate Center, Brazil; Senior Pastor, Presbyterian Church Barra Funda; author, *Law and Grace* and *The Origin of Idolatry*

"I don't remember who put *Nine Marks of a Healthy Church* in my hand almost twenty years ago, but it's a resource that shaped me deeply. I return to it frequently as I try to faithfully shepherd at the Village Church and plant healthy churches through Acts 29. The church needs a strong ecclesiology if she will faithfully fulfill her God-given mission, and this book is a foundational read for pastors across denominations and philosophies of ministry."

Matt Chandler, Lead Pastor, The Village Church

"From my early days as a football coach, my football mentor instilled in me a sense of urgency to be clear on what we were looking for as we set out to build championship teams. All championship teams own distinctive marks that we look to reproduce year after year. In my formative days as a pastor, Mark Dever has helped me gain biblical clarity on what a healthy local church looks like through *Nine Marks of a Healthy Church*. As leaders of our local churches, it is critical that we are clear on how Christ is building his church so that we can faithfully come alongside him in his work."

Rocky Seto, Senior Pastor, Evergreen Baptist Church of San Gabriel Valley

"Here are the timeless biblical truths that inform what the church is, how God creates and nurtures it, and how its pastors and members participate in that work. *Nine Marks of a Healthy Church* has helped me as a young pastor see through the fog of church growth models to the essential architecture of ecclesiology. This book is far and away the clearest and most biblical account of what the church is that I've come across. Most importantly, the vision of the church displayed here is so God-centered that it places the magnificent responsibility of sustaining and leading it back on the right shoulders, namely, his."

Samuel D. Ferguson, Rector, The Falls Church Anglican

"I was an ambitious Capitol Hill staffer when I was first handed this book twenty years ago. In retrospect, it was this moment that totally upended my estimation of the local church and changed the trajectory of my life toward ministry in it. The personal ambitions I had been aiming for began to seem insignificant compared to the growing desire for God's glory to be displayed through the local church. After now a decade of cross-cultural ministry in the Arab world, my understanding of a healthy church is continually shaped and sharpened by the principles of this book. Reader beware: this book could totally transform the way you see the seemingly ordinary local church."

Jenny Manley, pastor's wife, United Arab Emirates; author, *The Good Portion: Christ*

"My first conversation with Mark Dever was a memorable one. I'd asked why I should consider doing the pastoral internship program at his church. Mark's reply: 'Because too many pastors simply don't know about the church.' The statement struck me then and has stuck with me since—pastors of churches not knowing enough about the churches they pastor. But far from only harping on the problem, Mark has given his life to helping with the solution. How? With books like this one, pointing pastors and church members alike back to the Bible to recover a right understanding and practice of some of the most basic yet life-giving marks of a church. *Nine Marks of a Healthy Church* is not merely a manual for how to do church but a methodology of how to think about the church. Throughout its pages, the Bible is actually used, showing its authority and sufficiency, not simply talked about. The gospel is clearly communicated and celebrated, not simply assumed. Diverse voices from the past are consulted—whether African-American pastor Francis Grimké on preaching or African-Jamaican pastor Moses Hall on prayer—to instruct our practices in the present. And a pastoral heart is put on display, showing a love for God and his glory, and a love for God's people and their growth. Reading this book may not immediately change your church, but it might change you, causing you to more carefully, thoughtfully, and biblically consider how the Lord might use your faithfulness as a minister or a member to contribute to the greater health of your local church."

Omar Johnson, Pastor, Temple Hills Baptist Church, Temple Hills, MD

"The nine marks are as relevant and important for today's church as they've ever been. Whereas a combination of pragmatism, tradition, and cultural influences shape so much of modern Christianity, Dever refreshingly points us back to the foundational truths of the Bible that ought to drive all of our practices in the church. While the nine marks are so straightforwardly Scriptural that no faithful reader of the Bible could deny their significance, to actually implement them in our churches is to swim against the cultural current. To that end, this book is an invaluable resource for any pastor or congregant who desires to see God's glory more clearly manifest through Christ-centered, gospel-preaching, biblically sound churches."

Harry Fujiwara, Pastor, The First Baptist Church in the City of New York

"It is astonishing that the apostle Paul describes the local gathering of Christians as 'the church of God, which he obtained with his own blood' (Acts 20:28). That raises the stakes of church life and health and mission about as high as it can be. We are dealing with a blood-bought body of people. I do not want human ideas. I want God's word about the church. I turn with hope and confidence to Mark Dever's radically biblical commitment. Few people today have thought more or better about what makes a church biblical and healthy. I thank God for the book and for 9Marks ministries."

John Piper, Founder and Teacher, desiringGod.org; Chancellor, Bethlehem College & Seminary; author, *Desiring God*

"The future of biblical Christianity in the Western world is inextricably bound to the future of the local church. Mark Dever knows this, and his *Nine Marks of a Healthy Church* is a biblical prescription for faithfulness."

Ligon Duncan, Chancellor and CEO, Reformed Theological Seminary

Nine Marks of a Healthy Church

Crossway Books by Mark Dever

12 Challenges Churches Face

The Compelling Community: Where God's Power Makes a Church Attractive (coauthor)

Discipling: How to Help Others Follow Jesus

The Gospel and Personal Evangelism

How Can Our Church Find a Faithful Pastor?

How to Build a Healthy Church: A Practical Guide for Deliberate Leadership (coauthor)

In My Place Condemned He Stood: Celebrating the Glory of the Atonement (coauthor)

It Is Well: Expositions on Substitutionary Atonement (coauthor)

The Message of the New Testament: Promises Kept

The Message of the Old Testament: Promises Made

Nine Marks of a Healthy Church (4th edition)

Proclaiming a Cross-Centered Theology (coauthor)

The Unadjusted Gospel (coauthor)

What Does God Want of Us Anyway? A Quick Overview of the Whole Bible

What Is a Healthy Church?

Why Should I Join a Church?

Nine Marks of a Healthy Church

Fourth Edition

Mark Dever

Foreword by H. B. Charles Jr.

CROSSWAY®

WHEATON, ILLINOIS

Nine Marks of a Healthy Church, fourth edition

Published by Crossway
1300 Crescent Street
Wheaton, Illinois 60187

The first edition, published in 2000, was an expansion of a much short work published in 1997 by Founders Press.

Cover design: Jordan Singer

First printing 2021

Printed in the United States of America

All emphases in Scripture quotations have been added by the author.

Hardcover ISBN: 978-1-4335-7811-3
ePub ISBN: 978-1-4335-7813-7
PDF ISBN: 978-1-4335-7812-0
Mobipocket ISBN: 978-1-4335-7814-4

Library of Congress Cataloging-in-Publication Data

Names: Dever, Mark, author. | Charles, H. B., writer of foreword.
Title: Nine marks of a healthy church / Mark Dever ; foreword by H. B. Charles Jr.
Description: Fourth edition. | Wheaton, Illinois : Crossway, [2021] | Includes bibliographical references and index.
Identifiers: LCCN 2021008455 (print) | LCCN 2021008456 (ebook) | ISBN 9781433578113 (hardcover) | ISBN 9781433578120 (pdf) | ISBN 9781433578144 (mobi) | ISBN 9781433578137 (epub)
Subjects: LCSH: Church—Marks.
Classification: LCC BV601 .D48 2021 (print) | LCC BV601 (ebook) | DDC 250—dc23
LC record available at https://lccn.loc.gov/2021008455
LC ebook record available at https://lccn.loc.gov/2021008456

Crossway is a publishing ministry of Good News Publishers.

LB 30 29 28 27 26 25 24 23 22 21
15 14 13 12 11 10 9 8 7 6 5 4 3 2 1

Contents

Foreword

H. B. Charles Jr.

I WAS ON MY MONTHLY PILGRIMAGE to my favorite Christian bookstore. It was a large store with multiple sections. Each visit, I would browse my way through each section, strategically getting to the pastoral helps/church life area last. It was one of the smallest sections in the store. But I would spend the most time there, hoping to find resources to help me lead the established congregation I was called to serve.

One day, as I browsed the section, a book jumped out at me: *Nine Marks of a Healthy Church.* While only a young man and a new pastor, I was already burned out on church growth tricks, theories, and techniques. Not only had I read the material; I had tried out the novel ideas on my patient—but quickly becoming cynical—congregation. As I diligently read book after book, I unsuccessfully tried idea after idea. Three steps to . . . five keys to . . . seven ways to. . . .

Now someone had come up with nine marks!

"Here we go again," I thought, as I picked up the book virtually against my will. As I looked over the table of contents, I was more shocked than when I saw the title. The first mark of a healthy church was expositional preaching! The second mark was biblical theology! This was nothing like any church growth book I had ever read.

Nine Marks provided a biblical compass for the critical years of my pastoral ministry. It confronted me with the radical but obvious truth that the Lord Jesus Christ is the head of the church. The Word of God is to be the final authority in local church ministry—not pastoral vision, congregational tradition, statistical goals, ministry programs, or attendee preferences. The church is not a business, pastors are not executives, and ministry is not franchise-building.

Like many other pastors, I have benefited immensely from reading and rereading this biblical yet practical study of the church—and reading it again with fellow church leaders. The book became a ministry, which has served the church well by generously providing resources to help pastors, staff, and leaders think biblically about the local church.

I had devoured 9Marks resources for years, when the Lord blessed me with a personal friendship with Mark Dever. Getting to know him caused me to appreciate *Nine Marks of a Healthy Church* even more. These are not random ideas thrown together to sell a book. They are the Scripture-driven convictions of a pastor who loves Christ, the gospel, and the church. Dever has faithfully led Capitol Hill Baptist Church in Washington, DC, for decades. This local church, which embodies these nine marks, has influenced a generation of pastors and congregations to glorify the Lord by pursuing biblical church health.

I am excited that Mark Dever has labored to give us this updated and expanded version of *Nine Marks*. Some of the material in this edition has been rearranged. New chapters have been added on missions and prayer. But don't worry: this book is still the trusted friend you've come to love over the years. If this is your first time working through this material, prepare to meet a new friend that will be a helpful resource in the years to come. Read it. Practice the principles that will take you back to the basics of Christian ministry. Share it with colleagues and coworkers. Pray the Lord will raise up churches during these critical times that are devoted to Jesus Christ, biblical convictions, gospel proclamation, true community, and church health.

Preface to the Fourth Edition (2021)

SO MUCH HAS CHANGED since I first preached this series of messages in the 1990s, and yet so much has remained the same. Perhaps it's just my personal predisposition, but that which remains the same strikes me as greatly more important even than the most important changes we've seen. What doesn't change is what the Bible presents about a healthy church.

I go all over the country—and sometimes even outside of it—speaking to pastors and other Christians about what characterizes a sound, healthy local church. And yet, I realized some time ago that while I may often have an application or two about this topic in my normal Bible expositions, I hadn't addressed this issue in my preaching at Capitol Hill Baptist Church (CHBC) in any focused fashion since the 1990s!

As I talked about preaching on some of these same topics again, friends pressed me particularly on the topics of prayer and missions. It's not that they thought I had any novel theological breakthroughs to share, but they thought that some of the practices in our own church's life would be helpful and encouraging to other churches.

With that in mind, I decided to combine some messages. Decades of workshops on Nine Marks of a Healthy Church had led me to think some could be better handled that way. So I combined the messages on biblical theology and the gospel. That combined message is now "Gospel Doctrine" (chap. 2) in this edition. And because questions I received about conversion and evangelism were always interrelated, I combined those two messages. They are now a single chapter, "A Biblical Understanding of Conversion and Evangelism" (chap. 3). That left me free to take the two additional messages from the series of sermons given in November of 2015 and make them two new chapters: "A Biblical Understanding and Practice of Prayer" (chap. 8) and "A Biblical Understanding and Practice of Missions" (chap. 9).

Of course, I've never claimed that these are the only marks of health that a church should have; they are simply marks of health that need attention in many churches today. Over the years, you, dear reader, may see other marks that need to be investigated and championed. Perhaps our theology needs to be made more biblical. Or maybe our practice needs to be updated. I look forward to reading your further contributions on this vital, God-honoring topic. But, here in this fourth edition, I give you mine. I've scrubbed every chapter, omitting some things here and adding some things there. Some sections have been shortened, others expanded. And, of course, there are the larger changes mentioned above.

But the basic picture remains the same. In the years since this book first appeared, many other books on related themes have become available. Three may be of particular interest to you: the book I wrote called *The Church*; the book I wrote with Paul Alexander called *How to Build a Healthy Church*; and the book I wrote with Jamie Dunlop called *Compelling Community*. If you've liked this book, those other three titles would fit nicely in your reading and reflection.

Caleb Morell has been an outstanding assistant in preparing for these revisions. He's made my work much lighter. H. B. Charles Jr. was kind to agree to write a new foreword for this edition. And the friends at Crossway are always just that—friends—and colaborers in this regard. Their ability to produce and distribute books allows my private efforts to be of some public good. And yet, for all the help others have been in reading and writing and suggesting revisions and amendments to this book, as always, any errors you may find are mine alone.

Again, to God be the glory in all that lies within.

Mark Dever
Pastor, Capitol Hill Baptist Church, Washington, DC
President, 9Marks.org
July 2020

Preface to the Third Edition (2013)

FEW AUTHORS GET A THIRD CHANCE to try to get a message across to their readers. As I finish this revision, I'm now closing in on twenty years of pastoring the same congregation. When I first preached this series of sermons to our church, I hadn't been pastoring them even five years. My family was young. Our church was small and older. Now the church is larger and younger and my family is smaller and older. It is from this changing perspective that I take up the topic of church health yet again.

For this opportunity I am profoundly grateful to our friends at Crossway. Lane Dennis, Al Fisher, and many others have been allies in ministry since before they first approached me about doing this book some fifteen years ago.

The nine marks that I've chosen to cover seem every bit as relevant now as they did then. Many other aspects of the church can be fruitfully discussed, but I would like to continue pressing on these topics. Conversations with pastors and other church leaders in the intervening years have done nothing to cause me to think otherwise.

In this revised third edition, some arguments have been added (on, for example, expositional preaching, the nature of the gospel, and complementarianism), illustrations updated, and appendices changed and added. But the basic structure of the book remains the same.

Extensive help has been given to me in these revisions by friends too numerous to mention. Three that I cannot omit, however, because of the amount of attention they gave to this project and the help they were to me, are Mike McKinley, Bobby Jamieson, and Jaime Owens. Beyond that, my dear wife Connie reread the entire book, making thoughtful comments for the improvement of it throughout.

As with every edition, all errors of expression and judgment are my own. For any good done through it, all the glory goes to God.

Mark Dever
Senior Pastor, Capitol Hill Baptist Church
Washington, DC, September 2012

Preface to the Second Edition (2004)

Ten Years of Nine Marks

As I'm writing this preface to the new expanded edition of *Nine Marks of a Healthy Church*, I'm also about to celebrate ten years pastoring the same congregation. To some reading this sentence, that sounds like an eternity; to others, it may seem as if I've just begun. To be honest, to me it feels a bit like both.

I confess that pastoring a church sometimes feels like difficult work. There have been times when my tears have not been tears of joy, but of frustration, or sadness, or even worse. The people who are least happy and who leave have often been those who have required the most time, and who have talked the most to others as they have gone. And sometimes their talk has been neither edifying nor encouraging. They have little thought of how their actions affect others—the pastor, the pastor's family, those who have loved them and worked with them, young Christians who are confused, others to whom they talk wrongly. There are things I work for that don't work out, and things I care about that nobody else does. Some hopes go unfulfilled, and occasionally even tragedies intrude. It is in the nature of sheep to stray and of wolves to eat. I guess if I can't deal with that, I should just get out of undershepherding.

But most of my work is, to be honest, exhilarating! I thank God for those many times when I have known tears of joy. In God's grace, the number of people leaving the congregation unhappy has been dwarfed by the number of people leaving with tears of gratitude, and by those coming in. We have known growth in our congregation that hasn't been dramatic when considered in any one year, but which staggers me when I pause and look back. I've seen young men become converted and then eventually go into the ministry. While I'm writing this, two of the men now on our pastoral staff were first friends of mine when they were non-Christians. I studied the Gospel of Mark with them. By God's grace, I saw both of them come to know the Lord, and I now sit and listen to them preach the everlasting gospel to others. My eyes moisten even while I write these words.

The church as a whole has prospered. It seems clearly healthy. Strains in relationships are dealt with in godly ways. A culture of discipleship seems to have taken root. People go from here to seminary, or to their work as teachers, architects, or businessmen with more resolve in both their work and their evangelism. We've seen many marriages and young families begun. We've seen political types instructed in their worldviews; Christians in all walks of life helped in their understanding of the gospel; and discipline exercised to try to disabuse those who may be self-deceived. Pain has been exceeded by joy. God's grace toward us seems only to increase with every life encountered.

As God's Word has been taught, the congregation's appetite for good teaching has increased. A palpable sense of expectation has developed in the congregation. There is excitement as the congregation gathers. Older saints are cared for through their difficult days. One dear man's ninety-sixth birthday was celebrated by a bunch of the younger people in the church taking him to McDonald's (his favorite restaurant)! Wounded marriages have been helped; wounded people have found God's healing. Young people have come to appreciate hymns, and older people the vigorous singing of choruses. Countless hours have been given in quiet service to the building up of others. Courageous choices have been prayed for, made, and celebrated. New friendships are being made every day. Young men who have spent time with us here are now pastoring congregations in Kentucky and Michigan and Georgia and Connecticut and Illinois. They are preaching in Hawaii and Iowa. Missions giving has gone from a few thousand dollars a year to a few hundred thousand dollars a year. Our compassion for the lost has grown. I could go on. God has obviously been good to us. We have known health.

My Surprising Change

I didn't intend all of this when I came. I didn't come with a plan or program to bring all this about. I came with a commitment to God's Word, to give myself to knowing, believing, and teaching it. I had seen the blight of the unconverted church member, and was particularly concerned about that, but I didn't have a carefully worked out strategy to deal with the problem.

In God's providence, I had done a doctorate focusing on a Puritan (Richard Sibbes) whose writings about the individual Christian I loved, but whose concessions on the church came to seem increasingly unwise to me. Unhealthy churches cause few problems for the healthiest Christians; but they are cruel taxes on the growth of the youngest and weakest Christians. They prey on those who don't understand Scripture well. They mislead spiritual children. They even take the curious hopes of non-Christians that there might be another way to live, and seem to deny it. Bad churches are terribly effective antimissionary forces. I deeply lament sin in my own life, and sin's corporate magnification in the life of so many churches. They seem to make Jesus out to be a liar when he promised life to the full (John 10:10).

This all became more central to my life when, in 1994, I became the senior pastor of the congregation I now serve. The responsibility weighed on my mind. Texts such as James 3:1 ("judged more strictly") and Hebrews 13:17 ("must give an account") loomed larger in my mind. Circumstances conspired to emphasize to me the importance with which God regards the local church. I thought of a statement by nineteenth-century Scottish pastor and trainer of pastors, John Brown, who, in a letter of paternal counsel to one of his pupils newly ordained over a small congregation, wrote,

> I know the vanity of your heart, and that you will feel mortified that your congregation is very small, in comparison with those of your brethren around you; but assure yourself on the word of an old man, that when you come to give an account of them to the Lord Christ, at his judgment-seat, you will think you have had enough.[1]

As I looked out over the congregation I had charge of, I felt the weightiness of such an accounting to God.

But it was ultimately through preaching expositional sermons, serially going through book after book, that all of the Bible's teachings on the church became more central to me. It began to seem obviously a farce that we claimed to be Christians but didn't love each other. Sermons on John and 1 John, Wednesday night Bible studies going through James for three years, and conversations about membership and church covenants all came together.

The "each other" and "one another" passages began to come alive and enflesh the theological truths that I had known about God caring for his church. As I've preached through Ephesians 2–3, it has become clear to me that the church is the center of God's plan to display his wisdom to the heavenly beings. When Paul spoke to the Ephesian elders, he referred to the church as something that God "bought with his own blood" (Acts 20:28). And, of course, on the road to Damascus earlier, when Saul was interrupted on his course of persecuting Christians, the risen Christ did not ask Saul why he persecuted these Christians, or even the church; rather, Christ so identified with his church that the accusing question he put to Saul was, "Why do you persecute me?" (Acts 9:4). The church was clearly central in God's eternal plan, in his sacrifice, and in his continuing concern.

1 John Brown, cited by Alexander Grossart in *The Complete Works of Richard Sibbes*, vol. 1, ed. Alexander Grossart (1862–1864; reprint, Edinburgh: Banner of Truth Trust, 1979), 294.

I've come to see that love is largely local. And the local congregation is the place which claims to display this love for all the world to see. So Jesus taught his disciples in John 13:34–35, "A new command I give you: Love one another. As I have loved you, so you must love one another. By this all men will know that you are my disciples, if you love one another." I have seen friends and family alienated from Christ because they perceive this or that local church to have been such a terrible place. And, on the other hand, I have seen friends and family come to Christ because they have seen exactly this love that Jesus taught and lived—love for one another, the kind of selfless love that he showed—and they've felt the natural human attraction to it. So the congregation—the gathered people of God as the sounding board of the Word—has become more central to my understanding of evangelism, and of how we should pray and plan to evangelize. The local church is God's evangelism plan. The local church is God's evangelism program.

Over these last ten years, the congregation has also become more central to my understanding of how we are to discern true conversion in others, and how we are to have assurance of it ourselves. I remember being struck by 1 John 4:20–21 when preparing to preach on it: "If anyone says, 'I love God,' yet hates his brother, he is a liar. For anyone who does not love his brother, whom he has seen, cannot love God, whom he has not seen. . . . Whoever loves God must also love his brother." James 1 and 2 carries the same message. This love doesn't seem to be optional.

More recently, this consideration of the centrality of the congregation has brought about in my thinking a new respect for the local congregation's discipline—both formative and corrective. We've had some painful cases here, and some wonderful recoveries; and all of us are clearly still works in progress. But it has become crystal clear that if we are to depend upon each other in our congregations, discipline must be part of discipleship. And if there is to be the kind of discipline that we see in the New Testament, we must know and be known by others, and we must be committed to one another. We must also have some trust of authority. All the practicalities of trusting authority in marriage, home, and church are hammered out on the local level. Misunderstanding these matters and coming to dislike and resent authority seems very near to what the fall was all about. Conversely, understanding these matters seems very near to the heart of God's gracious work of reestablishing his relationship with us—a relationship of authority and love together. I've come to see that relationship with a local congregation is central to individual discipleship. The church isn't an optional extra; it's the shape of your following Jesus. I've come to understand that now in a way I never did before I came to this church. And I think that I'm seeing something of the health that God intends us to experience in a congregation.

What This Book Is Not

I should just say another word about what this book is not. Let me front-load your disappointment. This book leaves out a lot. Many of our favorite topics may not be covered. Rereading this book now, after a few years of others reading it too, I am even more aware of much I have not said. Friends have said to me, "What about prayer?" or "Where's worship?" John Piper asked, "Mark, why isn't missions in this?" I don't really like to disappoint friends who've taken the time to read the book; and I certainly don't like disappointing John Piper! But this book is not an exhaustive ecclesiology. We've been given good ideas for "more marks" that we could add. And a second edition might seem just the time to do this.

But we've decided not to. I continue to think that common errors in these particular nine matters are responsible for so much that goes wrong in our churches. It seems to me economical, strategic, faithful, and simply correct to continue to try to focus the attention of Christians on these particular matters. More missions, persevering prayer, wonderful worship—all will be best encouraged, I think, by tending better to these basic matters. Nobody is going to believe in the need that missions presupposes if they're not taught about that need from the Word. No one is going to go if they don't have an understanding of God's great plan to redeem a people for himself. And they won't do missions well if they don't understand the gospel.

If people do begin to think more carefully about conversion, it will affect their prayers. If we are more biblical in our practice of evangelism, we will find ourselves giving more of our prayer time to praying for non-Christians, and we will realize more of why we must pray for people to be converted. If we come to understand more about biblical church membership, we will find our corporate prayer times more central, better attended, more invigorating to our faith, and more challenging and reordering to our priorities.

If we begin to appreciate again the significance of church discipline, our times of corporate worship will be infused with more of a sense of awe at God's grace. If we find ourselves in churches that are increasingly marked by discipleship and spiritually flourishing members, the excitement and anticipation for singing praises and confessing sins together will grow. If we work to be led by those who meet the Bible's qualifications, we will find joy and confidence in our times together growing, we will be more free and enlivened in our times together, and our obedience will be more consistent.

This book isn't a complete inventory of every sign of health. It is intended to be a list of crucial marks that will lead to such a full experience.

An Outward-Looking Church

If I had to add one more mark to what you're about to read, it wouldn't be missions or prayer or worship; but it would touch on all of those things. I think that I would add that we want our congregations to be outward looking. We are to be upwardly focused—God centered. But we are also, I think, supposed to reflect God's own love as we look out on other people and on other congregations.

This can show itself in many ways. I long for our congregation to integrate better our vision for global missions and our efforts in local evangelism. If we have a commitment to help evangelize an unreached people group abroad, why haven't we done a better job in trying to find members of this people group in our metropolitan area? Why aren't our missions and evangelism better integrated?

We do pray in the pastoral prayer each Sunday morning for the prosperity of the gospel in other lands and through other local congregations. We're just now bringing someone on staff to help us plant another church. We as a church help to sponsor 9Marks, and through it work with many other churches for their benefit. We have "Weekenders" at which we welcome guest pastors and elders, seminarians, and other church leaders to be with us for a weekend. They sit in on a real elders meeting, in real membership classes. We put on special lectures and have attendees in our homes to eat and talk. We have internships for those preparing for the pastorate. We have curriculum we write and talks we give. All of this is for the building up of other congregations. As a pastor, I am certain that I need to realize that, under God, the local church is responsible for raising up the next generation of leaders. No Bible college, course, or seminary can do this. And such raising up of new leaders—for here and abroad—should be one of the goals of our church.

Looking back, I'm encouraged by how I've seen God's work here and in so many other congregations. In this congregation's life together I've seen evident, increasing, joyful, God-glorifying health.

Some people don't think this image of "health" is a good one. They may think that it's too man-centered, or too therapeutic. But as I've considered this, it seems to me more and more that health is actually a very good image for soundness, wholeness, correctness, and rightness.

Jesus talked of the health of our bodies as an image of our spiritual state (see Matt. 6:22–23 [Luke 11:33–34]; cf. Matt. 7:17–18). He said that, "It is not the healthy who need a doctor, but the sick" (Matt. 9:12 [Mark 2:17; Luke 5:31]). Jesus brought soundness to people's bodies to point to the soundness he offered for their souls (see Matt. 12:13; 14:35–36; 15:31; Mark 5:34; Luke 7:9–10; 15:27; John 7:23). The disciples in Acts continued the same health-giving Christ-exalting ministry (Acts 3:16; 4:10).

Paul used the image of the church as Christ's own body, and he described its prosperity in organic images of growth and health. For example, Paul wrote that "speaking the truth in love, we will in all things grow up into him who is the Head, that is, Christ. From him the whole body, joined and held together by every supporting ligament, grows and builds itself up in love, as each part does its work" (Eph. 4:15–16). Paul described correct doctrine in Titus 2:1 as "sound" or "healthy" doctrine. John greeted fellow Christians by telling them that, "I pray that you may enjoy good health and that all may go well with you, even as your soul is getting along well" (3 John 2).

None of this is to say that we can know it's God's will for his children to experience good physical health in this life, but simply to say that health is a natural image that God himself has sanctioned for that which is right and correct. As I said above, some Christians, out of concern over a wrongly therapeutic culture, shy away from using such images. But the abuse of the language shouldn't detract from its appropriate use. And with such understanding of health—its connection to life and prosperity; the objective norms of what is good and right that are presumed in it; the joy involved in it; the care to be taken over it—we can easily see the wisdom in our desiring to pursue the spiritual health of our own souls, and to work for healthy churches. It is to that end that this book was first written. And it is to that end that I pray that God will now use it in your life, and in the life of your church.

Mark Dever
Washington, DC, June 2004

Introduction

SOME TIME AGO, author and theologian David Wells reported some interesting findings of a survey taken in seven seminaries. One in particular struck me: "These students are dissatisfied with the current status of the church. They believe it has lost its vision, and they want more from it than it is giving them." Wells himself agreed: "Neither their desire nor their judgment in this regard is amiss. Indeed, it is not until we experience a holy dissatisfaction with things as they are that we can plant the seeds of reform. Of course, dissatisfaction alone is not enough."[1]

Dissatisfaction, indeed, is not enough. We find dissatisfaction with the church on every hand. Shelves groan under the weight of books with prescriptions for what ails her. Conference speakers live off the congregational diseases that always seem to survive their remedies. Pastors wrongly exult and tragically burn out. Confused and uncertain Christians are left to wander like sheep without a shepherd. But dissatisfaction is not enough. We need something more. We need positively to recover what the church is to be. What is the church in her nature and essence? What is to distinguish and mark the church?

For Historians

Christians often talk about "marks of the church." In his first published book, *Men with a Message*, John Stott summed up the teaching of Christ

1 David Wells, *God in the Wasteland: The Reality of Truth in a World of Fading Dreams* (Grand Rapids, MI: Eerdmans, 1994), 213.

to the churches in the book of Revelation this way: "These then are the marks of the ideal Church—love, suffering, holiness, sound doctrine, genuineness, evangelism and humility. They are what Christ desires to find in his churches as He walks among them."[2]

But this language has a more formal history as well, which must be acknowledged before engaging in the task of a book-length consideration of "nine marks of a healthy church."

Christians have long talked of the "marks of the church." Here, as in so much of the church's thinking, the question of how to distinguish true from false has led to a clearer definition of the true. The topic of the church did not become a center of widespread formal theological debate until the Reformation. Before the sixteenth century, the church was more assumed than discussed. It was considered to be the means of grace upon which the rest of theology rested. Roman Catholic theology uses the phrase "the mystery of the church" to refer to the depth of the reality of the church, which can never be fully explored. Practically, the church of Rome links its claim to being the true, visible church to the succession of Peter as the bishop of Rome.

With the advent of the radical criticisms of Martin Luther and others in the sixteenth century, however, discussion of the nature of the church itself became inevitable. As one scholar explains, "The Reformation made the gospel, not ecclesiastical organization, the test of the true church."[3] Calvin questioned Rome's claims to be the true church on the basis of apostolic succession: "Especially in the organization of the church nothing is more absurd than to lodge the succession in persons alone to the exclusion of teaching."[4] Since that time, therefore, the *notae*, *signa*, *symbola*, *criteria*, or *marks* of the church have been a necessary focus of discussion.

2 John Stott, *Men with a Message* (London: Longmans, 1954), 163–64. Reprinted in the United States as *Basic Introduction to the New Testament* (Grand Rapids, MI: Eerdmans, 1964).

3 Edmund Clowney, *The Church* (Downers Grove, IL: InterVarsity, 1995), 101.

4 John Calvin, *Institutes of the Christian Religion*, ed. John T. McNeill, trans. F. L. Battles (Philadelphia: Westminster, 1977), 4.2.3, 1045.

In 1530, Melanchthon drew up the Augsburg Confession, which in article 7 stated that "this Church is the congregation of the saints in which the gospel is rightly taught and the sacraments are rightly administered. And for that true unity of the Church it is enough to have unity of belief concerning the teaching of the gospel and the administration of the sacraments."[5] In his *Loci Communes* (1543), Melanchthon repeated the idea: "The marks which point out the church are the pure gospel and the proper use of the sacraments."[6] Since the Reformation, Protestants have typically viewed these two marks—the preaching of the gospel and the proper administering of the sacraments—as delineating the true church over against imposters.

In 1553 Thomas Cranmer produced the Forty-Two Articles of the Church of England. While not officially promulgated until later in the century as part of the Elizabethan Religious Settlement, they show the thinking of the great English Reformer concerning the church. Article 20 read (as Article 19 of the Thirty-Nine Articles still reads): "The visible Church of Christ is a congregation of faithful men in which the pure word of God is preached and the sacraments be duly administered, according to Christ's ordinance in all those things that of necessity are requisite to the same."[7]

John Calvin addressed the issue of distinguishing the false from the true church in his *Institutes*: "Wherever we see the Word of God purely preached and heard, and the sacraments administered according to Christ's institution, there, it is not to be doubted, a church of God exists."[8]

5 We could compare this with Luther's various writings about aspects that constitute a true church. See, e.g., his "Against Hanswurst," a treatise defending the Reformation from attacks by Henry, Duke of Braunschweig/Wolfenbuttel, in which Luther lays out what he considers to be ten characteristics of churches that are "faithful to the true ancient churches." Martin Luther, "Against Hanswurst," in *Church and Ministry III*, ed. Eric W. Gritsch, vol. 31 of *Luther's Works, American Edition*, eds. Jaroslav Pelikan and Helmut T. Lehmann (Philadelphia: Fortress, 1957), 194–98.

6 Philipp Melanchthon, *Loci Communes*, trans. J. A. O. Preus (St. Louis: Concordia, 1992), 137.

7 Gerald Bray, ed., *Documents of the English Reformation* (Cambridge, UK: James Clarke, 1994), 296.

8 Calvin, *Institutes*, 4.1.9. See also 4.1.7.

A third mark of the church, right discipline, has often been added since then, though it is widely acknowledged that this is implied in the second mark—the sacraments being rightly administered.[9] The Belgic Confession (1561), Article 29, said,

> The marks by which the true Church is known are these: If the pure doctrine of the gospel is preached therein; if she maintains the pure administration of the sacraments as instituted by Christ; if church discipline is exercised in punishing of sin; in short, if all things are managed according to the pure Word of God, all things contrary thereto rejected, and Jesus Christ acknowledged as the only Head of the Church.[10]

Edmund Clowney has summarized these marks as "true preaching of the Word; proper observance of the sacraments; and faithful exercise of church discipline."[11]

We can see in these two marks—gospel proclamation and observance of the sacraments—both the creation and the preservation of the church, the fountain of God's truth and the lovely vessel to contain and display it. The church is generated by the right preaching of God's Word; the church is contained and distinguished by the right administration of baptism and the Lord's Supper. (Presumed in this latter mark is that church discipline is being practiced.)

The Church Today Reflects the World

This book is a lesser thing than a consideration of these marks of the church. I accept the traditional Protestant understanding of the true

9 For an example of a modern popular treatment, see D. Martyn Lloyd-Jones, *The Church and the Last Things* (Wheaton, IL: Crossway, 1998), 13–18.

10 See A. C. Cochrane, ed., *Reformed Confessions of the Sixteenth Century* (Philadelphia: Westminster, 1966); and the Scottish Confession (1560), Article 18: "The trew preaching of the Worde of God . . . the right administration of the sacraments of Christ Jesus . . . Ecclesiastical discipline uprightlie ministered"; James Bulloch, trans., *The Scots Confession of 1560* (Edinburgh: St. Andrews College Press, 1993).

11 Clowney, *Church*, 101. On pages 99–115, Clowney has a good summary of the marks of the church considered biblically and historically, as well as in view of recent questions of distinguishing the church from the parachurch.

church being distinguished or marked off from the false by the right preaching of the Word and the right administration of the sacraments. But inside the set of all true local churches, some are more healthy and others less so. This book describes some marks that distinguish the more healthy churches from the true but more sickly ones. Therefore this book does not attempt to say everything that should be said about the church. To use theological language, it is not a full ecclesiology. To use an image, it is more a prescription than a course in general anatomy of the body of Christ.

Certainly no church is perfect. But, thank God, many imperfect churches are healthy. Nevertheless, I fear that many more are not—even among those that affirm the full deity of Christ and the full authority of Scripture. Why is this the case?

Some say the ill health of many churches today is related to various cultural conditions that have infested the church.

Some of the most common scapegoats have been the institutions that prepare people for the ministry. Richard Muller has described something of what he has seen of the seminaries' defaulting on their stewardship:

> Seminaries have been guilty of creating several generations of clergy and teachers who are fundamentally ignorant of the materials of the theological task and prepared to argue (in their own defense) the irrelevance of classical study to the practical operation of ministry. The sad result has been the loss, in many places, of the central, cultural function of the church in the West and the replacement of a culturally and intellectually rich clergy with a group of practitioners and operations-directors who can do almost anything except make sense of the church's theological message in the contemporary context.[12]

This book, then, is a plan for recovering biblical preaching and church leadership at a time when too many congregations are languishing in a

12 Richard A. Muller, *The Study of Theology* (Grand Rapids, MI: Zondervan, 1991), xiii.

notional and nominal Christianity, with all the resulting pragmatism and pettiness. The purpose of too many evangelical churches has fallen from glorifying God to growing larger, assuming that numerical growth, however achieved, must glorify God.

One problem, theologically and even practically, with lowering our vision is the self-defeating pragmatism that results. Neopaganism, secularization, pragmatism, and ignorance are all serious problems facing churches today. But I am convinced that the problem most fundamentally lies in the way Christians conceive of their churches. Too many churches misunderstand the priority that they are to give to God's revelation and to the nature of the regeneration he offers therein. Reevaluating these must be a part of any solution to the problems of today's churches.

Popular Models of the Church

Four models of the church are found today in my own association of churches (Southern Baptist Convention) and in many others as well. We might summarize these models as liberal, prosperity gospel, seeker-sensitive, and traditional.

Drawing with bold lines for a minute, we might conceive of the liberal model as having F. D. E. Schleiermacher as its patron saint. In an attempt to be successful in evangelism, Schleiermacher tried to rethink the gospel in contemporary terms.

The well-known preacher Benny Hinn might be an example of a second model, the prosperity gospel church. In an attempt to make the promises of physical healing equal to the promises of spiritual forgiveness, and to make the future fulfillment present, preachers like Hinn have built churches around what they claim are immediate displays of God's power. According to this model, all should be able to see and benefit from promised health and prosperity now.

We might find something of the same goal in the seeker-sensitive model, seen in the writing and ministry of Bill Hybels and his associates at Willow Creek and the many churches associated with them. They have tried to rethink the church, like the liberals, with the goal of evangelism always in mind—from the outside in, again, in an attempt to make the gospel's relevance obvious to all.

The patron saint of traditional evangelical churches could be said to be the late Billy Graham (or perhaps one of several other great evangelists of the present or preceding generation). Again, the motive is to be successful in evangelism, with the local church treated as a stationary evangelistic rally. Actually, the "traditional" evangelical church in America is much like the seeker-sensitive model, only to an older culture—the culture of fifty or a hundred years ago. So instead of Willow Creek skits, the First Baptist Women's Trio is regarded as the thing that will draw nonbelievers in.

While there are important doctrinal distinctions between these various kinds of churches, all four have important commonalities. All assume that evident relevance and response is the key indicator of success. The social ministries of the liberal church, the miracles of the prosperity gospel church, the music of the seeker-sensitive church, and the programs of the traditional evangelical church all must work well and work *now* to be considered relevant and successful. Depending on the type of church, success may mean so many fed, so many involved, or so many saved, but the assumption that all these kinds of churches share is that the fruit of a successful church is readily apparent.

From both a biblical and a historical standpoint, this assumption seems incalculably dangerous. Biblically, we find that God's Word is replete with images of delayed blessing. God, for his own inscrutable purposes, tests and tries his Jobs and his Josephs, his Jeremiahs, and even Jesus himself. The trials of Job, the beating and selling of Joseph, the imprisonment and mocking of Jeremiah, and the rejection and crucifixion of Jesus all remind us that God moves in mysterious ways. He calls us more fundamentally to a relationship of trust with him than to a full understanding of him and his ways. The parables of Jesus are full of stories of the kingdom of God beginning in surprisingly small ways but growing finally to a glorious prominence. Biblically, we must realize that the size of what our eyes see is rarely a good way to estimate the greatness of something in the eyes of God.

From a historical standpoint, we would do well to remember that looks can be deceiving. When a culture is saturated with Christianity and biblical knowledge, when God's general benevolence and even his special grace are spread widely, one might perceive obvious blessings. Biblical morality may be affirmed by all. The church may be widely esteemed. The Bible may be taught even in secular schools. In such a time, it may be hard to distinguish between the apparent and the real.

But in a time when Christianity is being widely and rapidly disowned, where evangelism is considered intolerant or even classified as a hate crime, we find the stakes are changed. On the one hand, the culture to which we would conform in order to be relevant becomes so inextricably entwined with antagonism to the gospel that to conform to it must result in a loss of the gospel itself. On the other hand, it is more difficult for nominal Christianity to thrive. In such a day, we must rehear the Bible and reimagine the concept of successful ministry not as necessarily immediately fruitful but as demonstrably faithful to God's Word.

Great missionaries who have gone to non-Christian cultures must have known this. When they went to places where there were no obvious "fields white unto harvest" but only years and even decades of rejection, they must have had some other motivation to keep them going. William Carey was faithful in India and Adoniram Judson in Burma not because their immediate success showed them that that they were being obviously relevant. They were faithful because the Spirit of God in them encouraged them to obedience and trust. We in the secular West must recover a sense of satisfaction in such biblical faithfulness. And we must recover it particularly in our lives together as Christians, in our churches.

Needed: A Different Model

We need a new model for the church. Actually, the model we need is an old one. Even though I'm writing a book about it, I'm not quite sure what to call it. Mere? Historic? Biblical?

Simply put, we need churches that are self-consciously distinct from the culture. We need churches in which the key indicator of success is not evident results but persevering biblical faithfulness.[13] We need churches that help us to recover those aspects of Christianity that are distinct from the world, and that unite us.

What follows is not intended to be a full portrait of this new (old) model of the church but a timely prescription. It focuses on two basic needs in our churches: preaching the message and leading disciples.

Preaching the Message

The first five marks of a healthy church that we will consider reflect the concern to preach rightly the Word of God. *Mark One* is about preaching itself. It is a defense of the primacy of expositional preaching as a reflection of the centrality of God's Word.

Why is his Word central? Why is it the instrument of creating faith? The Word is so central and so instrumental because the Word of the Lord holds out the object of our faith to us. It presents God's promise to us—from all kinds of individual promises (throughout the Bible) all the way to the great promise, the great hope, the great object of our faith, Christ himself. The Word presents that which we are to believe.

Then, in *Mark Two*, we consider the framework of this message: gospel doctrine. We must understand God's truth as a coherent whole, coming to us first and foremost as a revelation of himself. Questions of who God is and of what he is like can never be considered irrelevant to the practical matters of church life. How discerning are we in how we understand the gospel ourselves, how we teach it, and how we train others to know it? Is our message, though larded with Christian pieties, basically a message of self-salvation, or is there something more in it? Does our gospel consist only of universal ethical truths for our daily lives, or are there once-for-all, historical, special saving actions of God in Christ at the root of it?

That brings us to the reception of the message, *Mark Three*: a biblical understanding of conversion and evangelism. One of the most painful

13 See Mark Dever, "Endurance Needed: Strength for a Slow Reformation and the Dangerous Allure of Speed" (sermon, Together for the Gospel, Louisville, KY, 2016), http://t4g.org/resources/mark-dever/asl-endurance-needed-strength-slow-reformation-dangerous-allure-speed/.

tasks pastors face is trying to undo the damage of false converts who have been too quickly and thoughtlessly assured by an evangelist that they are indeed Christians. Such apparently charitable activity may lead to short bursts of excitement, involvement, and interest, but if an apparent conversion does not result in a changed life, then one begins to wonder at the unwitting cruelty of convincing such people that because they once prayed a prayer or were baptized spontaneously, they have fully investigated all the hope that God has for them in life. "If that failed," we may leave them to think, "then Christianity has nothing more to offer me. No more hope. No more life. I tried, and it didn't work." We need churches to understand and teach what the Bible teaches about conversion.

And this means that we must consider our evangelism. If, in our evangelism, we imply that becoming a Christian is something that we do ourselves, then we disastrously pass on our misunderstanding of the gospel and of conversion. In our evangelism we must be partners with the Holy Spirit, presenting the gospel but relying on the Holy Spirit of God to do the true convicting and convincing and converting. Are your church's or your own evangelistic practices in line with this great truth?

Leading the Disciples

The other nexus of problems in today's churches has to do with the right administration of the borders and markers of Christian identity. More generally put, we have problems in leading disciples.

First, in *Mark Four*, we address the question of the whole framework for discipleship: a biblical understanding of church membership. In this past century, Christians have all but ignored biblical teaching on the corporate nature of following Christ. Our churches are awash in self-centered narcissism, hyperindividualism thinly veiled in everything from "gift inventories" to "targeted churches" that "aren't for everybody." When we read 1 John or the Gospel of John, we see that Jesus never intended us to be lone Christians, and that our love for others who aren't just like us shows whether we truly love God.

Many churches today have problems with the basic definition of what it means to be a disciple. So in *Mark Five* we explore a biblical understanding of church discipline. Is there any behavior that churches should not tolerate? Are any teachings in our churches "beyond the pale"? Do our churches indicate a concern for anything beyond their own institutional survival and expansion? Do we evidence an understanding that we bear the name of God and live either to his honor or to his shame? We need churches to recover the loving, regular, and wise practice of church discipline.

In *Mark Six* we examine Christian discipleship and growth. Evangelism that does not result in discipleship is not only incomplete evangelism but is entirely misconceived. The solution is not that we need to do more evangelism but that we need to do it differently. We don't simply need to remember to tell people to come to church after we have prayed the prayer with them; we need to tell them to count the cost before they pray that prayer!

Mark Seven focuses on the need to recover a biblical understanding of church leadership. Leadership in the church should not be granted as a response to secular gifts or position, to family relationships, or in recognition of length of service in the church. Leadership in the church should be invested in those who seem to evidence in their own lives, and who are able to promote in the life of the congregation as a whole, the edifying and sanctifying work of the Holy Spirit.

Mark Eight examines the church's prayer life. How we pray reveals what we understand prayer to be. It reflects what we believe about God's sovereignty and our responsibility. It touches on how we deal with trials and how we will care for each other. When we consider how we pray in our times together as a local church, we reveal much of what is most important about us as a community.

Finally, *Mark Nine* focuses on the need to think about God's purposes in the world and the role he wants his church to play in bringing about those purposes. Few places in our life together does our theology show itself more than in our practice of missions. Our God is not a village god. He is not concerned only with us and our families, only with our city, or even only with our nation. God has a purpose as big as this world (and bigger!), and he wants to involve our churches in it deeply—in everything from our praying to our paying, from our sending to our staying.

The end and purpose of all this is the glory of God as we make him known. Throughout history, God has desired to make himself known. This is why he delivered Israel from Egypt in the exodus, and why he delivered them again from the Babylonian exile. Scores of passages in Scripture tell of God's desire to make himself known (e.g., Ex. 7:5; Deut. 4:34–35; Job 37:6–7; Pss. 22:21–22; 106:8; Isa. 49:22–23; 64:4; Ezek. 20:34–38; 28:25–26; 36:11; 37:6; John 17:26). He has created the world and has done all that he has done for his own praise. And it is right and good that he should do so.

Calvin called this world the theater of God's splendor. Others have referred to history as one great parade culminating in the glory of God. Mark Ross, who for decades pastored First Presbyterian Church in Columbia, SC, put it this way:

> We are one of God's chief pieces of evidence. . . . Paul's great concern [in Ephesians 4:1–16] for the church is that the church manifest and display the glory of God, thus vindicating God's character against all the slander of demonic realms, the slander that God is not worth living for. . . . God has entrusted to His church the glory of His own name.[14]

Everyone—those who are church leaders and those who are not—is made in the image of God. We are to be walking pictures of the moral nature and righteous character of God, reflecting it around the universe for all to see—especially in our union with God through Christ. This, therefore, is what God calls us to and why he calls us to it. He calls us to join together with him, and together in our congregations, not for our glory but for his own.

14 Mark Ross, unpublished sermon notes.

This Book

This book comes from a series of sermons. According to one church consultant, sermons should be easier to understand, less abstract, more spontaneous, shorter, filled with more stories of the preacher's personal experience, and allow for audience participation.[15] He is not alone in suggesting that we do something to mitigate the one-sidedness and the bare appeal to reason that marks so much preaching, particularly expositional preaching. But permit me to suggest that the one-sidedness of preaching is not only excusable but it is actually important. If in our preaching we stand in the place of God, giving his Word by his Spirit to his people, then surely it is appropriate that it be one-sided—not that it should be one-sided in the sense that the one preaching is never to be questioned; but, in the event of preaching itself, the univocal character of God's Word comes as a monologue to us, not hoping to elicit interest and participation but requiring that we respond. Something of this character must be retained. This does not mean that the sermon must be deliberately boring, obscure, or abstract. I hope that, in these sermons masquerading as chapters, something of a serious engagement with the great truths of the Bible and with today's context will come through for the blessing not only of you, but for your church as well. May it be so.

Other Resources

- For group study: *Built upon the Rock: The Church* (2012), by Bobby Jamieson, a six-week inductive Bible study.
- For pastoral application: *How to Build a Healthy Church: A Practical Guide for Deliberate Leadership* (2021), by Mark Dever and Paul Alexander.
- For handing out to church members: *What Is a Healthy Church?* (2007), by Mark Dever.

15 My summary from comments at a conference in Wheaton, Maryland, October 9, 1997.

What's Coming Up

Mark One: Expositional Preaching

Expositional Preaching

The Central Role of the Word of God

- The Role of God's Word in Bringing Life
- The Role of God's Word in Preaching
- The Role of God's Word in Sanctifying
- The Role of the Preacher of God's Word

Mark One

Expositional Preaching

THIS IS HOW I BEGAN my sermon one Sunday morning in January, several years ago:

> So, how's it going? Did you get enough sleep last night? Did you have trouble finding a good parking place this morning? Were the doors clearly marked? Did the people welcome you as you came in? Did the building seem nice and neat? I wonder, did the church's name make it more difficult for you to decide whether to come in? Or maybe that was part of the reason why you decided to come in.
>
> And when you did come in, were the people friendly and welcoming? Any trouble dropping the kids off? And what do you think about the stained glass? I know I have the best view of it, but it's really pretty, isn't it? Then again, maybe it's a little too traditional for you.
>
> Are the pews comfortable? Do you have a good view of all the activities from where you are sitting? Can you see clearly? Can you hear okay? Is it warm enough for you right now? Do you feel pretty comfortable?
>
> And how about the bulletin? Nice, clear, simple, pretty straightforward, wouldn't you say? Not too complicated. Maybe a little too staid. Did you notice all the announcements in it?

And what about the people sitting around you? Are they the kind you like to go to church with? Yeah, I know you're too nervous to look around you right now, but you know who they are. What do you think? Are they the right age? Are they the right race? Are they the right social class? Are they just like you?

And what about the service so far? There weren't too many announcements in the service, were there? I don't think so this morning. Have the prayers been involving? Have they engaged your heart and mind?

It is a bit unusual these days to read so much Scripture in church, isn't it? You don't often find that done.

And of course, there's the music. You know, we're still trying to get some things worked out, as you can tell—contemporary or traditional, classical or more modern, liturgical or more informal. As with every other church in America this very morning, there are probably some people who have come to this church in the past who this morning are out looking at other churches because they would like a different musical experience. And, you know, there are probably some people who are still here, in part, because they like this musical experience.

What are you doing here? Whether you've been coming to this church for fifty years or this is your first Sunday—why do you come?

And now, of course, well, you know what's coming now. Maybe it has already begun: the sermon! For some people, this is what you just have to sit through to get to the good bit—maybe some more singing, or meeting and talking to people afterward.

The preacher does have a difficult job, doesn't he? He has to be someone that you feel you could relate to and talk with and let your hair down with or trust in some measure. But he needs to seem holy, too. But not too holy. He needs to be knowledgeable, but not too knowledgeable. He needs to be confident, but not too confident. He needs to be compassionate, but not too compassionate. And his sermon needs to be good enough, relevant enough, entertaining and engaging enough, and certainly short enough.

There is so much to consider when you are evaluating a church, isn't there? Have you ever really stopped to think about it? There are so many different things to think of and, as much as Americans move these days, we have to evaluate churches. We have to ask ourselves what makes a really good church.

In my study I have shelf after shelf and stack after stack of books about exactly this question: What really makes a good church? You would be amazed at how widely the answers vary. They range from friendliness to financial planning to pristine bathrooms to pleasant surroundings to vibrant music to being sensitive to visitors to plentiful parking to exciting children's programs to elaborate Sunday school options to the right computer software to clear signage to homogeneous congregations.

So, what do you think? What makes for a healthy church? If you are a visitor today, looking for a church where you can come regularly and to which you can commit yourself, you need to consider this question. Even if you are already a member here, you need to consider this question—you might move, you know. And even if you don't ever move again, you need to know what constitutes a healthy church. If you're going to stay in the church and be a part of building it and shaping it, don't you need to know what you're trying to build? What you want it to look like? What you want to aim for? What should be foundational?

Be careful how you answer these questions. You'll find experts who will tell you the answer is everything from how religion-free your language is to how invisible your membership requirements are.

So, what do you think? Are secure nurseries and sparkling bathrooms, exciting music and look-alike congregations really the way to church growth and church health? Is that really what makes a good church?

And so I began the series of sermons that has become this book—*Nine Marks of a Healthy Church*. The purpose of this book is to ask and answer the question, What distinctively marks a really good church?

I suggest nine distinguishing marks of a healthy church. You can find them listed in the table of contents. These nine marks certainly are not the only attributes of a healthy church. They're not even necessarily the most important things that could be said about a church. For example, I address only in passing the topics of baptism and communion, even though these are essential aspects of a biblical church, commanded by Christ himself. This book is not a complete ecclesiology. It focuses on certain crucial aspects of healthy church life that have grown rare among churches today. Though they may often be misunderstood, baptism and the Lord's Supper have not vanished from most churches; but many of the attributes that we will consider in these pages *have* disappeared from many churches.

Of course, there is no such thing as a perfect church, and I certainly don't mean to suggest that any church I ever pastor will be a perfect church. But that doesn't mean our churches can't be more healthy. It is my goal to encourage such health.

Expositional Preaching

The first mark of a healthy church is expositional preaching. It is not only the first mark; it is far and away the most important of them all, because if you get this one right, all of the others should follow. This chapter will help you to understand what pastors are to give themselves to, and what congregations are to demand of them. My main role, and the main role of any pastor, is expositional preaching.

This is so important that if you were to miss this one and happen to get all the other eight marks right, in a sense they would be accidents. You would have just happened to get them right. They may be distorted, because they wouldn't have sprung from the Word, and they would not continually be reshaped and refreshed by it. But if you establish the priority of the Word, then you have in place the single most important aspect of the church's life, and growing health is virtually assured because God has decided to act by his Spirit through his Word.

So what is this all-important thing called expositional preaching? It is usually contrasted with topical preaching. A topical sermon is like this chapter—it takes a subject and talks about it, rather than taking a particular text of the Bible as its subject. The topical sermon begins with a particular matter that the preacher wants to preach about. The topic could be prayer or justice or parenting or holiness or even expositional preaching. Having established the topic, the preacher then assembles various texts from various parts of the Bible and combines them with illustrative stories and anecdotes. The material is combined and woven together around this one topic. The topical sermon is not built around one text of Scripture but around this one chosen theme or idea.

A topical sermon can be expositional. I could choose to preach on a topic and pick one passage of Scripture that addresses exactly this concern. Or I could preach with a number of texts that address this same theme. But it is still a topical sermon, because the preacher knows what he wants to say and he is going into the Bible to see what he can find to say about it. For example, when I preached a version of this material as a sermon, I largely knew when I set out what I wanted to say. When I preach expositionally, this is not usually the case. In preparing my normal expositional sermon, I am often a bit surprised by the things I find in the passage as I study it. Generally, I do not choose series of expositional sermons because of particular topics that I think the church needs to hear about. Rather, I assume that all of the Bible is relevant to us all of the time. Now, I trust that God may lead me to some particular books of the Bible, but very often when I'm working on a text and reading through it in my quiet times the week before preaching, and working with it very seriously on Friday, I will find things in it that I didn't expect to find at all. I will sometimes be surprised by the point of the passage and therefore by what must become the point of my message.

Expositional preaching is not simply producing a verbal commentary on some passage of Scripture. Rather, expositional preaching is preaching that takes for the point of a sermon the point of a particular passage of Scripture. That's it. The preacher opens the Word and unfolds it for the people of God. That is not what I'm doing in this chapter, but it is what I normally intend to do when I step into the pulpit on Sunday.[1]

Expositional preaching is preaching in service to the Word. It presumes a belief in the authority of Scripture—that the Bible is actually God's Word; but it is something much more than that. A commitment to expositional preaching is a commitment to *hear* God's Word—not just to affirm that it is God's Word but to actually submit to it. The Old Testament prophets and the New Testament apostles were given not a personal commission to go and speak, but a particular message to deliver. Likewise Christian preachers today have authority to speak from God only so long as they speak his message and unfold his words. As loquacious as some preachers may be, they are not commanded simply to go and preach. They are commanded specifically to go and preach the Word.

Many pastors happily accept the authority of God's Word and profess to believe in the inerrancy of the Bible; yet if they do not in practice regularly preach expositionally, I'm convinced that they will never preach more than they knew when they began the whole exercise. A preacher can take a piece of Scripture and exhort the congregation on a topic that is important, but that isn't really the point of that particular passage. You can pick your Bible up right now, close your eyes, open it to a certain place, put your finger down on a verse, open your eyes, and read that verse, and you can get a great blessing from it for your soul—but you still might not learn what God intended to say through that passage. What is most important in real estate is most important in understanding the Bible: location, location, location. You understand a text of Scripture where it is. You understand it in the context in which it was inspired.

1 See Mark Dever and Greg Gilbert, *Preach: Theology Meets Practice* (Nashville: B&H, 2012). For some careful cautions about the abuse of expositions of consecutive passages of Scripture, see Iain Murray, *Archibald G. Brown* (Carlisle, PA: Banner of Truth, 2011), 353–63. Murray wants to make sure that inspiring, gripping, converting preaching is not replaced by a wrong-headed commitment to a certain style of lecturing, which many label "expositional preaching."

A preacher should have his mind increasingly shaped by Scripture. He shouldn't use Scripture as an excuse for what he already knows he wants to say. When someone regularly preaches in a way that is not expositional, the sermons tend to be only on the topics that interest the preacher. The result is that the preacher and the congregation only hear in Scripture what they already thought before they came to the text. There's nothing new being added to their understanding. They're not continuing to be challenged by the Bible.

In being committed to preach a passage of Scripture in context, expositionally—that is, taking as the point of the message the point of the passage—we should hear from God things that we didn't intend to hear when we set out to study the passage. God surprises us sometimes. And from your repentance and conversion to the latest thing the Holy Spirit has been teaching you, isn't that what it means to be a Christian? Don't you again and again find God challenging you and convicting you of some things you would never have thought about a year ago, as he begins to unearth the truth of your heart and the truth of his Word? To charge someone with the spiritual oversight of a church who doesn't in practice show a commitment to hear and to teach God's Word is to hamper the growth of the church, in essence allowing it to grow only to the level of the pastor. The church will slowly be conformed to the pastor's mind rather than to God's mind. And what we want, what as Christians we crave, are God's words. We want to hear and know in our souls what he has said.

The Central Role of the Word of God

Preaching should always (or almost always) be expositional because the Word of God should be at its center, directing it. In fact, churches should have the Word at their center, directing them. God has chosen to use his Word to bring life. That's the pattern that we see in Scripture and in history.

At a reception I once attended, the conversation turned to a book that had recently been published. I had read it, because I was about to give a speech on the topic of the book. My host, a Roman Catholic, had also read it—for a review he was writing. I asked him what he thought.

"Oh, it was very good," he said, "except it was marred by the author's repeating that old Protestant error that the Bible created the church, when we all know that the church created the Bible." Well, I was in a bit of a quandary. It was his gathering and I was a guest. What should I say? I saw the whole Protestant Reformation flash before me!

I decided that if he could politely be so openly dismissive, then I could be as forthright and honest as I wished. So I came right out and said, "That's ridiculous!" Trying to be as pleasantly contradictory as I could, I continued, "God's people have never created God's Word. From the very beginning God's Word has always created his people! From Genesis 1, where God literally creates all that is, including his people, by his Word; to Genesis 12, where he calls Abraham out of Ur by the word of his promise; to Ezekiel 37, where God gives Ezekiel a vision to share with the Israelite exiles in Babylon about the great resurrection to life that would come about by God's Word; to the supreme sending of God's Word in Jesus Christ, the Word made flesh; to Romans 10, where we read that spiritual life comes to us by the Word—God has always created his people by his Word. It has never been the other way around. God's people have never created God's Word."

I can't remember exactly what happened in the rest of that conversation, but I remember that part very clearly because it helped to crystallize for me the absolute centrality of the Word.

Let's follow this path through the Scriptures and see what it tells us about the centrality of God's Word in our lives, and then consider what that means for the nature and importance of preaching in our churches. I want to focus on four points: the role of the Word in bringing us life; the role of God's Word in preaching; the role of the Word in sanctifying us; and, therefore, the role a preacher of God's Word should have in the church.

The Role of God's Word in Bringing Life

Let's start at the beginning, where the Bible starts. In Genesis 1, we see that it was by his Word that God created the world and all the life in it. He spoke, and it was so. In Genesis 3, we see the grim story of what happened next: the fall. There we see that our first parents sinned, and that after they sinned, they were cast out from God's presence. They quite literally lost sight of God. But in God's great grace they did not lose all hope. Though God was vanishing from their sight, he mercifully sent his voice to them so that they could hear the Word of promise. In Genesis 3:14–15, God cursed the serpent. He warned him that the offspring of the woman would crush him. That word is the first word of hope Adam and Eve had in the aftermath of their own sin.

In Genesis 12, we find that it was by God's Word that Abraham was called out of Ur of the Chaldeans. The word of God's promise, recorded in the first few verses of Genesis 12, was the attractive force, the drawing promise, literally calling Abraham out of Ur to follow after God. God's people were created—they became visible—by hearing that word of promise and by responding to it—by coming out after it. God's people were created by God's Word. Abraham never set up a committee to craft God's Word. No, he was made the father of God's people because God's Word came specially to him and he believed it. He trusted God for what he said. Then we read of how the children of Abraham expanded in the Promised Land and then went down into Egypt, eventually falling into slavery there for centuries. Just when that bondage looked so permanent, what did God do? He sent his Word. In Exodus 3:4, God began with Moses, calling out to him. A burning bush was an extraordinary thing to see, but a burning bush in and of itself wouldn't tell Moses anything. Even learned scholars disagree on the symbolism of the burning bush. The key is that God spoke out of the bush. He gave his words to Moses. He called out to him by his Word. God's Word came not just to Moses and his descendants but to the whole nation of Israel, calling them to be his people.

In Exodus 20, we find that God gave his law to his people, and by accepting God's law they became his people. It was by God's Word that the people of Israel were constituted as God's special people.

Continuing through the Old Testament, we see that God's Word plays both a seminal and a discriminating role, as some people hear it and others refuse to hear it. Consider, for example, the story of Elijah in 1 Kings 18: "After a long time, . . . the word of the LORD came to Elijah: 'Go and present yourself to Ahab, and I will send rain on the land'" (18:1). The phrase "the word of the LORD came" or its equivalents occurs more than 3,800 times in the Old Testament. The Word of the Lord came as he created and led his people. God's people were those who heard God's words of promise and responded in faith. In the Old Testament, God's Word always came as a means of faith. It was, in a sense, a secondary object of faith. God, of course, is always the primary object of our faith—we believe in God—but that doesn't mean very much if that object is not defined. And how do we define who God is and what he calls us to do? We could make it up, or our God could tell us. We believe that God has told us. We believe that God himself actually has spoken. His Word is to be trusted and relied upon with all the faith that we would invest in God himself. So we see in the Old Testament that God led his people by his Word.

Do you see why the Word of God is central as an instrument in creating faith? It presents God and his promises to us—from all kinds of individual promises throughout the Old and New Testaments, all the way to the great promise, the great hope, the great object of our faith, Christ himself. The Word shows us what we are to believe.

For the Christian, the speed of sound (the Word that we hear) is in a sense greater than the speed of light (the things we can actually see). It is as if, in this fallen world, we perceive the future first by our ears rather than by our eyes.

In the great vision of Ezekiel 37, we see most remarkably that life comes by the Word of God:

> The hand of the LORD was upon me, and he brought me out by the Spirit of the LORD and set me in the middle of a valley; it was full of bones. He led me back and forth among them, and I saw a great many bones on the floor of the valley, bones that were very dry. He asked me, "Son of man, can these bones live?"
>
> I said, "O Sovereign LORD, you alone know."
>
> Then he said to me, "Prophesy to these bones and say to them, 'Dry bones, hear the word of the LORD! This is what the Sovereign LORD says to these bones: I will make breath enter you, and you will come to life. I will attach tendons to you and make flesh come upon you and cover you with skin; I will put breath in you, and you will come to life. Then you will know that I am the LORD.'" (Ezek. 37:1–6)

This is one encouraging vision! If you have ever been called to pastor a church that looks like it might be on its last legs, or if you can recall your own feelings of spiritual hopelessness before you found salvation, then you can see why this is a great passage of hope.

In verses 7–10 we see what happens when Ezekiel responds in obedience to the vision:

> I prophesied as I was commanded. And as I was prophesying, there was a noise, a rattling sound, and the bones came together, bone to bone. I looked, and tendons and flesh appeared on them and skin covered them, but there was no breath in them.
>
> Then he said to me, "Prophesy to the breath; prophesy, son of man, and say to it, 'This is what the Sovereign LORD says: Come from the four winds, O breath, and breathe into these slain, that they may live.'" So I prophesied as he commanded me, and breath entered them; they came to life and stood up on their feet—a vast army. (Ezek. 37:7–10)

Then God interprets this vision for Ezekiel. He says that these bones stand for the whole house of Israel, who say, "Our hope is gone" (37:11).

God's answer to Israel, as it was to the dry bones, is: "I will put my Spirit in you and you will live" (37:14). And how does he do this? He does it *by his Word.* To make the point crystal clear, God calls Ezekiel to start preaching to this bunch of dry bones, and through that preaching of the Word God brings life to the bones. God has Ezekiel speak his Word to them while they are dead, and as he does so, they come to life!

The vision of the dry bones reflects the way God called Ezekiel to speak to a nation that wouldn't listen to him. It also reflects the way God himself spoke into the void and created his world—by the power of his Word. We are reminded, likewise, of what happened when God's Word came into the world in the person of Christ: "And though the world was made through him, the world did not recognize him" (John 1:10). Yet through that Word, through the Lord Jesus, God has begun creating his new society on earth.

God told Ezekiel to speak to the dry bones. Life came through breath; the Spirit traveled through speech; and that Word of God, his breath, gave life. Do you see the close connection between life, breath, spirit, speech, and word? It reminds us of times in Jesus's own ministry. For instance: "Some people brought to him a man who was deaf. . . . He looked up to heaven and with a deep sigh said to him, . . . 'Be opened!' . . . At this, the man's ears were opened" (Mark 7:32, 34–35). Jesus spoke to a deaf man, and his ears were opened. Life came back into his ears! Jesus called his people to himself in just the way that Ezekiel prophesied: "I will give you a new heart and put a new spirit in you; I will remove from you your heart of stone and give you a heart of flesh" (Ezek. 36:26).

This is the glorious reality that we Christians have experienced. As I once said to a Jehovah's Witness worker, Christians know that in and of ourselves we are spiritually dead, and that we need God to initiate his life in us. We need him to reach down and rip out our old, stony hearts and put in us new, fleshy hearts of love toward him—hearts that are soft and pliant to his Word. And that's just what Jesus Christ does for us. He is creating a different *kind* of people, a people who show the life of God in them as they hear his Word and as, by his grace, they respond to it.

This brings us to the supreme picture of God's Word bringing life:

> In the beginning was the Word, and the Word was with God, and the Word was God. . . .
>
> Through him all things were made; without him nothing was made that has been made. In him was life, and that life was the light of men. (John 1:1, 3–4)

It is in Christ that the Word of God has fully and finally come to us.

Jesus modeled that great reality in his own ministry. At the very beginning of his ministry, when his disciples told him that many people were looking for him because they wanted him to do some more miracles and to heal them, Jesus replied, "Let us go somewhere else . . . so I can *preach* there also. *That* is why I have come" (Mark 1:38). If we keep reading Mark's Gospel, we find that Jesus knew that he had come fundamentally to lay down his life for our sins (see 10:45); but in order for that event to be understood, he first had to teach.

It was God's Word that Peter preached at Pentecost in Acts 2. God brought life through his Word. Men and women heard the truth about God, their sins, and the provision God had sent in Jesus. And when they heard the message, they were cut to the heart, and they cried out, "Brothers, what shall we do?" (Acts 2:37). God's Word created his people. The church was founded by the Word.

I don't mean to give the impression that Christianity is only a bunch of words—but words are important. In the Bible, we see that God acts, but he doesn't stop there. After he acts, God speaks. He interprets what he has done so that we can understand it. God doesn't allow his acts to speak for themselves; he speaks, in order to interpret for us his great saving acts.

This "verbal" nature of God fits with the way he has made us. Consider our human relationships. How do we come to know each other?

We can get to know each other through just watching. Husbands and wives can learn about each other through physical intimacy. But there is a profound part of our knowing each other that can come only through some kind of cognitive communication. Words are important for our relationships.

You tell me you have a great relationship with your dog (he's man's best friend, after all!), and that you love your dog, though he could never speak to you or cognitively communicate with you. You come home, and he wags his tail. He rushes to you. He wants to lick you. You look in his eyes and see they're oh-so-sympathetic. He understands all of life and will never desert you. You figure this is love, so who needs words?

Well, words are important. If you went home one Sunday and your dog looked up at you and casually said, "So how was church today?" I submit that that would change your relationship with your dog! It would show you exactly how important words are in relationships.

Because we have separated ourselves from God by our sin, God must speak if we are to know him. God will not be known if he does not speak, and we cannot know him if he has not spoken a word that we can rely on. God must reveal himself. That's the point of the Bible. Because of our own sins, we could never know God otherwise. Either he speaks, or we are forever lost in the darkness of our own speculations.

We see this clearly throughout the New Testament. Consider Romans 10:17: "Consequently, faith comes from hearing the message, and the message is heard through the word of Christ." This "word of Christ" is the great message of the gospel: that God has made us to know him, but that we have sinned and separated ourselves from him; that therefore God in his great love has come in the person of Jesus Christ, who has lived a perfect life, taking on our flesh and our infirmities; that he died on the cross specifically as a substitute for all of those who would ever turn to him and trust in him; that he has been raised by God from the dead as a testimony that God has accepted this sacrifice; and that he calls us now to repent and to trust in him, even as Abraham trusted in the Word of God as it came to him in Ur of the Chaldeans so many centuries ago.

Paul writes just before this, in Romans 10:9, "If you confess with your mouth, 'Jesus is Lord,' and believe in your heart that God raised him from the dead, you will be saved."

Trusting in and relying on the truth of God's raising Jesus Christ is the way to salvation, the way to inclusion in the people of God. And so we see, once again, that God has always created his people by speaking his Word. And his greatest Word is Christ. As the writer to the Hebrews began his letter, "In the past God spoke to our forefathers through the prophets at many times and in various ways, but in these last days he has spoken to us by his Son, whom he appointed heir of all things, and through whom he made the universe" (Heb. 1:1–2).

As believers living after the fall but before the heavenly city, we are in a time when faith is central, and so the Word must be central—because God's Holy Spirit creates his people by his Word! We can create a people by other means, and this is the great temptation of churches. We can create a people around a certain ethnicity. We can create a people around a fully graded choir program. We can find people who will get excited about a building project or a denominational identity. We can create a people around a series of care groups, where everyone feels loved and cared for. We can create a people around a community service project. We can create a people around social opportunities for young mothers or Caribbean cruises for singles. We can create a people around men's groups. We can even create a people around the personality of a preacher. And God can surely use all of these things. But in the final analysis, the people of God, the church of God, can only be created around the Word of God.[2]

2 See Mark Dever and Jamie Dunlop, *The Compelling Community: Where God's Power Makes a Church Attractive* (Wheaton, IL: Crossway, 2015).

Asked about his accomplishments as a Reformer, Martin Luther said, "I simply taught, preached, wrote God's Word: otherwise I did nothing. . . . The Word did it all."[3] The Word of God brings life.[4]

The Role of God's Word in Preaching

The most extended treatment in the New Testament of what the Christian gathering should be like is in 1 Corinthians 11–14. Paul's chief concern is well summarized in 14:26: "All of these must be done for the strengthening of the church." Throughout 1 Corinthians, this is Paul's standard for deciding what should be done in the congregation. It follows then, that such a standard of usefulness in edification should especially be applied to that which we have said is central to the Christian congregation—preaching. What preaching will most edify the church? The answer must certainly be teaching that exposes God's Word to God's people.

Certainly not all preaching is biblical. Do you have any doubt that expositional preaching should be the basic diet of preaching in your congregation? When God gave Moses instructions for the kings that would surely come in Israel, do you remember what God required of them? "When he takes the throne of his kingdom, he is to write for himself on a scroll a copy of this law, taken from that of the priests, who are Levites. It is to be with him, and he is to read it all the days of his life so that he may learn to revere the Lord his God and follow carefully all the words of this law and these decrees and not consider himself better than his brothers and turn from the law to the right or to the left" (Deut. 17:18–20). And what marks the righteous man in Psalm 1? "His delight is in the law of the Lord, / and on his law he meditates day and night" (1:2). This delight is echoed in stanza after

3 Martin Luther, *Sermons I*, ed. John W. Doberstein; vol. 51 of *Luther's Works, American Edition*, ed. Jaroslav Pelikan and Helmut T. Lehmann (Philadelphia: Fortress, 1966), 77.

4 For more on the trustworthiness of the Bible as God's Word, see Greg Gilbert, *Why Trust the Bible?* (Wheaton, IL: Crossway, 2015) or Michael J. Kruger, *Canon Revisited: Establishing the Origins and Authority of the New Testament Books* (Wheaton, IL: Crossway, 2012).

stanza of the great Psalm 119: "Seven times a day I praise you / for your righteous laws. . . . I obey your statutes, / for I love them greatly. . . . Your law is my delight" (119:164, 167, 174). Given this delight in God's Word, delivering that word is to be the wonderful burden of Christian preaching.[5]

Furthermore, we live in a literate age, where the printed word is familiar to us all and where God's Word has been chapterized and versified and translated and made readily available. Why would we *not* take advantage of that in our preaching? In earlier times, when preachers had few of these advantages, Chrysostom, Augustine, and others preached consecutive series of sermons through portions of Scripture. In his *Third Sermon: Lazarus and the Rich Man,* Chrysostom said, "I often tell you many days in advance the subject of what I am going to say, in order that you may take up the book in the intervening days, go over the whole passage, learn both what is said and what is left out, and so make your understanding more ready to learn when you hear what I will say afterwards."[6]

To cite a more recent example from my own city, Francis Grimké (1878–1928), pastor for fifty years of Fifteenth Street Presbyterian Church in Washington, DC, once said, "I have stuck close to the preaching of the word of God. From the beginning, and all along, I have felt that my mission was to preach the gospel, to expound the Bible as the Word of God."[7]

In holding to such a commitment to bring God's Word to God's people, pastors like Chrysostom and Grimké have followed in the footsteps of Moses, whom Jethro charged with teaching the people the law (see Ex. 18:19–20). And Moses was leading the way for Josiah, who "read in [the people's] hearing all the words of the Book of the Covenant, which had been found in the temple of the LORD" (2 Chron. 34:30). And Josiah was leading the way for Ezra and the returning

5 See Mark Dever's sermon on Psalm 119 "In Praise of God's Word," in *One Foundation Essays on the Sufficiency of Scripture* (Valencia, CA: Grace to You, 2019), 105–23.

6 John Chrysostom, *On Wealth and Poverty* (Yonkers, NY: St. Vladimir's Seminary Press, 1999), 58.

7 Francis Grimké, *Meditations on Preaching* (Madison, MS: Log College Press, 2018), 47.

Levites who "read from the Book of the Law of God, making it clear and giving the meaning so that the people could understand what was being read" (Neh. 8:8).

This pattern of making the teaching of God's Word central to the gathering of God's people continued into the time of Christ. The synagogues of Jesus's day would read through the Scriptures in lectionary cycles of a year or two. Readers of God's Word would make comments on the text, as Jesus did in Luke 4. Exactly how much the first churches were modeled after the synagogue meetings of the time is impossible to determine. But the expositional series that survive from Chrysostom and other earlier Christian preachers suggest that the consecutive, expositional pattern was widespread. So when John Calvin was called back from Strasbourg a few years after having been banished from Geneva, he picked up in his sermon series right where he left off, saying "I resumed the exposition at the place where I stopped: by doing so, I showed that I had been interrupted for a time, rather than resigned from my teaching office."[8]

The sermons (or summaries of sermons) in the New Testament are few in number, and they are concerned with the hearers' cultural setting—but even more fundamentally they are clearly rooted in the Scriptures. Of course, the early Christians lacked some of our advantages. They did not have the text of Scriptures available to be examined during the sermon, so the mechanics of expositional preaching would more often rely on mnemonic devices, like the repetition of the lectionary. Peter's sermon at Pentecost was substantially a meditation, exposition, and application of portions of Joel 2 and Psalms 16 and 110. The writer to the Hebrews also spends long sections instructing on Psalms 95 (chaps. 3–4) and 110 (chap. 7).

In all of this, we see that it is good to preach the truth; it is even better to preach in such a way that people can see where they can get the

8 John Calvin, *CO* 11:366, quoted in Mark Earngey, "*Soli Deo Gloria*: The Reformation of Worship," in *Reformation Worship*, eds. Jonathan Gibson and Mark Earngey (Greensboro, NC: New Growth Press, 2018), 31.

truth. To again quote Francis Grimké, "As a general thing, it is always best for a minister to take a text or portion of Scripture, and stick to it, endeavoring faithfully to get out of it all there is in it, or so much of it as he wishes to use at that particular time."[9] This is true whether the texts are from the Old Testament or the New, whether they are single verses or long passages. "In this way," Grimké continues, "there will be variety in his preaching and growth in his knowledge of the Word of God. Merely to make a text as a hook upon which to string a number of unconnected things is not a wise thing to do."[10]

The Role of God's Word in Sanctifying

We must also consider the role of God's Word in sanctifying us. The Word of God must be central to our lives as individuals and as a church because God's Spirit uses the Word to create faith in us and to make us grow. We won't explore this point as carefully as the last because we will deal with this more in coming chapters. But the Word's role in our growth is just as clear in Scripture. As Jesus replied to Satan, quoting from Deuteronomy, "Man does not live on bread alone, but on every word that comes from the mouth of God" (Matt. 4:4; quoting Deut. 8:3). We know also those famous words of the psalmist, "Your word is a lamp to my feet / and a light for my path" (Ps. 119:105).

When we look at the history of Israel and Judah in the Old Testament, we see the sanctifying power of God's Word again and again. During the reign of King Josiah, in the declining days of Judah (2 Chron. 34), the Law—the written Word of God—was rediscovered and read to him. Josiah's response was to tear his clothes in repentance and then to read the Word to the people. A national recovery came as God's Word went out. God uses his Word to sanctify his people and to make them more like himself.

This is what the Lord Jesus taught, too. In his high priestly prayer he prayed, "Sanctify them by the truth; your word is truth" (John 17:17).

9 Grimké, *Meditations on Preaching*, 88.

10 Grimké, *Meditations on Preaching*, 88.

And Paul wrote that "Christ loved the church and gave himself up for her to make her holy, cleansing her by the washing with water through the word" (Eph. 5:25–26). We need God's Word to be saved, but we also need it to continually challenge and shape us. His Word not only gives us life; it also gives us direction as it keeps molding and shaping us in the image of the God who is speaking to us.

At the time of the Reformation, the Roman Catholic Church had a Latin phrase that became something of a motto: *semper idem*. It means "always the same." Well, the Reformed churches, too, had a "semper" motto: *ecclesia reformata, semper reformanda secundum verbum Dei*. "The church reformed, always being reformed according to the Word of God." A healthy church is a church that hears the Word of God and continues to hear the Word of God. Such a church is composed of individual Christians who hear the Word of God and continue to hear the Word of God, always being refashioned and reshaped by it, constantly being washed in the Word and sanctified by God's truth.

For our own health, individually as Christians and corporately as a church, we must continue to be shaped in new and deeper ways by God's agenda in our lives, rather than by our own agendas. God makes us more like himself through his Word, washing over us, refreshing us, reshaping us. That brings us to a fourth important point.

The Role of the Preacher of God's Word

If you are looking for a good church, the role of the preacher of God's Word is the most important thing to consider. I don't care how friendly you think the church members are. I don't care how good you think the music is. Those things can change. But the congregation's commitment to the centrality of the Word coming from the front, from the preacher, the one specially gifted by God and called to that ministry, is the most important thing you can look for in a church.

Preachers are not called to preach what's popular according to the polls. People already know all that. What life does that bring? We're not called to preach merely moral exhortations or history lessons or social commentaries (though any of those things may be a part of good preaching). We are called to preach the Word of God to the church of God and to everyone in his creation. This is how God brings life. Each person who is reading this book—and I, the one who has written it—is flawed and has faults and has sinned against God. And the terrible thing about our fallen natures is that we are greedy for ways to justify our sins against God. Every single one of us wants to know how we can defend ourselves against God's charges. Therefore we desperately need to hear God's Word brought honestly to us, so that we don't just hear what we want to hear but rather what God has actually said.

All of this is important, remember, because God's Holy Spirit creates his people by his Word.

This is why Paul told Timothy to "form a committee." Right? Of course not! "Take a survey"? No! Paul never told anyone to take a survey. "Spend yourself in visiting"? "Read a book"? No! Paul never told young Timothy to do any of those things.

Paul told Timothy, straight and clear, to "preach the word" (2 Tim. 4:2). This is the great imperative. This is why the apostles earlier had determined that, even though there were problems with the equitable distribution of financial aid in Jerusalem, the church would have to find others to solve their problems, because: "We . . . will give our attention to prayer and the ministry of the word" (Acts 6:3–4). Why this priority? Because this Word is "the word of life" (Phil. 2:16). The great task of the preacher is to "hold out the word of life" to people who need it for their souls.

Today some critics suggest that we need a less rational, more artistic, less authoritarian and elitist, more communal and participatory way of communicating God's truth than this ancient method of one person standing up front and talking in a monologue to others. We need video clips, they say, and dialogues and liturgical dance. And yet there's something right and good about this ancient method that makes it appropriate, perhaps even especially appropriate, for our culture today. In our isolatingly subjectivist culture where everyone is just into their own thing, in this anti-authority culture where everyone is confused and confusing, it is appropriate for us to gather together and listen to one who is standing in the place of God, giving his Word to us as we contribute nothing to it other than hearing and heeding it. There is an important symbol in this process in and of itself. The sermon as monologue—one person speaking with others sitting with mouths closed and ears open—is both an accurate and a powerful symbol of our spiritual state. One person speaking God's Word—reading it and explaining it, illustrating and applying it for the benefit of the hearers—is a depiction of God's self-disclosure and our salvation being a gift.

Of course there will come a day when faith will give way to sight and sermons will be no more. And let me tell you there is no one who looks forward to that more than I and most of my fellow preachers. When you don't need faith anymore because you can see the Lord—that's the climax of the Bible. "They will see his face" (Rev. 22:4). At that point this old cane of faith can be cast aside as we run and see him with our own eyes.

But we're not there yet. We're still laboring under the results of the sins of our first parents and of our own sins. On that day, faith will finally give way to sight, but for now we are in a different time—but by God's grace this is not a time of total despair. He gives us his Word and he gives us faith. We are in a day of faith. And so, like our first parents before us, like Noah and Abraham, the Israelites and the ancient apostles, we rely on God's Word.

What does all this mean for our churches? The preaching of the Word must be absolutely central. Sound, expositional preaching is often the fountainhead of growth in a church. Let a good expositional ministry be established, and watch what happens. Forget what the experts say. Watch hungry people have their lives transformed as the living God speaks to them through the power of his Word. As it was in Martin

Luther's own experience, such careful attention to God's Word is the way to salvation and is often the beginning of reformation. As Paul said, "Since in the wisdom of God the world through its wisdom did not know him, God was pleased through the foolishness of what was preached to save those who believe" (1 Cor. 1:21).

This doesn't mean that such a ministry will always be popular and blessed with increasing numbers of people hearing and being baptized. But it does mean that such a ministry will always be right. And it will feed God's children with the food they need. "Man does not live on bread alone but on every word that comes from the mouth of the Lord" (Deut. 8:3).

Are you in a job where you get a lot of emails? Some of those emails you know you don't ever have to reply to. Some of them you know you can deal with sometime in the next week or month. But some of those emails are of such a nature that you look at the message and know you need to respond right away. What if the Lord himself emailed you? I think you would snap right to it. We say that we believe the Bible is actually God's Word, God speaking to us, and yet so often we ignore it and set it aside and refuse to give time to thinking about it. Instead, our lives are absorbed by things such as going out to dinner with a friend, watching Netflix, or reading books other than the Bible. None of those things are bad. But what does it mean when we say that the Bible is the Word of God? It means that we must hear it and heed it.

In these strange days, even people who say that the Bible is the Word of God don't intend to follow it. It is not surprising, then, to hear that 35 percent of self-professed born-again Christians say they are still searching for the meaning of life—the very same percentage as non-Christians. What good does it do you to think you have the Word of God but refuse to give it any attention, read it, pray over it, or put your life under it? Preaching should have a certain content, a certain transparency of form. The people listening to preaching should know they are hearing God's Word preached. Church members should encourage preachers to spend time studying and preparing their sermons;

they should pray for their pastors in this, and look for such preaching, thanking God for it when it comes. It is good to preach the truth, and to preach it in such a way that people can see where the truth is coming from. That, more than anything else, is what Christians need.

So what makes a really good church? Even more than parking and pews and greetings and programs and nursery and music and all the things that I asked you about at the beginning of this chapter, even more than the preacher, it is what is preached—the Word of God. Because "man does not live on bread alone, but on every word that comes from the mouth of God" (Matt. 4:4).

Other Resources

- For group study: *Hearing God's Word: Expositional Preaching* (2012), by Bobby Jamieson, a six-week inductive Bible study.
- For deeper study: *Preach: Theology Meets Practice* (2012), by Mark Dever and Greg Gilbert.
- For further meditation: *Word-Centered Church: How Scripture Brings Life and Growth to God's People* (2017), by Jonathan Leeman.
- See also C. H. Spurgeon, *Lectures to My Students* (1869); D. Martyn Lloyd-Jones, *Preaching and Preachers* (1971); John Stott, *Between Two Worlds: The Challenge of Preaching Today* (1982); and David R. Helm, *Expositional Preaching: How We Speak God's Word Today* (2014).

Mark Two

Gospel Doctrine

I ONCE MADE A STATEMENT in a doctoral seminar about God. Bill, a student, responded politely but firmly that he liked to think of God differently. For several minutes Bill painted a picture of a friendly deity. He said that he liked to think of God as wise, but not meddling; compassionate, but not overpowering; resourceful, but never interrupting. After going on for a bit, he concluded, "This is how I like to think of God."

My reply was perhaps somewhat sharper than it should have been. "Thank you, Bill," I said, "for telling us so much about *yourself*, but we are concerned to know what God is really like, not simply about our own desires. Why would we ever assume that merely because we want something to be a certain way, it therefore must be that way?"

The seminar went silent for a moment. The students were taking in my potential breach of politeness, but they were also considering my point. Then we got on with our discussion about the nature and character of God as revealed in the Bible.

When you hear the word *God*, what do you think of? I am not asking how you *like* to think of God, but how, for instance, do you reconcile in your mind the warm and loving God of Christmas with the God of the final judgment? To some, this whole discussion may sound nonsensical. Why expend any energy at all over what various people believe about an invisible being? But Christians know that it is important to understand what God is like.

Today people *believe* to be true simply what they *desire* to be true. Long-held Christian beliefs about everything from the nature of God to morality are being reshaped or even jettisoned in the name of making Christianity more relevant, more palatable, and more acceptable to today's hearer. B. B. Warfield warned against this when he wrote, "It is not a matter of small importance for the servant of Christ to begin to seek to please men in the gospel which he offers them. Doing so, he ceases to be Christ's servant, performing his will; and becomes the slave of men. . . . So doing, he is no longer the teacher of the truth to men, but the learner of falsehood from men."[1]

Does all this seem unimportant to you? How relevant are your own beliefs to your daily life? When you last sat in church, how much did you examine the words of the prayers you heard? How much did you think about the words of the songs you sang? Or how about the words you heard from Scripture? Does it really matter to you if what you said or sang in church was true?

How much does it really matter, anyway? If I attend church, am friendly, and feel encouraged, and if I give my time to being there and even give my money, how much does it really matter if, in my heart of hearts, I really don't believe what the people around me say, and maybe even what I say? How important are religious beliefs?

According to the Bible, the truth about how we should live is not just about how we treat each other. The most important things about us are what we know and believe to be true about God. It's what we know and believe about him that determines how we relate to him, and then how we in turn relate to one another. Another way to say this is that according to the Bible, theology is really important. In our churches, we need to be clear about the good news that saves us. Christianity is all about news. It's the good news—the best news the world has ever

1 B. B. Warfield, "The Dogmatic Spirit," in *Selected Shorter Writings of Benjamin B. Warfield*, ed. John E. Meeter, 2 vols. (Nutley, NJ: P&R, 1970), 2:666.

heard. And yet this news is too often scrambled and confused. Too often it becomes a thin veneer spread lightly over our culture's values, being shaped and formed to the contours of our culture rather than to the truth about God.

In this chapter I want to make a simple point. Expositional preaching serves a church and helps to make it more healthy only if what is preached is true. What is preached must truly be what the Bible says. For example, some evangelical churches today say that homosexuality is fine. Many of them even claim to preach expositionally. But expositional preaching is preaching that teaches what the Bible actually says. As a sinner who deserves hell and is saved only by God's grace, I have an interest in hearing when and what the Bible speaks against me. The last thing I need is a church that flatters me. I am already inclined toward self-flattery. I need a church that will clearly tell me, "Do not deceive yourself!" The least valuable thing in the world is a church that echoes what I already think. What we need today more than ever are churches that preach the truth about God and the gospel.

This idea of the good news wasn't some later Christian packaging of Christianity. Jesus himself talked about the good news, reaching back to the language of Isaiah from hundreds of years earlier (Isa. 52:7; 61:1). However Jesus may have expressed it in Aramaic, the way his followers heard and remembered the good news was with the Greek word *evangel*, which literally means "good news" or "gospel."

So what is the gospel? The good news is the truth that the one and only God, who is holy, has made us in his image to know him. But we have sinned and cut ourselves off from him. In his great love, God became a man in Jesus, lived a perfect life, and died on the cross, thus fulfilling the law in himself and taking on himself the punishment for the sins of all those who would ever turn from their sins and trust in him. All of those sins he bore as a sacrifice. He rose again from the dead, ascended to heaven, and presented his completed work to his heavenly Father, who accepted Christ's sacrifice, thus declaring his wrath against all of his own people exhausted. God now sends out his Spirit to call us through this message of repentance and faith to trust in Christ alone for our forgiveness. If we repent of our sins and trust in Christ only, then we are born again into a new life, an eternal life with God. That is the good news. This is far from being something that Christians later invented; when we read the Gospels, we see that this is exactly what Jesus taught. And this is far from being a departure from anything taught before; when we read the Prophets and the Law, we find that this is what was being assembled and prefigured for 1,500 years in the history of the people of Israel.

All of this makes sense when it is placed in the context of the whole Bible. A few years ago, I visited my favorite building in the world: King's College Chapel in Cambridge, England. It is a beautiful example of fifteenth-century Gothic architecture, with stained glass windows twenty times as large as those of Capitol Hill Baptist Church and four hundred years older. They are the finest collection of Renaissance stained glass in the world. During World War II the stained glass panels were removed from the windows to protect them from the bombings. (The Brits did not know that Hitler had given instructions not to bomb Cambridge.) These huge panels were hidden in barns and places in the ground in East Anglia. After the war the glass was reinstalled in the chapel. During the reconstruction, large black drapes covered the building, both to protect the glass and the workmen and to cover the project until it was completed. When the chapel was ready, students gathered in the main courtyard and placed spotlights inside the chapel. That night they dropped the curtains and turned on the spotlights, revealing these magnificent windows for the first time since the beginning of the war.

In the same way, the Old Testament is the floodlight shedding light on the glories of the New Testament. That effect of light coming through those stained glass windows is like the experience of understanding the Old Testament and then coming to the New. While it is possible to be a Christian who mainly reads the New Testament, this will enable you to see only the basic pictures in the window. But if you give time to understanding the whole big picture of the Bible, you will find that understanding the Old Testament will flood the New with deeper meaning. Suddenly, you will begin to see even more of the surprising details and the amazing intricacy of God's plan. And the gospel will become deeper, more meaningful, and sweeter to you.

That is why biblical theology and the gospel fit together. Biblical theology is the theology of the Bible, particularly as it is considered in the sweep of its history. Biblical doctrine is gospel doctrine.

What are the main lines of the great story of the Bible? If we can hear and see those main lines more clearly—if we have a framework in mind—then we will understand the God of the Bible more clearly, and especially the good news he gives to us in Jesus. There are many ways this can be done. One of the simplest, I think, is the way I explained the Bible to a Jewish friend. He had read some of the Hebrew Scriptures but nothing of the New Testament. So I said, "The Scriptures may likely seem like a bunch of disconnected books to you, but did you know that they actually have one main message?" He seemed interested, so I explained further: "The Scriptures are about the exodus." I talked with him about how the exodus was central to the Old Testament and then explained how, as a Christian, I understand that the New Testament, which might seem like twenty-seven disconnected books, is actually about one main thing: the cross. And the whole purpose of the exodus was to point to the cross. The exodus was a prefigurement of the deliverance that God would accomplish through Christ.

Just from this one example, do you see how understanding the big picture of the Bible enables you to better understand and explain the gospel? When you see the big picture, the Bible goes from being a confusing series of unrelated events that you are never going to be able to remember, to suddenly reflecting the glorious radiance of the gospel, like those stained glass windows in England.

Another helpful way we can summarize the main storyline of the Bible is by using just five words. The Bible teaches us that God is *creating*; he is *holy*; he is *faithful*; he is *loving*; and he is *sovereign*. We will consider how the Bible presents each of these truths. Pay attention to the difference it would make if God were not any of these five things. Doing so will help you recognize afresh how important theology really is.

The God of the Bible Is a Creating God

First, beginning where the Bible begins, we see that God is a creating God. He creates the world, and he creates a special people in the world.

The Bible is sometimes represented as a collection of noble ethical sentiments. But when people describe it like that, I can only assume they have never read it. If you have read the Bible at all, you know that it is full of history. The Bible is a long story about what goes on with God and the world he has made. I know that some people are bored by history the minute you mention the word. But the story of the Bible is anything but boring. It is an amazing story! It begins with nothing. And then nothing becomes something. That's the most amazing thing ever conceived of! Then, after nothing has become something, God makes the first inanimate creation. After that then come living beings, as God makes man and woman in his own image. We find the account of the garden of Eden and then the fall. And then things go downhill. It is all disintegration, from Cain down to Noah. Then comes the flood, and after Noah there is disintegration again, down to the time of the Tower of Babel.

Then God calls Abraham. And that is where the story of the Bible, in a sense, really begins—the very special story of God creating a particular people for himself. After a brief time of prosperity, Israel falls into centuries of slavery, until the exodus, when they are led out of slavery, are given the Law, and enter the Promised Land.

There is the time of confusion under the judges, and then the kingdom is established under Saul and David. David's son Solomon takes the throne upon David's death, and then Solomon's son Rehoboam takes the throne. Next we find the nation divided into two, the northern kingdom and the southern kingdom. Idolatry becomes more and more common. God through the Assyrians destroys the northern kingdom of Israel in 722 BC and then destroys the southern kingdom of Judah through the Babylonians a little more than a century later. The Hebrews are exiled to Babylon for several decades, until they return to Judah and rebuild Jerusalem and the temple.

And that's where the Old Testament ends, with the story of this remnant of Israelites—needy, pitiful, reduced to complete, utter dependence on God. That is the story of the Old Testament. It is not a disembodied theology about God or a list of philosophical ideas. It is a specific, earthy revelation of who God is and what he is like.

You might know what it's like to get a résumé from a prospective employee. It is one thing to look at a résumé; it is another thing to actually work with a person. That's why prospective employers will call the references—to hear what it is like to actually interact with this person. In the Old Testament, God hasn't just sent us a résumé of some abstract truths about himself. No, we have an account of what it is like to actually live with God, what it is like to know and interact with him. In this history, we see much of what it means to be God's people, and we see much of what God is like.

The history recorded in the Bible shows us very plainly that God is both a creating God and an electing God. Every bit as much as God's creating this world, his choosing some out of it reveals God to be the unique initiator and beginner of life, and of our new life in Christ. Even if we cannot fully understand everything about this truth, we cannot deny that this is what the Bible teaches. It may have implications that we don't fully understand, but it is important. If we know that our salvation ultimately comes from God rather than from ourselves, then that knowledge affects how we understand God. It affects how we understand ourselves. It even affects how we understand our churches.

We must acknowledge that God is the great initiator, the great giver, the Creator of the world, the Creator of his people, the author of our faith. That is what God is like. That is who God is.

We especially see God as Creator in the gospel because he initiates. Just as God spoke the world into being and re-created his people by calling Abram (Gen. 12), God also called his people into existence by calling Moses (Ex. 4) and then taking the nation of Israel as his special people at Mount Sinai (Ex. 20). We see a dramatic picture of God creating life in the vision of the valley of dry bones in Ezekiel 37. And all of that prepares us for the coming of the Word made flesh in the incarnation of the Son of God, Jesus (John 1). So is it any surprise that it is the Word in us that gives us new life by creating faith in him (Rom. 10:17)?

Christians are the objects of God's special re-creating work! We are born again by his Spirit (John 3), living a new life (Rom. 6) worthy of the kingdom (1 Thess. 2:12), shining like stars (Phil. 2:15). We are even said to be colaborers with God (1 Cor. 3:9).

In the most profound sense, the gospel is not something that we do but something that we proclaim. And the good news we proclaim is not about what we're doing; it's about what God has done, is doing, and will continue to do. We must know that God has given us new life through Christ.

The God of the Bible Is a Holy God

If we are to understand the whole story of the Bible, then we must not only understand that God is a creating God, but we must also understand that this creating God is not morally indifferent. Some view God to be like a clockmaker: he built the clock, wound it up, and then walked off and let it run. But when you read the pages of the Bible, you see a God who has a passion for holiness. He is completely good. Period. God has never done anything wrong. If you look for anything wrong with God, you will come up empty. His holiness shows itself in his love, in his righteousness, and in his truthfulness. There is no defect in God's character. He is morally pure and perfect. And he is always, without question, just. Even his perfect knowledge of everything reflects his holiness, his perfection. All of our best attributes are dim reflections of God's eternal and complete holiness. All of his attributes—his love and faithfulness, his kindness and wisdom—reflect his holiness, his utter goodness.

Yet the very fact that God is perfectly good makes the whole story of the Bible more complicated—and surprising—because we are not. This is where the Bible is so much smarter than the secular college you may have gone to. University campuses today are populated by professors who are not too adept at understanding human reality. They either think that people are basically good and just need to be tinkered with a little to function properly, or they are quite cynical and think that people are basically bad. But those are at best "one-eyed" ways to look at the world God has made. To know the truth about ourselves and the world God has made, we need to know the Bible. It is a lot smarter than most college professors.

The truth is that God is holy and we are not. We need to know this. We need to know the good that we should do and the bad that we should not do. If we don't, we will have a rude awakening at death. God does not take a casual attitude toward sin. God cares about what the people made in his image are advertising him to be like. Yes, all seven billion people who are currently drawing breath on this planet are advertising something about God. All of us, in one way or another, are lying about God. That is why we need something more than just a book of laws or a prophet. We need a Savior. God shows us in his holiness that we are sinful. And our sins reveal that something deeper is going on in us than simply individual sins. Our sins reveal that something is morally broken in our nature, our very self.

According to the Bible, God has not merely created us, but he jealously loves us. He wants all of us. When we think that we can disregard him, simply setting him and his ways aside when it suits us, it reveals that we have not understood the nature of our relationship with God at all. The way we relate to God is as a subject to a Lord, as a son to a father. He is the one who has made us, the one we can trust completely.

We cannot claim to be believers and yet knowingly, repeatedly, and happily break his law. If I were to knowingly, repeatedly, and happily fail to do things I tell my wife I will do, then our relationship would be harmed. If that is true on a human level in marriage, how much more so in our relationship with the God who made us and therefore deserves so much more from us? We cannot choose to only selectively obey the God who deserves our entire allegiance without it indicting our professed relationship to him. It shows that we are not relating to him in love. But this is in fact the state we find ourselves in. We not only *feel* guilt, but we *are* guilty before him. We not only *feel* conflicted in ourselves, but we actually are in conflict with God. We break God's laws again and again because, as Paul reminds us, we are dead in our sins and transgressions (Eph. 2). The New Testament book of Romans begins with an argument about this dilemma, concluding in chapter 3 by exclaiming,

> What shall we conclude then? Are we any better? Not at all! We have already made the charge that Jews and Gentiles alike are all under sin. As it is written:
>
> "There is no one righteous, not even one;"
>
> . . . Now we know that whatever the law says, it says to those who are under the law, so that every mouth may be silenced and the whole world held accountable to God. Therefore no one will be declared righteous in his sight by observing the law; rather, through the law we become conscious of sin. (Rom. 3:9–10, 19–20)

Now, all of this may seem much too grim to have anything to do with something called the "good news." But an accurate understanding of where you are is essential to getting to where you need to be. You know this from using your phone for directions. Your phone can only help you get to where you want to be if it knows your present location. You have to start by letting the app know your present location. That's how the journey starts. The same is true of our Christian life. Knowing the intended destination is of no use if you do not know your current location morally before God.

One of the early stages of becoming a Christian involves beginning to realize that my problem fundamentally is not that I have messed up my own life or that I have failed to realize my own potential, but that I have sinned, not primarily against myself or even against someone else, but against God. And because of that, I begin to realize that I am myself rightly the object of God's wrath, of his judgment. I deserve death, hell, separation from God, spiritual alienation from him, and even his active punishment now and forever.

At this point I need to resolve to keep reading the Bible, because it is this lava-meets-the-water combination of God encountering our sin that creates the most surprising and breathtaking views of God's character in the whole Bible.

It is in God's holiness that we discover our need for atonement, and it is in God's holiness that we find God able to meet that need. The Old Testament helps us here. Our English word *atonement* literally means "at-one-ment." Two parties who were separated are brought together. Atonement is needed because we need to be reconciled to—become at one with—this holy God. And here we come to the deepest part of the Bible's story, *the gospel*, the good news. And this good news is centrally concerned with the idea of *sacrifice*. In the Old Testament atonement is linked with sacrifice. Sacrifice is the way God provides for us to make reparation and to restore our relationship with him. We're not pitifully trying to placate some volcano, like something we've seen in a movie. It isn't like that at all. The Old Testament idea of sacrifice does not involve human efforts to win God's favor. Rather, it is God's own revelation to his people of how we can come to know him, of how we can find our way to him despite our sin.

This idea of sacrifice is innate in the Bible. Cain and Abel offered sacrifices. When God takes the people of Israel out of Egypt, the entire exodus centers on the sacrifice of the Passover lamb (Ex. 12). It was to be without defect, and it was to be slaughtered. Its blood was to mark the houses God would save. The lives of the firstborn (who represented the whole family) would be required. God said, "When I see the blood . . ." (Ex. 12:13). The object of this sacrifice was clearly God's own satisfaction. The Old Testament sacrifices showed something of the seriousness of sin; it costs life. All the offerings had to be voluntary and costly, from the offerer's own property. What was God doing there? Perhaps God was implanting in his people's minds the idea of the innocent being given in place of the guilty.

We see further symbolism in God's design of the temple. Access to the Holy of Holies was restricted, showing that sin hinders access to a holy God, purification is needed, and sin is so serious that death is required to atone for it. Salvation and forgiveness are costly.

We see this especially in the Day of Atonement, the one day of fasting prescribed for all of Israel. The Day of Atonement centered on a special sin offering for the whole nation. It served as a reminder that all the other regular sin offerings throughout the year did not completely atone for sin (see Lev. 16). The high priest, as representative of the people, entered the Holy of Holies one day of the year for access to God because this atonement had to be made in the very presence of God. The high priest bore the blood of the goat, the sin offering (see Heb. 9:7). First he made atonement for himself—because he himself had to be clean—and then he made atonement for the people. And when he brought that blood into the Holy of Holies, who could see it? Only God. The blood was shed *for God.* The point of this sacrifice, the point of the atonement, was for God to be reconciled to his people.

It is noteworthy that this sacrifice of atonement was repeated annually. You see, other nations would go into frenzies of sacrifices whenever they thought things were going badly for them. But God had taught Israel that regardless of how good or how bad their circumstances, they were to make this sacrifice annually. They needed to be reminded that they were continuously in a state of sin, that sin separates people from God, that they could never offer a perfect sacrifice, and that God himself provides the way of access to him as he forgives our sins. God possessing holiness means sinners need atonement; but God giving holiness means sinners receive atonement.

What does all this mean for us today? Are we as bad as the people in the Old Testament must have been to require this intricate system of sacrifices? What kind of people are we? How you answer that question will determine what kind of church you set up. If you think people are basically good, then a church is simply a place where we seek encouragement or perhaps the enhancement of our self-esteem. We need simply to take the good that's in us and build on it. However, if you think that something is radically wrong with us humans—if you think that we are spiritually dead, guilty before God, separated from him, and under his judgment and wrath—then you are going to build a very different kind of church. You're going to build a church where you pray for God to move supernaturally, where the gospel is presented clearly, and where people are regularly called to believe in Christ. Churches need to call people not merely to improve but to repent, and not to believe in ourselves but to believe in Christ!

We should never try to change the gospel to make it more pleasant. The God of the Bible is a holy God, and no "gospel" that ignores God's holiness is the true gospel.

The God of the Bible Is a Faithful God

God is a creating God and a holy God. He is also a faithful God. Some may find it surprising that the focus of each New Testament Gospel's account of the life of Christ is his death. That death was God's certainty that he was effectively dealing with the claims of both his love and his justice. So Christ isn't just our friend. To call him that as his supreme title is to damn him with "faint praise." Christ is our friend, but he is so much more. By his death on the cross, Christ has become the Lamb that was slain for us, our Redeemer, the one who has made peace between us and God, who has taken on our guilt, who has conquered death, and who has assuaged the well-deserved wrath of God. And with each title, the promises God made to his people in the Old Testament are fulfilled in the New.

We find one such title in Exodus 34:6–7, where the Lord is speaking to Moses. What he says is amazing, especially when we consider that God is the great Creator who made the world and that our sin ruptured his creation. The Lord reveals himself and his character: "The Lord, the Lord, the compassionate and gracious God, slow to anger, abounding in love and faithfulness, maintaining love to thousands, and forgiving wickedness, rebellion and sin. Yet he does not leave the guilty unpunished." That last sentence might not seem to fit with the previous. How can the Lord be "abounding in love and faithfulness, maintaining love to thousands, and forgiving wickedness, rebellion and sin" and yet "he does not leave the guilty unpunished"?

How can he both "forgive wickedness" and "not leave the guilty unpunished"? How can God be faithful to such contradictory promises? The riddle of the Old Testament is the riddle of our lives, isn't it? How could God be both of these to us? The answer to that mystery wasn't found in these Israelites, but in God and his promise—particularly in the person he promised to send. In the Old Testament, hope required an atoning sacrifice, a propitiation to assuage the righteous wrath of God. It required a substitution of suffering and death on the part of the innocent for the deserved punishment of the guilty. And it seemed to require some relationship between the offerer and the victim.

In the time of Christ, people were not wondering whether or not a Messiah would come. They took that for granted. You can tell by the early chapters of each of the Gospels that people were looking for a Messiah. No, the question everyone was asking was, How will God fulfill his promises? What will this Messiah be like? The Lord had said through Moses that he would raise up a prophet (see Deut. 18:15–19). But when this prophet came, he took everyone by surprise, because he—Jesus—presented himself not just as the fulfillment of the kingly prophecies of the Messiah (which the people were all quite comfortable with) but as the fulfillment of the suffering one, as one who came to be rejected and to suffer in the place of his people. Jesus brought together the prophecies about the Messiah as King with other prophecies about the Messiah as the one who would suffer in the place of his people. He brought those two strands of prophecy together. Both the Old and the New Testaments teach us that this kingly, suffering Messiah is our only hope. Jesus is the answer to the riddle of Exodus 34. He reveals how God can forgive our wickedness while at the same time punishing the guilty.

At the heart of understanding Jesus Christ is understanding what he came to do. He came as the one by whom you and I can have a restored relationship with God. Where Adam and Israel had failed and been unfaithful, and where we have each failed, Jesus was faithful, enduring temptations without sin. Here is the Prophet promised by Moses, the King prefigured by David, and even the divine "son of man" of Daniel 7. These all had come in Jesus of Nazareth. He was the Word of God made flesh. He was the Lamb of God, slain for the sins of his people. All of those promises were faithfully fulfilled in Jesus according to God's promise.

So we see that our creating God and our holy God is also an amazingly faithful God. The God of the Bible is also a loving God.

The God of the Bible Is a Loving God

Even many non-Christians can quote from memory "God is love" (1 John 4:8). But by itself, "God is love" is not a great summary of the Bible. It is not a great summary of the gospel. We need to press further and ask, What is God's love like?

God's love is closely tied to his faithfulness. He is the God of love who has a special love for his covenant people. God has made us to reflect his image. He has made us to be in covenant with him. So how could the Lord "forgive wickedness" and yet "not leave the guilty unpunished"? The answer, of course, is found in Jesus. He is the one who, though not guilty himself, took on our guilt and was punished for it. This is what Jesus taught his disciples in Luke 24: "Beginning with Moses and all the Prophets, he explained to them what was said in all the Scriptures concerning himself. . . . Then he opened their minds so they could understand the Scriptures. He told them, 'This is what is written: The Christ will suffer and rise from the dead on the third day, and repentance and forgiveness of sins will be preached in his name to all nations, beginning at Jerusalem'" (Luke 24:27, 45–47).

"This is what is written," this is what the Lord had prophesied—that he would show his love to his people in this particular way. Remember the prophecies from Isaiah 53:

> Surely he took up our infirmities
>   and carried our sorrows,
> yet we considered him stricken by God,
>   smitten by him, and afflicted.
> But he was pierced for our transgressions,
>   he was crushed for our iniquities;
> the punishment that brought us peace was upon him,
>   and by his wounds we are healed.
> We all, like sheep, have gone astray,
>   each of us has turned to his own way;
> and the LORD has laid on him
>   the iniquity of us all. (Isa. 53:4–6)

This is what Christ did in his love! As he taught his disciples, "The Son of Man did not come to be served, but to serve, and to give his life as a ransom for many" (Mark 10:45).

Paul, too, described Christ Jesus as the one "who, being in very nature God, / did not consider equality with God something to be grasped, / but made himself nothing, / taking the very nature of a servant, / being made in human likeness. / And being found in appearance as a man, / he humbled himself / and became obedient to death— / even death on a cross!" (Phil. 2:6–8). And on the third day he rose again! As Peter said, "But God raised him from the dead, freeing him from the agony of death, because it was impossible for death to keep its hold on him" (Acts 2:24).

In the New Testament then, we find that God faithfully keeps all of his promises because of his covenant love for his people. And if we are Christians today, it is because God continues to keep those promises. Christ takes away our sins and gives us his righteousness instead.

What does it mean to become a part of God's covenant people, to be a Christian? What happens when someone becomes a Christian? Is it simply a matter of making a decision? Is it simply a matter of praying a prayer? Do we need to repent? Do we need to believe? If we do repent and believe, how is it that we're able to do that—if we're as bad as Scripture says we are? If we are dead in our sins and transgressions, how do we all of a sudden repent and believe?

The Relationship between Faith and Repentance

According to the New Testament, we repent of our sins and we trust in Christ. That is why we often find repentance and belief mentioned together in the New Testament. As Paul was meeting with the leaders of the church in Ephesus, he summarized the message he had preached in this way: "I have declared to both Jews and Greeks that they must turn to God in repentance and have faith in our Lord Jesus" (Acts 20:21). This is the message we see clearly throughout the New Testament: repent of sins and trust in Christ. That is the basic message that Jesus gave, that his disciples gave, and that every true church around the world gives. Once you have heard the truth about your sin and God's holiness, about his love in sending Christ, and about Christ's death and resurrection for our justification, then you are called to respond.

And what is the prescribed response to this message of Christ's love for us—of his giving himself for us as a sacrifice on the cross in the place of all of us who would turn to him in trust? Is it to walk down an aisle? Is it to fill out a card or to lift up a hand? Is it to make an appointment with a preacher or to decide to be baptized and join the church? While any of those things may be involved, none of them necessarily is. The response to the good news—the message that Paul preached and other Christians preached throughout the New Testament—is to repent and believe.[2] As instructed by the first words of Jesus recorded in Mark's Gospel, our response is to "repent and believe the good news!" (Mark 1:15). What is repentance? It is simply turning from our sin. To repent is to recognize that I'm a sinner and to renounce that sin.

Along with repentance comes belief, faith. Once we honestly think that what the gospel says is true, we must begin fully relying on Christ for salvation. We must come to grips with the fact that we are unable to satisfy God's demands on us no matter how morally we live. We don't trust a little in ourselves and a little in God; we must rely on God fully, to trust in Christ alone for our salvation.

True belief and full reliance on God make a difference. This belief demands not only faith but also repentance; it demands that our lives actually change. Repentance and faith are two sides of the same coin. It is not as though you can have the basic model (belief) and then, if you really want to get holy at some later time, you can start adding some repentance to it. No, that's an anti-Bible message. *Repent* is what you do when you begin thinking rightly about God and yourself—belief without this kind of change is counterfeit. Repentance is change rooted in a deep, supernaturally given trust in our good God. As John wrote, "This is love: not that we loved God, but that he loved us and sent his Son as an atoning sacrifice for our sins. . . . We love because he first loved us" (1 John 4:10, 19).

The God of the Bible is a God of amazing love!

The God of the Bible Is a Sovereign God

Finally, we find that God is a sovereign God and that, in his sovereignty, all of creation is to be involved in his renewing love. The prayer that Jesus taught his disciples roots their faith firmly in the rule and reign of God—whose will should be done. "Your kingdom come, your will be done on earth as it is in heaven" (Matt. 6:10). Have you ever wondered what that means?

2 See Greg Gilbert, "What Is (and Isn't) the Gospel" (sermon, Together for the Gospel, Louisville, KY, 2020), https://t4g.org/resources/greg-gilbert/what-is-and-isnt-the-gospel/.

Some people limit their hopes very deliberately to today, to things that they can promise and fulfill in their own power and strength—things that they know they can be certain of. They don't want to put their hearts on anything else. They want to be careful and guarded with their hearts. They've been burned too many times. They're not going to put their trust in some promise whose fulfillment they cannot guarantee themselves.

But Christianity has never been like that. We Christians have always had a hope that extends beyond ourselves and exceeds what we could ever do in our own power. Peter wrote, "We are looking forward to a new heaven and a new earth, the home of righteousness" (2 Pet. 3:13). This points to the fulfillment of that first and final hope of the Bible—the hope of the whole world being put right, as God's sovereign plan extends from Christ to his covenant people to creation itself.

We find this hope at the very end of the Bible. The book of Revelation picks up the prophetic tradition of the Old Testament, but with some changes. Revelation is presented as the consummation of God's sovereign plan to have a people in right relationship with himself. As the church militant becomes the church triumphant, the heavens and the earth are re-created (see Rev. 21:1–4; 21:22–22:5). We see the climax of the fulfillment of all of God's promises to his people. The holiness of God's people is finally complete. Finally God's people are truly holy and with him. The garden of Eden is restored. The presence of God is once again with his people. The Holy City (Rev. 21:2) is in the shape of a cube, like the Holy of Holies in the Old Testament, where God's presence was. But now the whole world becomes the Holy of Holies, an eternal garden home filled with God's presence and including all of his people, from all times and places.

This is the great news that Christians have to offer. This is our vision of the future—not because we thought it up or because some committee somewhere came up with it. Not because it's simply what we wish to be the case, like my friend and student Bill, whom I mentioned at the beginning of this chapter, but because this is what God has revealed.

In light of these promises for the future, the present is a time of *waiting.* This is the natural posture of the Christian: a riveted, expectant, looking to God while anticipating that he will fulfill all of his promises. We know he has already fulfilled some of them, and like a kid on Christmas morning, we are excited for the fulfillment of the rest of them. In our waiting time, it is appropriate that the New Testament closes with the book of Revelation. Revelation was not written by someone who was on top of the world. It was written by an old man whose life was just about over. John was in exile, utterly desperate and dependent, with no friends around him. Yet he was full of hope in a sovereign God because he knew that regardless of whoever sat on the world's thrones, they did not finally decide what would happen in the world. He knew that there was a God in heaven who would bring to fulfillment all of his promises. John could sit on the island of Patmos full of hope, because he knew what this God was like. He is the highest authority, the God who has revealed himself to his people as the Lord of lords, the sovereign God.

This kind of biblical theology is practical. It makes a difference. God's promise to fill the earth with the knowledge of its Creator would be kept in his new creation. The God of the Bible makes promises, and the God of the Bible sovereignly keeps them.

Do you see the importance of this? As Christians, we need to know that God will continue to care for us, and that his continuing care is based not on our faithfulness but on his. It may be exciting for a little while to run around pretending that the world is some great spiritual laser-tag contest between the forces of darkness and the forces of light. And certainly there are very real evil forces that we as Christians come up against in the world and in our own hearts. But the outcome does not hang in the balance. Our God is a sovereign God. John the Revelator had hope, not because he knew what *he* would do but because he knew what *God* would do.

These questions about God's sovereignty are not matters only for bookish theologians or young seminary students. They are important

What's Coming Up

Mark Two: Gospel Doctrine

The God of the Bible Is a Creating God
The God of the Bible Is a Holy God
The God of the Bible Is a Faithful God
The God of the Bible Is a Loving God
The God of the Bible Is a Sovereign God

for all Christians. How you think about God impacts the way you live and the kind of church you build. You must have a biblical understanding of God in order to understand the gospel. And without the gospel, you have no hope, no Christian life, and certainly no real church.

Pastors especially need to know that the biblical God is creating, holy, faithful, loving, and sovereign. If we change our thoughts about any one of these attributes of God, we would change the way we do our job. We would shepherd differently. Faithfulness to Scripture demands that we speak about these issues with clarity and authority. We will understand nothing about the Bible if we do not understand the God of whom it is about.

We have seen that the biblical God is creating, holy, faithful, loving, and sovereign. This last attribute, his sovereignty, is often denied even within the church. But we must be very careful here. For confessing Christians to resist the idea of God's sovereignty in creation or salvation is to flirt with pious paganism. Many faithful Christians have honest questions about God's sovereignty, such as how God's sovereignty and our free will work together. But a sustained, tenacious denial of God's sovereignty should concern us. To baptize a person who is antagonistic to God's sovereignty may be to baptize someone whose heart still is not quite willing to trust God completely. That, after all, is the issue when it comes to God's sovereignty. Are we willing to trust him? Are we willing to acknowledge that we are not God? That we are not the Judge? That we are not the one who determines what is fair and unfair? Are we willing to put our whole lives in God's hands and truly trust him?

As dangerous as resistance to the idea of God's sovereignty is for the spiritual life of any Christian, it is even more dangerous in the leader of a congregation. To appoint a leader who doubts God's sovereignty, or who seriously misunderstands the Bible's teaching on it, is to set up as an example a person who in his own heart may well be deeply unwilling to trust God. That is bound to hinder the church as it tries to trust the Lord together.

If we are to be a healthy church, we must be especially careful to pray for leaders in the church to have a biblical grasp of and an experiential trust in the sovereignty of God. Sound doctrine, in its full, biblical glory, marks a healthy church.

Conclusion

We can be disinclined to trust. Sometimes we don't trust because we have been disappointed too often. But disappointments have their purpose. The ruins of our own cherished plans are often the steps to finding the true God and the good that he has for us. The Bible is full of stories like this. Israel's hopes for the Messiah again and again drove her to the point of needing to trust God fully. Paul's "thorn in the flesh" drove him to be used by God, to trust his Savior and rely on him and so to find him reliable in a way Paul never would have without that thorn.

And it is the same for us. We are at our most dangerous point spiritually when we think everything is fine. We need to know that God is entirely right to condemn us eternally. And we need to know that God in Christ has offered us another way, if we rely not on our own righteousness and our own goodness and merit but on Christ alone. That is the way to peace with God.

If we're honest, we know that such trust is not our natural tendency. We cling with all our might to what we have in this world, as if it were going to last forever. But nothing that we physically possess in our lives right now will last forever in the state that it is in.

And yet, if we are God's children, we know that he has something even better prepared for us. As good as the best things may be in our lives right now, the best is still to come.

In the last paragraph of the last book of the Chronicles of Narnia, C. S. Lewis writes,

> And as [Aslan] spoke, he no longer looked to them like a lion; but the things that began to happen after that were so great and beauti-

> ful that I cannot write them. And for us this is the end of all the stories, and we can most truly say that they all lived happily ever after. But for them it was only the beginning of the real story. All their life in this world and all their adventures in Narnia had only been the cover and the title page: now at last they were beginning Chapter One of the Great Story, which no one on earth has read: which goes on forever: in which every chapter is better than the one before.[3]

If you are God's child, the conclusion he has in mind for you is unimaginably good. As John wrote, "Dear friends, now we are children of God, and what we will be has not yet been made known. But we know that when he appears, we shall be like him, for we shall see him as he is" (1 John 3:2). The apostle Paul, thinking about the same things, just dissolved into doxology: "Oh, the depth of the riches of the wisdom and knowledge of God! How unsearchable his judgments, / and his paths beyond tracing out!" (Rom. 11:33).

This is the God of the Bible—the creating, holy, faithful, loving, sovereign God of the Bible. The Bible, in fact, is all about this God. It is about promises made by God and promises kept by God. And in the Bible God calls out for us to respond to him by trusting in him and his Word by believing his gospel.

In the Bible we see God giving us his Word—his promises—and we respond to him by trusting him—just as Adam and Eve did *not* do in the garden of Eden; just as Jesus *did* in the garden of Gethsemane. And as we hear and believe God's Word, we begin again to have that relationship with him that we were made to have. This is the God whom we can trust and should trust, because his Word will not disappoint. This is the good news that the Bible is all about.

At the very center of the gospel stands the great exchange of Christ's righteousness and our sin. His substitutionary, in-our-place death on

3 C. S. Lewis, *The Last Battle* (New York: Macmillan, 1956), 183.

the cross is the heart of the message. It is meaningless to speak of loving God if it does not include believing this truth and relying on Christ completely and alone for our salvation. The good news is about our being united, by faith, to Christ, who took our punishment and gave us his life!

Bill Sykes was a poor, irreligious fruit seller in London in the nineteenth century.[4] As he lay at home sick, nearing death, a Christian began calling on him and sharing the gospel with him. At first, Sykes showed little interest. Then the worker shared with him Isaiah 43:25: "I, even I, am he who blots out / your transgressions, for my own sake, / and remembers your sins no more," and he explained this great exchange. "I see it now," Sykes said. "Christ suffered for me then." Later, the Christian worker recounted, "I have no hesitation in saying that Bill Sykes entered into peace."

After a few more visits, the worker met Bill's son, sitting at his father's bedside. Bill said to the Christian worker, "Give him that little bit." "What bit?" the visitor asked. "That little bit about Christ taking my place, and how he had my punishment for me. That's the bit."

Bill was a better theologian than many seminary professors today. That dying man on his bed understood the main point of the Bible that he needed to reach out and grasp as death drew close. Bill Sykes heard a lot of theology—he heard the gospel! Is this the gospel preached in your church? Is this what is central in your preaching and in your services? Not a soothing word about your goodness, or about God's acceptance, or about Jesus's inoffensive willingness to befriend all and sundry, or even some convicting word about getting rid of some sin in your life—but the Bible's great message about God and us? Does it sound like the best news you've ever heard? Old sins forgiven! New life begun! A personal relationship with your God, your Creator, now and forever! This is the news God has for you today in his Word.

What better news could you hear?

4 Th[illegible] ry is recounted in Iain Murray [illegible] *Archibald G. Brown* (Carlisle, PA: Banner of Truth, 2011), [illegible]-76.

Other Resources

- For group study: Bobby Jamieson's *The Whole Truth about God: Biblical Theology* (2012), a six-week inductive Bible study; and *God's Good News: The Gospel* (2012), a seven-week inductive Bible study.
- For deeper reflection: *Sound Doctrine: How a Church Grows in the Love and Holiness of God* (2013), by Bobby Jamieson and *Biblical Theology in the Life of the Church: A Guide for Ministry* (2010), by Michael Lawrence.
- See also D. Martyn Lloyd-Jones, *The Plight of Man and the Power of God* (1943); J. I. Packer, *Knowing God* (1973); Edmund Clowney, *The Unfolding Mystery: Discovering Christ in the Old Testament* (1989); John MacArthur, *The Gospel According to Jesus: What Is Authentic Faith?* (1994); Graeme Goldsworthy, *Gospel and Kingdom* (2002); Mark Dever, *The Message of the New Testament: Promises Kept* (2005), *The Message of the Old Testament: Promises Made* (2006), and *What Does God Want of Us Anyway? A Quick Overview of the Whole Bible* (2010); J. I. Packer and Mark Dever, *In My Place Condemned He Stood: Celebrating the Glory of the Atonement* (2008); Mark Dever and Michael Lawrence, *It Is Well: Expositions on Substitutionary Atonement* (2010); Russell S. Woodbridge and David W. Jones, *Health, Wealth & Happiness: Has the Prosperity Gospel Overshadowed the Gospel of Christ?* (2010); Michael Reeves, *The Unquenchable Flame: Discovering the Heart of the Reformation* (2010); Greg Gilbert, *Who Is Jesus?* (2015) and *What Is the Gospel?* (2010); Greg Gilbert and Kevin DeYoung, *What Is the Mission of the Church? Making Sense of Social Justice, Shalom, and the Great Commission* (2011); Nick Roark and Robert Cline, *Biblical Theology: How the Church Faithfully Teaches the Gospel* (2018); Costi Hinn, *God, Greed, and the (Prosperity) Gospel: How Truth Overwhelmed a Life Built on Lies* (2019); and Dane Ortlund, *Gentle and Lowly: The Heart of Christ for Sinners and Sufferers* (2020).

What's Coming Up

Mark Three: A Biblical Understanding of Conversion and Evangelism

A Biblical Understanding of Conversion

A Biblical Understanding of Evangelism

What Is Evangelism?

Why Should We Evangelize?

How Should We Evangelize?

Evangelism Is Not Marketing

Mark Three

A Biblical Understanding of Conversion and Evangelism

WHAT DO YOU THINK when you hear the word *conversion*? For that matter, what do you think of the whole category of personal change? Many people today are skeptical that anyone can really change. Politicians, lawyers, preachers, professors, reporters, and lobbyists all have their predetermined vices, don't they?

For such people, wisdom is seen as learning to accept your internal circumstances and adapt to them rather than trying to fundamentally change them. The die is cast, the lot is fixed, our personality is assigned and, except for some terrible trauma, the assumption is that the leopard does not change his spots, the anxious person his personality, or the insecure person his psyche. "That's the way it is!" Maturity—even virtue—comes from facing up to the truth about yourself and resigning yourself to it.

Any suggestion that you can change *deeply* is regarded with serious suspicion. Any such suggestion is taken to be a potentially sinister tool of manipulation in the hands of those who would coerce you into conformity to their standards, cultivating in you self-hatred and a loathing of some characteristic of yourself, whether it be your sexual desires, your vocational ambitions, your ethical standards, or your religious beliefs.

We are who we are, so they say, and rather than question our innate desires, we should be proud of it and even promote it!

But for all of this uncertainty and suspicion about the possibility of change, people do have a deep longing for change. There's a restlessness about the "slings and arrows of outrageous fortune" and, if the truth were known, a dissatisfaction with ourselves that is as widespread as it is deep-seated. We are not content, so we rearrange the furniture, paint the hallway, or buy new clothes. If things then just get worse, we wonder about changing where we live. We ask for flexible hours at our job, or even to change jobs. Sometimes we might even long for changing our spouse. Today even those more traditionally fixed boundaries of gender, sexuality, and of life itself are transgressed in a vain attempt to find satisfaction. And yet, as work conditions and jobs, marriages and families, and even gender and death become subject to our own choices, as state after state begins to legalize medical murder, we seem to find ourselves defeated, trapped, and hopeless. So are the cynics right? Is any real change impossible?

What does the Bible say about deep, real, meaningful change? In the context of this book, of course, we are talking about the great change that takes place in conversion. Conversion is literally turning: turning from sinning to repenting of our sins and turning from trusting in ourselves to trusting only in Christ to reconcile us to God (see Paul's summary of his preaching in Acts 20:21).

If we think conversion is something that we alone do, then we will evangelize one way. If we think that conversion is something that most fundamentally God does, then we will evangelize another way. And how we evangelize will determine, in no small part, our church's health as surely as what food you're buying at the store affects your physical body's fitness. Anemic evangelism will starve us, and we will waste away. Careless evangelism will stuff us with false converts, and our church will become sick, unsound, and dysfunctional, and perhaps it will even die. But a biblical understanding of conversion will encourage us to a biblical practice of evangelism. A biblical understanding of conversion and of evangelism is a mark of a healthy church.

Understanding these matters biblically will free us to tell all we can of the good news of Jesus Christ, as we seek to show people with our lives and persuade them with our words what it means to be changed by God. God has always promised that his Word works! God promises through the prophet Isaiah that his Word "shall not return to me empty, / but it shall accomplish that which I purpose, / and shall succeed in the thing for which I sent it" (Isa. 55:11).

So, first, let's think a little more about conversion. Do people really need to be converted, to be changed?

A Biblical Understanding of Conversion

This basic question of whether conversion is even necessary is increasingly an obstacle when it comes to biblical Christianity. A lot of what passes for religion today is simply an affirmation of ourselves, leading many to choose complacency about our human condition over biblical change. When confronted with the idea that they might need some great alteration in their life, they simply say, "Why change? You shouldn't impose your ideas on others, you know. Besides, you're surely not suggesting that *your* way of living, *your* way of looking at the world, is any better than mine? If you are suggesting that, you must be some kind of self-righteous hypocrite! I'll kindly thank you to manage your own neuroses and leave me to mine!"

But the Bible clearly teaches that change is needed, that we are not "just fine." In fact, the Bible teaches that we are in trouble.

Years ago, a reporter asked basketball star Sam Perkins, "How will you rebound from your thirty-five-point loss?"

Perkins replied, "We just have to maintain our consistency."

Of course, consistency in losing won't do. Consistency in our dead spiritual state simply will not help us. We have to remind ourselves of Jesus's understanding of the natural state of people in this world: "The light has come into the world, and people loved the darkness rather than the light because their deeds were evil. For everyone who does wicked things hates the light and does not come to the light, lest his works should be exposed" (John 3:19–20).

Paul reminded the Ephesian Christians that before they were converted, they were dead in their sins and transgressions (Eph. 2:1). Paul taught clearly that this spiritual death is shared by all humanity. If you have any doubt as to whether conversion is important to the Bible, read Romans 2–3. The truth is that we have all sinned against God. Paul quotes the Old Testament in a sweeping denunciation of any claim we might make to being righteous in and of ourselves: "None is righteous, no, not one" (Rom. 3:10). The Bible teaches that we are totally depraved, not in the sense that we are as bad as we can be but in the sense that every part of our being has been touched by rebellion against God. All aspects of our selves are marked by this sin—this spiritual death. Even our tongues are used to deceive (Rom. 3:13). Thus Paul concludes that "by the works of the law no human being will be justified in [God's] sight" (Rom. 3:20). Any church that is not clear on this is not serving you well. We must be clear as to what the basic problem is in order to know how the church is to be deployed.

The Bible gives us radical images to show us the state of our human nature. It says we are in debt, enslaved, bankrupt, and even dead. This is our condition. We are in a disastrous situation. Clearly, a change is needed—a change that only Jesus can bring.

Consider these twin truths: we are in desperate need of God's grace, yet God owes his grace to no one. That's the very nature of grace—it is not something owed. What God owes us is justice for our sins. And that justice is what Jesus has taken as a substitute for all who will believe. So when Jesus calls us through his Spirit, we turn from our sins to faith in him.

And when God's Spirit begins powerfully to call us to turn from our sins, we experience a great sense of conviction. We begin to sense something of the seriousness of sin, particularly the seriousness of its deadly character as an act of revolt against God himself. We no longer just feel like "I shouldn't have done that" or "Oh, my conscience is bothered by that." Rather, we begin to see what our sins reveal about our lack of trust in God, our lack of prioritizing what God prioritizes, and our lack of caring about what God cares about. We begin to see the ugly nature of sin. We begin to feel like the adulterer David who prayed, "Against you, you only, have I sinned / and done what is evil in your sight, / so that you may be justified in your words / and blameless in your judgment" (Ps. 51:4).

According to the Bible, this is a crucial part of the good news: we need to be converted. Our state by nature is not good. The change we need is not merely to "discover" ourselves and our possibilities, but to *turn.* You don't need a better you; you need a new you! And that is what God provides for us in Christ. In conversion, we resign our claim to be the final judges and governors of our own lives, and we acknowledge that that role belongs to God alone. Our past sins need to be forgiven. Our present lives need to be reoriented. Our future destiny needs to be changed from the hell of God's good judgment to the heaven of God's gracious forgiveness and acceptance of us in Christ. Perhaps every other religion on the planet preaches self-salvation, but Christianity does not. Christianity preaches that we need to be radically changed.

True conversion is a change of mind, but it is not just a change of mind. It is a change of heart, though not a mindless emotional experience. As God converts the heart and gives new birth, new actions flow from our new identity as those who are united to Christ by faith.

I regularly pray that our congregation's collective witness will be more successful than our witness as individuals. Of course, it is true that God's Spirit should be at work in each of us. Yet while each one of us may be a fine witness for Jesus on our own, I pray that as a collective whole, we would actually be confusing to the non-Christian friends who begin to interact with us and get to know our congregation—nine hundred examples of imperfect people that God's Spirit has made new. And while none of us is perfect, upon closer examination it becomes apparent that he is doing real work in us. We have really changed, and his Spirit really is giving us the new life described in Romans 6.

According to the Bible, the real change of Christian conversion involves relying on Christ alone. We are not simply to try to justify ourselves before God or improve our life a little bit here and there, and think that somehow such changes will hide our sins from God or make our hearts appear righteous before him. In true conversion we begin to rest in Christ, to trust in him and rely on his merit alone before God. This great change is all about realizing that we can never go to church enough, we can never teach enough Sunday school classes, we can never give enough money, we can never be kind enough or beautiful enough or happy enough or contented with our religious lives enough to merit God's good will toward us.

We must realize that because of our sin, we are truly desperate before God. Our only hope comes in understanding that God has taken on flesh in Christ, that Christ lived a perfect life and died on the cross in the place of all those who would ever turn and trust in him, and that he rose in victory over our sins and now offers to pour out his Holy Spirit into our hearts. Beginning to have this reliance upon God and trusting in him alone is the nature of the great change that takes place in conversion.

We must repent of our sins and trust in Christ. And we can do that only by the power of God's Spirit, who takes the words we read and hear and uses them to create life and faith in our previously dark and dead souls. We need God to give us life. We need God to give us new hearts. Scripture tells us that is exactly what God has promised to do: "And I will give them one heart, and a new spirit I will put within them. I will remove the heart of stone from their flesh and give them a heart of flesh" (Ezek. 11:19). We find this idea throughout the Bible. This kind of heart transplanting is God's work. He alone can do it. And he must work this change in us if we are to accept the spiritual truths of the Bible (see 1 Cor. 2:14). As Jesus said, "No one can come to me unless the Father who sent me draws him" (John 6:44).

Christians sometimes talk about being "born again." Have you ever thought about that language? We get that language from Jesus himself. It wasn't a marketing ploy of the Southern Baptist Convention back in the 1970s. No, it comes right from Jesus in John 3. There we read of a very religious leader named Nicodemus who came to speak to Jesus with a specific question in mind.

> "Rabbi, we know that you are a teacher come from God, for no one can do these signs that you do unless God is with him." Jesus answered him, "Truly, truly, I say to you, unless one is born again he cannot see the kingdom of God." Nicodemus said to him, "How can a man be born when he is old? Can he enter a second time into his mother's womb and be born?" Jesus answered, "Truly, truly, I say to you, unless one is born of water and the Spirit, he cannot enter the kingdom of God." (John 3:2–5)

This religious leader wanted to know what he had to do to see the kingdom of God. Jesus didn't say that he should simply keep up the good work, keep living a good, moral, religious life, or keep teaching. No, Jesus said that this virtuous leader needed a whole new life. Nicodemus asked Jesus how anyone could get such a new life. Jesus said that only God could give it, and so Nicodemus must simply believe in Jesus and live by the truth.

Jesus taught clearly that we must act, but he also taught that we can act only if God's actions are behind our own. In so teaching, Jesus reflected the Old Testament. For example, consider the book of Joel. Joel was a prophet through whom the Lord prophesied great judgment. But Joel also offered words of hope: "Everyone who calls on the name of the LORD shall be saved" (Joel 2:32). Paul quotes that verse in Romans 10, and if you have ever shared the gospel with anyone, you may very well have quoted that verse yourself. Now, Joel had just been writing for two chapters about the judgment that would come upon the Israelites for their unbelief. But why would such unbelievers call on the Lord in this saving way? We find the answer in the rest of Joel 2:32: "Everyone who calls on the name of the LORD shall be saved. For in Mount Zion and in Jerusalem there shall be those who escape, as the LORD has said, and among the survivors shall be those whom the LORD calls." Who calls on the name of the Lord? Those whom the Lord calls!

Do you see why understanding this is important for your own spiritual health, and for the spiritual health of any church you would be involved with? If our conversion, our turning, is understood as something we do ourselves instead of something God does in us, then we misunderstand it. Conversion certainly includes our own actions. We must make a sincere commitment. We must make a self-conscious decision. Even so, real conversion is more than that. Scripture is clear that we are not all journeying toward God. Instead, Scripture presents us as needing to have our hearts replaced, our minds transformed, and our spirits given life. We can do none of this for ourselves. True conversion is a work of God's Spirit, and it bears different fruit than the flesh. So if you want to see if you are truly converted, there is a test you can take; it's found in Galatians 5:19–24. There Paul, by the inspiration of the Holy Spirit, specifically lays out the fruit of the flesh and the fruit of the Spirit. You can look and see which of those two lists looks like your life.

Every human needs this change, regardless of how one may outwardly appear. And this change is so radical that only God can bring it about. So, in order to have a healthy church, we need to be converted and we need to know that God converts us.

But the fact that we need God to convert us shouldn't lead us to conclude that we don't need people to evangelize! God's Word clearly teaches the importance of evangelism.

A Biblical Understanding of Evangelism

A friend of mine was raised in a Muslim country in a family known for its zealous observance of Islam. While studying outside of his native country, he had a dream of Jesus appearing to him and telling him to go talk to a Christian minister he had never even heard of. He was scared by the dream and ignored it. But the dream happened again and again and again. After ignoring the dream for some time, he finally went to find the minister, spoke to him about Jesus, and was converted!

I have heard or read many similar testimonies from the Muslim world—angels appearing in dreams telling people to go and speak to Christians. I'm always interested to note that God sends the dream, but then he sends the dreamer to another human messenger, who tells the dreamer the good news.

In these stories, who is the evangelist—the angel in the dream or the Christian the dreamer goes to talk to? The answer is, the Christian the person goes to talk to. In this case, it was the minister who shared the good news with my friend. And that's what evangelism is. God has reserved evangelism as a service—a privilege—for us! As Paul reasons in Romans 10:14, "How are they to believe in him of whom they have never heard?" In other words, if we don't tell others, they won't know. God has committed this great task to us! That's why the risen Christ taught his disciples, "Go . . . and make disciples of all nations" (Matt. 28:19). When we look at the book of Acts, we see that not just the apostles but all Christians are involved in the work of church planting and evangelism.

To help us understand and practice evangelism, we will consider a few simple questions: What is evangelism? Why should we evangelize? How should we evangelize?

Book Recommendations on Evangelism

For a short and accessible book to give out to your congregation, you won't find a better book than Isaac Adams's *What If I'm Discouraged in My Evangelism?* (2020).

Mack Stiles's books are all good, but especially his *Evangelism: How the Whole Church Speaks of Jesus* (2014). Mack's books are filled with good stories of how you can actually, practically talk to your friends about Jesus. In this book he shows how the local church is a surprisingly powerful tool for evangelism.

Iain Murray's *Revival and Revivalism: The Making and Marring of American Evangelicalism, 1750–1858* (1994) is a heavier read but well worth the effort. Murray examines how the practice of evangelism in America changed from 1750 to 1850 and how those changes continue to affect us today.

For a greater grasp of the biblical and theological foundations of evangelism, see J. I. Packer's *Evangelism and the Sovereignty of God* (2008). It has only four chapters and less than a hundred pages, but people consistently find it helpful in answering basic questions about biblical evangelism.

To think about how persuasion is a part of our discipleship, Os Guiness's *Fool's Talk: Recovering the Art of Christian Persuasion* (2015) is encouraging and thought-provoking.

And finally, I've written a book on evangelism that expands the ideas in this chapter. *The Gospel and Personal Evangelism* (2007) is intended to be an introduction to evangelism.

What Is Evangelism?

Evangelism is one person telling another person the good news of how he or she can be reconciled to God through faith in Jesus Christ. One of the best ways to understand this is to think about some common ways evangelism is often misunderstood. Let me mention six ways.

1. Evangelism is not an imposition of our beliefs on others. Probably the most common objection to evangelism these days is "Isn't it wrong to impose our beliefs on others?" Some people think evangelism is an imposition. And the way evangelism is sometimes done, I can understand the confusion. But when you understand what the Bible presents as evangelism, you understand that it's really not a matter of imposing your beliefs.

First, you must understand that the things you believe in as a Christian are facts. They are not mere beliefs or opinions. You can no more "impose" the gospel on someone than you can "impose" the law of gravity on someone. Like gravity, the objective truth of the gospel exists apart from our subjective perception of it.

Second, these facts are not *yours* in the sense that they uniquely pertain to you or your perspective or experience, or in the sense that you made them up on your own. When you evangelize, you are presenting the facts of the Christian gospel.

In biblical evangelism we don't *impose* anything. In fact we really can't. According to the Bible, evangelism is simply telling the good news; it does not include making sure that the other person responds to it correctly. I wish we could make people respond to the gospel, but we cannot. According to the Bible, the fruit of evangelism comes from God, not from our clever techniques or our personal passion for what we are doing. As Paul wrote to the Corinthians, "What then is Apollos? What is Paul? Servants through whom you believed, as the Lord assigned to each. I planted, Apollos watered, but God gave the growth. So neither he who plants nor he who waters is anything, but only God who gives the growth" (1 Cor. 3:5–7; see 2 Cor. 3:5–6).

This is an important point for us to grasp, especially in a world that is so hostile to evangelism. Years ago at Cambridge I was talking with a Lebanese Muslim friend of mine about a mutual friend who was a fairly secular Muslim. My friend wanted him to embrace a more faithful Muslim lifestyle, and I wanted him to become a Christian. So, in a strange way, he and I had something in common. We were both concerned about our friend's drunkenness, though we had very different solutions for his problem. We commiserated on the difficulty of living in a secular British culture. Then my friend remarked on the corruption of this Christian country. I responded that Great Britain is not a Christian country, that in fact there is no such thing as a Christian country. "That," my friend said, quickly seizing the opportunity, "is the problem with Christianity, compared to Islam. Christianity does not provide answers and guidelines for all of the complexities of real life," he maintained. "It has no overarching sociopolitical pattern to offer people for the real questions they come up against in life."

I thought for a moment about how I should respond, and then said, "Christianity is simply more realistic about the human condition than Islam." He asked me what I meant. I said, "To speak frankly, Islam is shallow in thinking that the human problem is simply a matter of behavior. According to Islam, it is merely a question of the will. But Christianity teaches that there is a much deeper problem, and this is a more accurate understanding of the human situation. Christianity includes a frank admission of human sinfulness not merely as an aggregate, a collection, of bad actions, but as an expression of a bad heart, a heart in rebellion against God. Christianity recognizes our problem as a matter of character, of human nature. Christianity has no comprehensive political program because the real human problem cannot ultimately be dealt with by political power."

To make it clear, I said to my friend, "Look, I could put a sword to a person's throat and make him at least a sufficiently good Muslim."

He agreed that that was true.

"But," I continued, "I could never put a sword to a person's throat and make him a Christian. There has to be a change that occurs *within* the person. Becoming a Christian is not merely a matter of your doing this and not doing that, or of your following that law and not doing that thing. To be a Christian is to have your life transformed by God. The Bible presents the human problem as something that could never be solved by coercive force or human imposition. All I can do is to present the good news accurately to you, live a life of love toward you, and pray that God will convict you of your sins. I can pray for God to show you your need of a Savior, and to give you the gifts of repentance and faith. But I can't make you a Christian."

Christian evangelism by its very nature involves no coercion, only loving persuasion. We are to present the gospel freely to all; we cannot manipulate anyone to truly accept it. True biblical evangelism is never an imposition.

2. Evangelism is not simply a personal testimony. Some people assume that evangelism can be reduced to sharing about a personal experience of an encounter with God. Certainly a testimony of what God has done in our lives may include sharing the good news, but it may not. In our pluralistic age, people are happy for you to get all the hope you can from anything in the world. You can get all the hope you can from the lampstand in your room, and they're fine with that, as long as you don't say anything about their lives. But the moment you move from what God has done in your life to these truths about Jesus Christ, and the implications they have for the life of the person you're talking to, that's when people say, "You don't judge me," or, "That's not your place." Evangelism can include your testimony of what God has done in your life, but it is not only that. Evangelism has to move on to the objective, indisputable, necessarily confrontational facts of the gospel.

3. Evangelism is not the same thing as social action or political involvement. Today, horizontal problems—problems between people—often obscure the fundamental vertical problem between us and God. Too often, what passes for evangelism may really be campaigns for public virtue, programs of compassion, or advocacy for social change. People refer broadly to "partnering with God" and "redeeming our communities." But evangelism is not about redeeming society; it's about redeeming sinners. Evangelism is a declaration of the gospel to individual men and women. Societies are challenged and changed when, through this gospel, the Lord brings individual men and women together in churches, to display his character in the interactions of those whom he has saved.

As individual sinners are born again, their faithful following of God's calling on their lives will lead them to love their neighbors and work for justice in thousands of various ways.[1] Sometimes, members of the same church will disagree about the best means of loving our neighbor.[2] But our goals will have been set by the commands of God, even as the means of achieving them are left to our own varying and imperfect plans. For instance, every Christian should oppose racism. But members of the same church can debate how to best oppose racism, or even disagree about the nature of racism in our culture, without debating the gospel or the necessity of sharing it with others. Since evangelism is not the same as social action, churches and church members can partner together in evangelism even while not agreeing on every social question.

4. Evangelism is not simply encouraging positive thinking. Some people think of evangelism as promoting "positive thinking" or sharing Bible verses that appear to promise prosperity. As the almost unbelievably well-named Creflo Dollar tweeted, "Jesus bled and died for us so that we can lay claim to the promise of financial prosperity."[3] Of course, health and wealth are things that everyone wants, but, contrary to what Mr. Dollar says, Jesus never promised health and wealth in this life. In fact, what he seemed to promise was trouble, rejection, and even persecution (see John 15:20). When we follow someone, we shouldn't be surprised if we end up where he ended up. Some preachers may celebrate owning private jets and claim that thousands of followers love them. Maybe you're tempted to believe that everyone who follows this kind of leader will also find success. But if you follow Jesus, you can't be surprised when you end up where he did—taking up your cross *and*

1 See Jonathan Leeman's chapter "Soteriological Mission: Focusing in on the Mission of Redemption," in *Four Views on the Church's Mission*, ed. Jason S. Sexton (Nashville, TN: Zondervan Academic, 2017), 17–45, as well as Leeman's *How the Nations Rage: Rethinking Faith and Politics in a Divided Age* (Nashville, TN: Thomas Nelson, 2018) and Robert Benne's *Good and Bad Ways to Think about Religion and Politics* (Grand Rapids, MI: Eerdmans, 2010).

2 For a discussion about disagreements between believers over matters of conscience, see Jonathan Leeman and Andy Naselli's short book *How Can I Love Church Members with Different Politics?* (Wheaton, IL: Crossway, 2020). For an in-depth study of the Bible's teaching on the conscience, see Andy Naselli and J. D. Crowley, *Conscience: What It Is, How to Train It, and Loving Those Who Differ* (Wheaton, IL: Crossway, 2016).

3 This tweet has since been deleted from his Twitter account.

being accepted by God himself. That's the eternal health and wealth that we should most care about, not the passing riches of this world.

5. Evangelism is not the same as apologetics. The term *apologetics* refers to the process of answering questions and objections people may have about our Christian faith. As with sharing your testimony, such question-answering and defending may often be a part of your conversations with others about Christ, and may include evangelism. But it is not the same thing as evangelism. I can defend the inerrancy of the Bible without sharing the gospel. I can defend the virgin birth of Christ or the historicity of the resurrection, and that is very important, but it is not evangelism. Whereas apologetics responds to the agenda that others set, evangelism follows the agenda that Christ has set: giving out the news about him. Evangelism is the positive act of telling the good news about Jesus Christ and the way of salvation through him.

6. Evangelism is not to be confused with the results of evangelism. Finally, one of the most common and dangerous mistakes is to confuse *the results of evangelism* with evangelism itself. This may be the most subtle of the misunderstandings. Evangelism must not be confused with the fruit of evangelism. If you combine this misunderstanding—thinking evangelism is the fruit of evangelism—with an unbiblical understanding of the gospel and conversion, then it is very possible to end up thinking not only that evangelism is simply seeing others converted, but also thinking that it is within your own power to convert others. This kind of thinking may lead you to become manipulative.

Many Christians and churches today focus on rapid growth. But rapid growth is not necessarily good growth—or even real growth. In fact, rapid growth can be cancerous. We all know that children need to eat in order to live. Imagine a couple, then, concludes that more food equals more life. They find what their children want and give it to them. The children eat it all happily and quickly, and then demand more. Rapid growth sets in—but probably not the kind the parents really want! Diets of ice cream and french fries can sustain life for a while, but they don't give children healthy growth.

The sudden advances of gospel work we find in the Bible are few—the exodus, the incarnation, the resurrection, Pentecost. But the quiet daily work of faithfulness is indicated on the majority of pages in Scripture, and in the vast majority of the lives of the people of God. Why do we think that we will harvest all we sow—or more? Is there any possibility that our devotion to rapid growth actually undermines real growth? Is this why so much of the work done in the name of evangelism in this country and overseas seems to result in weeds rather than in oaks? Can it be that this is the case because we are determined only to plant things that grow quickly?[4]

According to the Bible, evangelism must not be defined in terms of results but only in terms of faithfulness to the message preached. In the book of Acts Paul preached the gospel many times, and few responded. But he writes, "For we are the aroma of Christ to God among those who are being saved and among those who are perishing, to one a fragrance from death to death, to the other, a fragrance from life to life" (2 Cor. 2:15–16).

Paul is not saying that he gave out two different messages. He could not look out onto a crowd and say, "I can see who the elect are. To you I'm going to preach one message. Now, to all of those who are not becoming Christians, let me preach another message." No. Paul preached the same gospel to everyone, and yet, in evangelizing the same way to everyone, he was to some an aroma of life and to others the smell of death. The same ministry had two different effects.

Jesus taught something similar in his parable of the soils (Matt. 13:1–23). In this parable, the sower scattered the same seed on several different kinds of soil. The parable says nothing about the methods of the sower. Presumably he used the same method each time. The message of the parable is that some people will respond to the gospel and some will not, even though all hear the same message. We cannot finally judge the correctness of what we do in evangelism by the

4 See the forthcoming book by Matt Rhodes on this topic, *No Shortcut to Success: A Manifesto for Modern Missions* (Wheaton, IL: Crossway, 2022).

immediate response that we see. If missions organizations in North America understood this, a great gospel advance would surely take place. Failure to understand this truth can distract well-meaning churches into pragmatic, results-oriented endeavors and can transform pastors into neurotic people-manipulators. We make a terrible mistake when we misunderstand evangelism so badly that we think we can tell from the immediate results whether we are evangelizing properly. As Christians, we should know that even if we are faithful in telling the gospel, people still may not respond. Their lack of acceptance of the gospel does not necessarily mean that we have been wrong in how we have presented the gospel.

Misunderstanding this point can cripple individual Christians with a deep sense of personal failure and, ironically, can cause an aversion to evangelism itself. "I don't see any fruit from evangelism," some may say, "so I don't want to evangelize anymore." Imagine the guilt some Christians feel because they have shared the gospel for thirty years with a particular person who hasn't come to know Christ. They may feel that it must somehow be their fault. But the Bible teaches that conversions do not occur merely by our evangelistic prowess and proficiencies, just as resistance to the gospel is not merely a reflection of our evangelistic failures. Successful evangelism is not fundamentally a matter of our methods but of our faithfulness in proclamation.

Some of us became Christians through presentations of the gospel that may have been terrible in a number of ways. The person who shared the gospel with us may have been scared, stuttering, forgetful, intimidating, pushy, or even obnoxious. But somehow the truth was there amid all the errors, and God's Holy Spirit used the encounter to bring us to repentance and faith. If God can use someone else's sputtering attempt, surely he can use you! Tell people about Jesus.

God is sovereign in evangelism. A heart that one day might be as hard as concrete may, by the action of God, turn into fertile soil for the gospel the next day. The doctrine of election scares some people. But when Paul was discouraged, the Lord used a statement about election to encourage him to continue proclaiming the gospel: "And the Lord said to Paul one night in a vision, 'Do not be afraid, but go on speaking and do not be silent, for I am with you, and no one will attack you to harm you, for I have many in this city who are my people'" (Acts 18:9–10). God wasn't referring to the population of Corinth, but to the fact that he had many people whom he had chosen to save at some point in the future! God used the doctrine of election as an encouragement to Paul in evangelism. His preaching would not be in vain.

Why Should We Evangelize?

When you understand that evangelism isn't converting people but that it is telling them the wonderful truth about God, the great news about Jesus Christ, then obedience to the call to evangelize can become certain and joyful. Understanding this increases evangelism, because we stop viewing it as a burden and instead see it as a joyful privilege. Christians love hearing the gospel—it builds us up and encourages us—and we love telling it. It is beautiful to be able to tell someone else such good news, isn't it?

Every Christian is commanded to love God and love our neighbor. How could we better love God than to share these amazing truths about his justice being met and his love being extended in the gospel? And how can we better love others than to invite them to know God's forgiving and reconciling love? What is best can be hard and awkward. This is a matter of obedience as Christians. So we glorify God when we evangelize, even if we don't see immediate results.

All Christians, not just professional clergy, are to spread the good news. Part of our evangelistic activity has to do with the way we relate to each other as believers. Jesus said, "By this all people will know that you are my disciples, if you have love for one another" (John 13:35). Ultimately, this love for God leads to a desire to see him glorified. Throughout the Bible, God makes himself known to his creation. We share the gospel to glorify God as the truth about him is made known to his creation. The call to evangelism is a call to turn our lives outward, to stop focusing on ourselves and our needs and to start focusing on God and the world he has made. This includes loving people who are made in God's image and yet are at enmity with him, alienated from him and in need of salvation from sin and guilt. We bring God glory when we tell the great thing he has done in Christ for these creatures made in his image.

Sometimes, however, if we're honest, the main reason we don't evangelize is because we're not exactly sure how to do it.

How Should We Evangelize?

We evangelize by preaching the Word, by spreading the message, by telling the good news. Biblically, that's the basic answer to how we evangelize.

We can spread the Word publicly through social media, television, or through public meetings, and we can spread it privately, too, through personal conversations. Whatever the context, whether through print or preaching, through conversation or evangelistic Bible study, here are eight guidelines to consider when we evangelize.

1. Pray. Prayer is important because salvation is the work of God. We depend on him utterly and completely in seeing the spiritual resurrection of non-Christians being converted. Paul writes, "My heart's desire and prayer to God for them is that they may be saved" (Rom. 10:1). Pray regularly for your non-Christian friends and neighbors. This is what we do at our church every Sunday evening as we gather for a time of singing, prayer, and a brief reflection from God's Word. If you're a pastor, do you regularly lead your church in praying for specific evangelistic opportunities in the lives of members? Model praying regularly for both evangelism and conversions.

2. Tell people with honesty that if they repent and believe they will be saved—but it will be costly. We must be accurate in what we say, not holding back any important parts of the message out of a fear that those parts are too awkward or difficult to explain. Many people don't like including anything negative in a presentation of the good news. Talking about sin and guilt and repentance and sacrifice is thought to be too negative for our age of self-esteem. But we must die to self.

According to the Bible, making people aware of their lost and sinful condition is part and parcel of sharing the good news of Jesus Christ. When you are sick, a good doctor will tell you what is wrong with you. A bad doctor will blow sweet nothings at you while your body is being eaten up by disease. But you need the good doctor who tells you the truth and what can be done about it.

In the early chapters of the book of Acts, Peter is breathtakingly honest about the sinfulness of those to whom he is talking. Holding back important and unpalatable parts of the truth is manipulative. It amounts to selling a false bill of goods.

3. Tell people with urgency that if they repent and believe they will be saved—but they must decide now. We must make clear the urgency of the message, and that our listeners certainly should not wait until a "better deal" comes along.

Are you the kind of person who spends a lot of time comparison shopping online to get the best prices? What about your cell phone plan? You could use up a good portion of your life trying to find the best deals. But when it comes to the gospel, there is no point in waiting for a better deal. According to the New Testament, Jesus is the only way to God (John 14:6; Acts 4:12; Rom. 10). How else would you suggest that sinners and the holy God be reconciled? There is no other way than Christ, and if Christ is the only way, then what are you waiting for? As the Bible warns, "Today, if you hear his voice, / do not harden your hearts" (Heb. 4:7; quoting Ps. 95:7–8). It is not manipulative or insensitive to bring up such urgent warnings. It is simply the truth. None of us has an unlimited amount of time in which to decide whether to follow Christ. We need to be clear about the urgency.

4. Tell people with joy that if they repent and believe the good news, they will be saved. Hebrews 11 recounts the stories of those who suffered hard things for the faith and yet endured. The pinnacle comes in Hebrews 12:2, where we read that Jesus himself endured the cross "for the joy that was set before him." We are to consider all of our human sufferings as "light momentary affliction" (2 Cor. 4:17) compared to what we gain in Christ. So being honest and truthful about the cost should never make us grim evangelists! Following Christ does cost a lot, but it costs things that you don't want to keep anyway. And what you embrace instead is unbelievably wonderful and never, never ends. As martyred missionary Jim Elliot said, "He is no fool who gives what he cannot keep to gain what he cannot lose."[5]

What do we gain in coming to Christ? We gain a relationship with God himself. We gain forgiveness, meaning, purpose, freedom, community, certainty, and hope. Being honest about the difficulties when we're sharing the gospel doesn't mean we have to mask the blessings. For all of the difficulties we may face, it is infinitely more than worth it to make the decision to die to self and to follow Christ.

5. Use the Bible. The Bible isn't only for public preaching. Learn the Bible for yourself, and in evangelism share it with others. They will see that your message isn't from your own thoughts or ideas. As an example, in Acts 8 Philip shares the good news with an Ethiopian official. Philip uses the Old Testament he was reading to tell the Ethiopian about Jesus. Because God reveals himself through his Word, we should use the Bible in evangelism.

6. Realize that the lives of individual Christians and of the church as a whole are central to evangelism. Our lives, individually and as a congregation, should give credibility to the gospel we proclaim. This is one reason why church membership is so important. We as a church bear a corporate responsibility to present to the world what it means to be a Christian. When a group of people representing different life stages, different ethnicities, different backgrounds, and demographic differences come together to worship the same God, this action carries

5 Jim Elliot's October 28, 1949, journal entry, quoted in Elisabeth Elliot, *Shadow of the Almighty: The Life and Testament of Jim Elliot* (New York: Harper & Brothers, 1958), 108.

a weight and significance that none of us can muster on our own.[6] We should understand clearly what church membership means, and we should help our fellow believers understand it as well. God is glorified not only when we speak the message but also when we live consistently with it. It's true that we can't live perfectly, but we can try to live in a way that commends the gospel. Remember Jesus's words in the Sermon on the Mount: "Let your light shine before others, so that they may see your good works and give glory to your Father who is in heaven" (Matt. 5:16; see 1 Pet. 2:12). You can live in such a way that your life brings glory to God as others who observe you begin to believe the gospel.

Again, remember the words of Jesus: "A new commandment I give to you, that you love one another: just as I have loved you, you also are to love one another. By this all people will know that you are my disciples, if you have love for one another" (John 13:34–35).

Live a life of committed love to the other members of your local church, as a fundamental part of your own sanctification and of your evangelistic ministry. Our individual lives alone are not a sufficient witness. Our lives together as church communities are the confirming echo of our witness.

7. Build relationships with non-Christians. All the guidelines above can apply to all the situations in which you share the gospel: the person next to you in an elevator, or on a bus, or on a plane. But one category of evangelism includes those people whom you already know—friends or family—who aren't Christians. It includes people whom you could get to know if you were to give a little time and forethought to going to the places where you might meet people who don't know Christ, intending to build relationships with them. (Pastors, this means our

6 See Mark Dever, "Regaining Meaningful Church Membership," in *Restoring Integrity in Baptist Churches*, ed. Thomas White et al. (Grand Rapids, MI: Kregel, 2008), 45–61; Mack Stiles, *Evangelism: How the Whole Church Speaks of Jesus* (Wheaton, IL: Crossway, 2014); and Mark Dever and Jamie Dunlop, *The Compelling Community: Where God's Power Makes a Church Attractive* (Wheaton, IL: Crossway, 2015).

churches can't keep people so busy with meetings and activities that they have no time to build relationships with non-Christians.)

Let's do some evangelistic "contact tracing." Write down all the non-Christians you've spoken to this last week. Which of them will you probably see again? Which could you see again with a little planning and forethought? Make it a priority to share the gospel with them and pray for their conversion.

8. Work together with other Christians to take the gospel to those who don't live around any Christians. This is an extension of the previous point—deliberately building relationships with non-Christians—but it takes our initiative to another level. We need to reckon with the fact that there are people who simply do not know any Christians. Since God's plan is that the whole world would know about this good news, and since he has committed the task of telling others into our hands, then we must send and we must go (Matt. 28:18–20; Rom. 10:14–15)! Why would we want anyone made in God's image to live in ignorance of God's love in Christ? A healthy local church will see its concern for evangelism informing its love not merely for those around them, in their own community, but for those they've never met, for those who've never heard. One test for your local church is to consider whether your church's budget sufficiently emphasizes bringing the gospel to the nations. We'll return to this topic in chapter 9.

Evangelism Is Not Marketing

I want to address one more thing. For the last couple of centuries the practice of praying a particular prayer of initial faith in Christ—something that is not expressly commanded in the New Testament—has been almost universal in some circles. The "sinner's prayer" has been as standard as baptism, and perhaps more universally agreed upon. Recently, it has come under some criticism from younger ministers as being merely a human tradition and not a biblical command. It has been negatively characterized as a magical incantation or spell, and confidence in it has been undermined. Many have discarded the practice altogether, usually in the name of trying to be more faithful, and often, of trying to stop practices that generate false converts.

Some of these critics of the sinner's prayer err, however, in their adoption of the practice of "spontaneous baptism." Less spectacular and mysterious than spontaneous combustion, spontaneous baptism is still surprising to many. Historically, churches have scheduled baptisms weeks or even months in advance, often requiring some course of preparation for those to be baptized. But in recent years, some churches have begun conducting large public services where the baptismal pool is opened and all who wish to are invited forward to be baptized. This practice is based on a misunderstanding of the book of Acts.[7]

Are spontaneous baptisms much different from the sinner's prayer they seem to have replaced? In the New Testament, baptism is a sign of God's saving grace that incorporates someone into God's kingdom. But spontaneous baptisms may often represent hasty decisions—and perhaps not even reflect decisions about salvation!

A pastor friend was invited to participate in a time of spontaneous baptisms at a church where he was the guest preacher. He agreed, but was surprised when a young woman asked him to baptize her "for her mother, who was sick." My friend was horrified at the thought of so wrongly using baptism, and politely declined, encouraging the young woman to speak to one of the pastors of the church.

Later, after the service, the regular pastor approached my friend, upset that he hadn't baptized the woman. Evidently, many of their "baptisms" were no more than wet prayer requests! But how confusing will the New Testament's language about baptism be to those who have been so "baptized"—never really intending themselves to say anything about salvation but simply doing a religious ritual in the hope of gaining God's blessing.

7 See Caleb Morell, "Does the Book of Acts Teach Spontaneous Baptisms?," 9Marks website, March 10, 2020, https://www.9marks.org/article/does-the-book-of-acts-teach-spontaneous-baptisms/.

We can't know why people come forward for spontaneous baptism. Perhaps some have heard the good news and have themselves been converted and so wish to be baptized. But there could also be other practices which would make such baptisms even less reflective of those who have truly repented and believed. One church plants "baptism counselors" among the congregation—much like the Billy Graham rallies of the past did with evangelism counselors—instructing them to come forward as soon as the invitation is given. The intention is to prime the pump, to create a stream of people going forward, to make it more comfortable for others to choose to come forward and be baptized. Another church even published their instructions concerning this online, advising baptism counselors to "move intentionally through the highest visibility areas and the longest walk." Why the highest visibility areas and the longest walk? Because the purpose is not only for those people to come forward to counsel those seeking baptism, but it is also to provoke many others to come forward. Again, the intention is to make it easier to walk forward and be baptized. But there is nothing in the New Testament that encourages us to want to try to make adopting the symbol and sign of discipleship any easier than discipleship itself. To do that is to invite more people to wrongly think that they have been converted when they haven't been. It recreates the very error some of these same pastors wished to eliminate when they stopped using the sinner's prayer.

Such social pressure can create larger churches, but not healthier ones. A biblical understanding of conversion prevents us from understanding evangelism merely as marketing, where we refine our techniques until we find what most reliably gets us to "yes"!

A few years ago, after a Sunday morning service, a visitor came up to me, took me by the hand, pulled me uncomfortably close, and said, "Dr. Dever, I just want you to know that was one of the best sales presentations I've ever heard in my life. But there was only one problem: you didn't close the sale!"

I didn't really know how to respond to him. I didn't say much. But what I thought was, "Friend, I know what kind of sales I can close, and I know what kind I can't close, and the redemption of an eternal soul is one sale that I, in my own strength, cannot accomplish."

I need to understand this not so that I won't preach the gospel, but so that I won't allow my presentation of the gospel to be molded by what I think will finally get a response and "close a sale." Rather than using all of my human powers to convict and change the sinner, while God stands back quietly waiting for the spiritual corpse, his declared spiritual enemy, to invite him into his heart, I'm going to preach the gospel, trying to persuade but knowing that I can't convert, and then stand back while God uses all of his divine powers to convict and convert and change the sinner. Then we'll see clearly just who can really call the dead to life. That's the good news we want to see our churches built on—not what *we* can do, but what God has done and will do, if you believe in Christ!

Christians should tell everyone the good news. We should all evangelize. We should do so with honesty, urgency, and joy, living a life that backs up our message and praying that the people we share with will be truly converted. All glory to God as people are saved and healthy churches are built up.

Other Resources

- For group study: Bobby Jamieson's *Real Change: Conversion* (2012), a seven-week inductive Bible study; *Reaching the Lost: Evangelism* (2012), a six-week inductive Bible study; and *God's Good News: The Gospel* (2012), a seven-week inductive Bible study.
- For handing out to Christians and non-Christians: *What Is the Gospel?* (2010) and *Who Is Jesus?* (2015) by Greg Gilbert.

- See also Joseph Alleine, *A Sure Guide to Heaven* (1671); J. I. Packer, *Evangelism and the Sovereignty of God* (1961); Will Metzger, *Tell the Truth: The Whole Gospel Wholly by Grace Communicated Truthfully and Lovingly* (1984); David F. Wells, *God the Evangelist: How the Holy Spirit Works to Bring Men* (1987) and *Turning to God: Biblical Conversion in the Modern World* (1989); Donald S. Whitney, *How Can I Be Sure I'm a Christian? What the Bible Says about Assurance of Salvation* (1994); Iain Murray, *Revival and Revivalism* (1994); Mark Dever, *The Gospel and Personal Evangelism* (2007); John Piper, *Finally Alive* (2009); Mike McKinley, *Am I Really a Christian?* (2011); J. Mack Stiles, *Evangelism: How the Whole Church Speaks of Jesus* (2014); Os Guinness, *Fool's Talk: Recovering the Art of Christian Persuasion* (2015); and Greg Gilbert, *Assured: Discover Grace, Let Go of Guilt, and Rest in Your Salvation* (2019).

What's Coming Up

Mark Four: A Biblical Understanding of Church Membership

What Is a Church?

Why Join a Church?

1. To Assure Ourselves
2. To Evangelize the World
3. To Expose False Gospels
4. To Edify the Church
5. To Glorify God

What Does Church Membership Entail?

1. In Action, Initially by Baptism
2. In Writing, by Signing a Statement of Faith and Church Covenant

Special Responsibilities of Membership at Capitol Hill Baptist Church

Mark Four

A Biblical Understanding of Church Membership

ALL THE STATISTICS SEEM TO point to our age being an era of "commitment-phobia." Commitment-phobia is the fear that in promising to do something good we will miss out on getting something even better. And so, although we see many good things we could be doing, we would rather just "keep our options open." Surely that is the wisdom of our time. One writer has observed:

> Public-opinion research points to a deepening paradox in society: the combination of commitment to religion with a deepening moral relativism. For example, while 91 percent of the American people consider religion very important in their lives, 63 percent reject the concept of absolutes.[1]

Can you be afraid of commitment and be a Christian, too? I'm not asking if a Christian can be uncertain about things. Most Christians have doubts. But what could be more "options-closing" than following Jesus, who told his disciples that anyone who would follow him must "take up his cross" (Matt. 16:24)?

1 Don E. Eberly, *Restoring the Good Society: A New Vision for Politics and Culture* (Grand Rapids, MI: Baker, 1994), 38.

Add to this the problem of lone-rangerism: Why depend on someone else if you can do it yourself? We are concerned today with ease and simplicity. Why entangle ourselves with others? We may be a burden to them; they certainly may be a burden to us.

Put these tendencies together and you get a culture that is fairly hostile to New Testament Christianity, and certainly not very comfortable with a commitment like church membership.

Isn't the whole idea of church membership counterproductive? Isn't it unfriendly, and maybe even elitist, to say that we're in and you're out? Can we go so far as to say that it is unbiblical and un-Christian? The end of Acts 2 says that "the Lord added to their number . . . those who were being saved" (Acts 2:47). Isn't that all there is to it? Isn't the church simply a reality created by our salvation? For example, when the Ethiopian official responded to the gospel and was baptized, wasn't he automatically a member of the church (see Acts 8)?

I'm convinced that getting this concept of membership right is a key step in revitalizing our churches, evangelizing our nation, furthering the cause of Christ around the world, and so bringing glory to God. Remember that this chapter is part of a book called *Nine Marks of a Healthy Church*. This book is not meant to include everything there is to say about a healthy church, but in these nine chapters I am trying to call attention to some important aspects of church life that have been overlooked or even forgotten in so many places today.

My own fellowship of churches is a prime example. According to one recent Southern Baptist Convention study, the typical Southern Baptist church has 176 members, only 69 of whom are present at the typical Sunday morning worship service.[2] Where are the other 107 members? Are they all at home sick, in a rest home, or at college? Are they on vacation or deployed with the military? Maybe some are, but all 107 of them? What do such churches convey about Christianity to the world around us? What do we understand this to mean about

2 SBC 2011 Annual Church Profile. Thanks to Ed Stetzer for providing this information.

the importance of Christianity in our lives? And what is the spiritual state of those people who haven't attended church for months or even longer? Is their nonattendance really any of our business?

In this chapter, we will consider three questions:

1. What is a church?
2. Why join a church?
3. What does church membership entail?

What Is a Church?

The word *church* does not simply refer to an organizational unit of any particular religion. You won't hear anyone speak of Buddhist "churches" or Jewish "churches." In that sense, *church* is a thoroughly Christian word. *Church* does not fundamentally mean a building; only in a secondary sense is it that. The building is simply where the church meets—thus the New England Puritan name for the church building was "meeting house." The earliest New England churches looked like large houses from the outside—they were the houses where the church met.

According to the New Testament, the church is primarily a body of people who profess and give evidence that they have been saved by God's grace alone, for his glory alone, through faith alone, in Christ alone. This is what a New Testament church is; it is not a building. The early Christians didn't have buildings for almost three hundred years after the church began. A church is a local collection of people committed to Christ, to regularly assemble, and to have his Word preached and obeyed, including Christ's commands to baptize and to celebrate the Lord's Supper.

A few passages in the New Testament seem to refer to the church in the abstract, or universally, but the overwhelming majority of references to the church are to a local, living, and loving collection of people who are committed to Christ and to each other. That's what the word *church* means again and again in the New Testament. It is a body from which you can be excluded and in which, therefore, you can clearly be included. Consider this: if there is no way for you to be *excluded* from the local church you are currently attending, perhaps that's because you have not *included* yourself in it as the Bible intends.

One interesting sidenote for historians: the idea of the church being a covenanted community of believers—and not just for everyone who lives in a particular locality—is an important contribution that Baptists particularly have made to our nation's religious liberty. The church is not finally something that's for you and every member of your family by physical, natural descent, or that is yours as a citizen of this nation. Though all are welcome to attend, the New Testament teaches that the church in its purpose and membership is for believers, for those to whom God's Holy Spirit has given the new birth and who join together in a covenanted community. America today has laws that allow such churches to operate in liberty. Some nonbelievers fear that Christians are seeking some kind of official or "established" church in America. But Christians who have inherited this Baptist understanding of the church are actually the firmest foes of such an established church. Our very understanding of the church will not allow that. Rather, we desire the evangelization of our nation through churches that are allowed to freely cooperate as believers in Christ.

If you read the story of the early churches recorded in the book of Acts, you will find no evidence that any of them meant to have anyone other than believers as members. When you read the letters of Paul, it seems clear that Paul too wrote as if the churches were composed entirely of believers; thus he addressed them as saints—those whom God has specially chosen. The church is the body of Christ, the local collection of Christians committed to Christ and to each other.

Why Join a Church?

Any church growth specialist would tell me that inviting people to join a church is exactly the wrong thing to do today. They would warn me, "Mark, you might just cause them to be disaffected. Why don't you just not mention this topic?" But I think that this topic is a must for our churches, and for us as Christians today. Church membership is a crucial topic for understanding what Christ is calling us to as his disciples. Joining a church will not save us any more than our good works, education, culture, friendships, financial contributions, or baptism will save us. Non-Christians should not seek to join a church, but to learn more about what it means to be a Christian.

But for those who are confessing Christians, what does it mean to live the Christian life? Do we live the Christian life alone? Is it merely a matter of our individual, isolated virtues or spiritual disciplines that we work on—the fact that we're honest at work, that we don't cheat on our spouse, that we believe certain things to be true?

Or maybe that does not describe you. Maybe you know that the Christian life is to include others. But who are these others? Are they the other people at work or the other women in your women's Bible study or your friends from back in school days or your fellowship group at college? Which Christians are we called to relate to? The church is for everyone who is a Christian. The church is not a homogeneous group, centered around one subtask such as evangelizing college students or publishing a magazine. A Christian church is not just for you and your friends; it's for all believers.

The responsibilities and duties of members of a Christian church are simply the responsibilities and duties of Christians.[3] Church members, like Christians, are to be baptized and to regularly attend the Lord's Table. We are to hear God's Word and to obey it. We are to regularly fellowship together for mutual edification. We are to love God, one another, and those outside our fellowship, and we are to evidence the fruit of the Spirit (Gal. 5:22–23). We are to worship God in all the

3 For more on the duties of church members, see the contributions by Benjamin Keach, Benjamin Griffith, the Charleston Association, Samuel Jones, W. B. Johnson, Joseph S. Baker, and Eleazer Savage in Mark Dever, ed., *Polity: Biblical Arguments on How to Conduct Church Life: Some Historic Baptist Documents* (Washington, DC: 9Marks, 2000), 65–69, 103–05, 125–26, 148–51, 221–22, 276–79, 510–11. While the book is currently out of print, it is available for free online at https://www.9marks.org/.

activities of our home, work, community, and life.[4] Christians also have particular duties in relation to the congregation. As Millard Erickson writes, "Christianity is a corporate matter, and the Christian life can be fully realized only in relationship to others."[5] The most fundamental duty Christians have in relation to the congregation is the duty to regularly attend gatherings of the congregation (see Heb. 10:25; see Ps. 84:4, 10; Acts 2:42). In general, membership duties can be divided into duties toward other members and duties toward pastors.

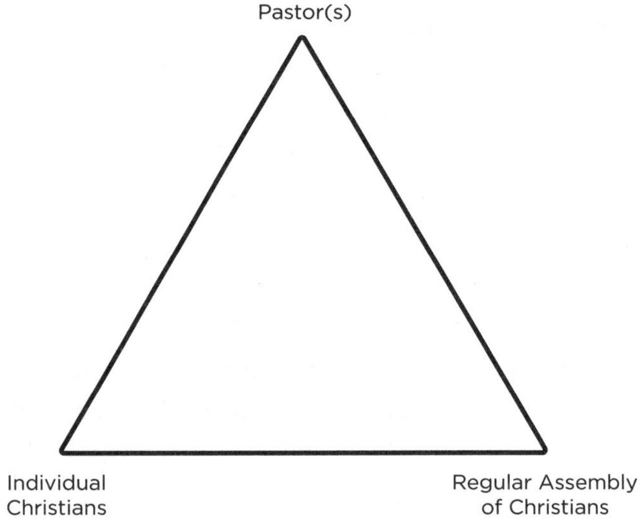

Church membership puts into practice what the Bible teaches about the self-conscious commitments that should exist within a church—the commitments between an individual Christian, his or her pastors, and a defined gathering of Christians.

4 For more on church membership, see Jonathan Leeman, *Church Membership: How the World Knows Who Represents Jesus* (Wheaton, IL: Crossway, 2012). Also see articles in the May–June 2011 *9Marks Journal* at https://www.9marks.org/journal/church-membership-holding-body-together/. See also John S. Hammett and Benjamin L. Merkle, eds., *Those Who Must Give an Account: A Study of Church Membership and Church Discipline* (Nashville, TN: B&H Academic, 2011).

5 Millard J. Erickson, *Christian Theology* (2nd ed., Grand Rapids, MI: Baker, 1998), 1058. For a careful study of the Christian's corporate duties in Paul's epistles, see James Samra, *Being Conformed to Christ in Community: A Study of Maturity, Maturation and the Local Church in the Undisputed Pauline Epistles* (London; T&T Clark, 2006), esp. 133–70.

The duties and responsibilities church members have *toward one another* summarize the life of the new society that is the church. As followers of Jesus Christ, Christians are obliged to love one another (John 13:34–35; 15:12–17; Rom. 12:9–10; 13:8–10; Gal. 5:14; 6:10; Eph. 1:15; 1 Pet. 1:22; 2:17; 3:8; 4:8; 1 John 3:16; 4:7–12; see Ps. 133). Christians are members of one family, even of one another (1 Cor. 12:13–27). Absent a life of love for one another, what other duty of church members is satisfying or worthwhile? Love obligates the members of the church to avoid anything that "tends to cool love."[6] By this love, the nature of the gospel itself is demonstrated.

Church members are also obliged to seek peace and unity within their congregation (Rom. 12:16; 14:19; 1 Cor. 13:7; 2 Cor. 12:20; Eph. 4:3–6; Phil. 2:3; 1 Thess. 5:13; 2 Thess. 3:11; James 3:18; 4:11). The desire for peace and unity should follow naturally from the obligation to love (Rom. 15:6; 1 Cor. 1:10–11; Eph. 4:5, 13; Phil. 2:2; see Zeph. 3:9). Further, if Christians share the same spirit and mind—the Spirit of Christ—then unity is a natural expression of that Spirit. Given the sin which remains in believers in this life, however, unity often requires effort. Thus Christians "stand firm in one spirit, contending as one man for the faith of the gospel" (Phil. 1:27). Strife should be actively avoided (Prov. 17:14; Matt. 5:9; 1 Cor. 10:32; 11:16; 2 Cor. 13:11; Phil. 2:1–3). Love is expressed and unity is cultivated when church members actively sympathize with one another. As Paul exhorts the congregation in Rome, "Rejoice with those who rejoice; mourn with those who mourn" (Rom. 12:15; see Job 2:11; Isa. 63:9; 1 Cor. 12:26; Gal. 6:2; 1 Thess. 5:14; Heb. 4:15; 12:3). Church members are also required to do the following.

- Care for one another physically and spiritually (Matt. 25:40; John 12:8; Acts 15:36; Rom. 12:13; 15:26; 1 Cor. 16:1–2; Gal. 2:10; 6:10; Heb. 13:16; James 1:27; 1 John 3:17; Deut. 15:7–8, 11)

6 Samuel Jones, "Treatise of Church Discipline," in Dever, *Polity*, 150; see 2 Cor. 12:20; 1 Tim. 5:13; 6:4; James 4:11.

- Watch over one another and hold one another accountable (Rom. 15:14; Gal. 6:1–2; Phil. 2:3–4; 2 Thess. 3:15; Heb. 12:15; see Lev. 19:17; Ps. 141:5)
- Edify one another (1 Cor. 14:12–26; Eph. 2:21–22; 4:12–29; 1 Thess. 5:11; 1 Pet. 4:10; 2 Pet. 3:18)
- Bear with one another (Matt. 18:21–22; Mark 11:25; Rom. 15:1; Gal. 6:2; Col. 3:12), including not suing one another (1 Cor. 6:1–7)
- Pray for one another (Eph. 6:18; James 5:16)
- Keep away from those who would destroy the church (Rom. 16:17; 1 Tim. 6:3–5; Titus 3:10; 2 John 10–11)
- Reject evaluating people by worldly standards (Matt. 20:26–27; Rom. 12:10–16; James 2:1–13)
- Contend together for the gospel (Phil. 1:27; Jude 3)
- Be examples to one another (Phil. 2:1–18)

Church members also have particular responsibilities toward the leaders of the church, even as the leaders do to them. As Paul said to the Corinthians, "Men ought to regard us as servants of Christ and as those entrusted with the secret things of God" (1 Cor. 4:1). Leaders in the church should be respected, held in the highest regard, and honored (Phil. 2:29; 1 Thess. 5:12–13). If Christians expect their pastor to fulfill his biblical responsibilities, church members must make themselves known to him. They must regard him as a gift from Christ sent to the church for their good. This is similar to the way the apostles were to be regarded as delegates of Christ (Luke 10:16; see 1 Cor. 16:10). The minister of the Word is a steward of God's household and an undershepherd of God's flock. He serves willingly and eagerly (1 Pet. 5:1–3). His reputation can and should be defended, his word believed, and his instructions obeyed unless Scripture is contradicted or facts are plainly distorted (Heb. 13:17, 22; 1 Tim. 5:17–19). The faithful minister should be so regarded simply because he brings God's Word to his people; he does not replace it with his own.

Church members should remember their leaders and imitate their life and faith (1 Cor. 4:16; 11:1; Phil. 3:17; Heb. 13:7). Good preachers and teachers are worthy of being doubly honored, according to Paul in 1 Timothy 5:17, which includes material support. (The word used in 1 Tim. 5:17 for "honor" has a clear financial connotation. See also Acts 6:4; 1 Cor. 9:7–14; Gal. 6:6.) And church members should give themselves both to praying for their ministers and to assisting them in every way they can (Eph. 6:18–20; Col. 4:3–4; 2 Thess. 3:1; Heb. 13:18–19). Ministers of the Word have been given the task of bringing God's Word to God's people. As Paul said to the Corinthians, "We are therefore Christ's ambassadors, as though God were making his appeal through us. We implore you on Christ's behalf: Be reconciled to God" (2 Cor. 5:20).

Not convinced? Let me break this down a little bit more. Below are five good reasons (you can probably think of more) to join a church that preaches the gospel and models Christian living.

1. To Assure Ourselves

You should not join the church in order to *be* saved, but you may want to join the church to help you in making certain that you *are* saved. Remember the words of Jesus:

> Whoever has my commands and obeys them, he is the one who loves me. He who loves me will be loved by my Father, and I too will love him and show myself to him. . . .
>
> If you obey my commands, you will remain in my love, just as I have obeyed my Father's commands and remain in his love. . . . You are my friends if you do what I command. . . .
>
> Now that you know these things, you will be blessed if you do them. (John 14:21; 15:10, 14; 13:17)

I could quote many more words from Jesus that teach us how we are to follow him, and how we must be careful not to delude ourselves. In joining a church, we are asking our brothers and sisters to hold us accountable to live according to what we speak with our mouths. We ask the brothers and sisters around us to encourage us, sometimes by reminding us of ways that we have seen God work in our lives, and other times by challenging us when we may be moving away from obeying him.[7]

It is easy to fool ourselves into thinking we're Christians simply because at one time we made a tearful decision and then joined a church. Perhaps we've gone along with the life of the church for years, supporting its organizations, making friendships based around activities, liking some of the hymns and complaining about others, but never really knowing Christ. Do you have a vital relationship with Christ that changes your life and the lives of those around you?

How can you tell if you do? One of the ways you can discover the truth about your own life is to ask this question: Do I understand that following Christ fundamentally involves how I treat other people, especially other people who are members of my church? Have I covenanted together to love them, and do I give myself to that?

Or, have you claimed that you know a love from God in Christ and yet live in a way that contradicts that claim? Do you claim that you know this kind of love that knows no bounds, and yet in loving others you set bounds, saying in effect, "I'll go this far but no farther"?

Such a claim to love, without a life backing it up, is a bad sign. And yet, if you just hang out by yourself and refuse to join a church, other Christians can't help you. You're sailing your own little ship your own little way. You'll come to church when you like the sermons, you'll come when you like the music or when you like something else that the church does, then you'll sail on out to wherever else you may go when you want something else.

Membership in a local church is not an antiquated, outdated, unnecessary add-on to true membership in the universal body of Christ;

7 For more on this topic, see Mike McKinley, *Am I Really a Christian?: The Most Important Question You're Not Asking* (Wheaton, IL: Crossway, 2011) and Greg Gilbert, *Assured: Discover Grace, Let Go of Guilt, and Rest in Your Salvation* (Grand Rapids, MI: Baker Books, 2019).

membership in a local church is intended to be a testimony to our membership in the universal church. Church membership does not save, but it is a reflection of salvation. And if there is no reflection of our salvation, how can we be sure that we are truly saved? As John explains, "If anyone says, 'I love God,' yet hates his brother, he is a liar. For anyone who does not love his brother, whom he has seen, cannot love God, whom he has not seen" (1 John 4:20).

In becoming a member of the church, we are grasping hands with each other to know and be known by each other. We are agreeing to help and encourage each other when we need to be reminded of God's work in our lives or when we need to be challenged about major discrepancies between our talk and our walk.

2. To Evangelize the World

Another reason you should join a local church is for the sake of evangelizing the world. When we act together, we can better spread the gospel at home and abroad. We can do this by our words, as we share the good news with others, and as we help others to do so. A local church is, by nature, a missionary organization. We back up this missionary outreach with our actions as we show God's love by meeting the physical needs of orphans and those otherwise disadvantaged.

We promote the gospel by cooperating to take it to those who have not yet heard it, and by making the gospel visible to the world through how we live. Those not yet saved may see us, and they may see something of the gospel. As imperfect as we are, if God's Spirit is genuinely at work in us, he will use our lives to help demonstrate to others the truth of his gospel. This is a special role we have now that we won't have in heaven—to be part of God's plan, and to take his gospel to the world. If you are reading this but haven't yet joined in that great task, do so today.

3. To Expose False Gospels

As we interact with other Christians, we show the world what Christianity really is; we dispel the false notion that Christians are nauseatingly self-righteous people who are worried that someone somewhere might be having fun, and who believe, above all else, in their own goodness. This is how many non-Christians think of Christianity. We can combat that false image by having a church that is not marked by such an attitude.

Some years ago I visited a relative whom I hadn't seen since childhood. My announcement that I was planning to be a Baptist preacher didn't go over very well. She paused, looked down at her coffee, and said, "I've given up on organized religion. I think I've decided that churches are just pits of vipers."

"Really?" I replied. She said, "Yep."

I said, "Do you really think the world outside is so much better?" She thought for a second and said, "Well, I guess not. They're vipers too. But at least they *know* they're vipers."

I said, "You might be surprised how much I agree with you. I know the world outside is a pit of vipers. And I know the church is a pit of vipers, too. But the difference is, I don't really think the world outside knows that they are. And I think Christians know that we are, and that's why we come to church—because we know we need help. Because we know that we're dependent on God, that we're saved by his grace alone." Then I added, with a smile, "We've always got room for one more to slither in."

All we can bring to our salvation is our sins. It must be God's love in Christ that saves us. He came and lived a perfect life for us, died on the cross in the place of all those who would ever turn and trust in him, and rose in victory over death and over sin. Our faith in him alone is the instrument by which we are saved.

So join a church that believes in *that* gospel. Join with other Christians in covenanting to make the truth known.

4. To Edify the Church

A fourth reason you should join the church is to help in the edification or building up of other believers. Joining a church will help counter our wrong individualism, and it will help us to realize the corporate nature of Christianity.

We need to give up trying to live the Christian life on our own. We need to covenant together with others to follow Christ. Christians must stop being selfish in their understanding of the Christian life. The Christian life is not just about you and those you are personally trying to reach with the gospel. God also intends for you to be a committed part of helping to make disciples out of the flock of sheep he has already saved.

If you commit to a church, you commit to a local body of people who will try to help you work through challenges and problems. So, for example, if it is found that you have a problem with gossip, your brothers and sisters will try to talk with you about that. If you're getting discouraged and falling away, your brothers and sisters will try to encourage you.

The New Testament clearly shows that our following Jesus is supposed to involve care and concern for each other. That is part of what it means to be a Christian. And though we do it imperfectly, we should be committed to building each other up, and, in so doing, building up the church.

I once had a friend who worked for a campus Christian ministry while attending a church where I was a member. He would always slip in right after the hymns, sit there for the sermon, and then leave. I asked him one day why he didn't come for the whole service. "Well," he said, "I don't get anything out of the rest of it." "Have you ever thought about joining the church?" I responded. He thought that was an absurd comment. He said, "Why would I join the church? If I join them, I think they would just slow me down spiritually."

I asked, "Have you ever considered that maybe God wants you to link arms with those other people, and that perhaps even though they might slow you down a little, you might help to speed them up—and that that's part of God's plan for how we're supposed to live as Christians together? Perhaps God cares about more than just you or me as individuals—maybe he also cares about the whole of the church together."

Of course you don't join a church because you're perfect and you're only going to bring benefits to the church. Whenever you join a church, you will bring problems into that church! But don't let that stop you—the church has problems already! That's why Christians are in a church. I've got problems; you've got problems. But we know that Jesus is Lord, and that his Spirit in us has already begun to work on those problems. Let's say, for example, that you're paranoid—that you don't really trust anyone. In Christ, God can begin to show you that he is trustworthy and that other people can be trustworthy too. Problem after problem, you will see God working in your life. Slowly, imperceptibly sometimes, but deliberately he will work on your problems, and most likely he will do that through his church.

It simply will not do for Christians to be self-centered, even in the name of Christ. God is not only concerned about the length and regularity of your quiet time each morning; he is also concerned about how you treat others—and that includes how you treat others with whom you have nothing in common except for Jesus Christ. That's why you need to invest your life in others and allow others to invest their lives in you. Being a member of a church should inculcate in you a committed concern for others. Growing as a Christian is not merely an individual matter; rather, it is a matter for the whole church.

Hebrews 10:19–25 has been called the "lettuce patch" of the New Testament. The writer keeps saying "let us . . . let us" throughout the passage. These are good verses to meditate on in our individualistic age:

> Therefore, brothers, since we have confidence to enter the Most Holy Place by the blood of Jesus, by a new and living way opened for us through the curtain, that is, his body, and since we have a great priest over the house of God, let us draw near to God with a sincere heart in full assurance of faith, having our hearts sprinkled to cleanse us from a guilty conscience and having our bodies washed with pure water. Let

> us hold unswervingly to the hope we profess, for he who promised is faithful. And let us consider how we may spur one another on toward love and good deeds. Let us not give up meeting together, as some are in the habit of doing, but let us encourage one another—and all the more as you see the Day approaching. (Heb. 10:19–25)

Church membership is our opportunity to grasp hold of each other in responsibility and love. By identifying ourselves with a particular church, we let the pastors and other members know that we intend to be committed in attendance, giving, prayer, and service. We allow fellow believers to have greater expectations of us in these areas, and we make it known that we are the responsibility of the local church. We assure the church of our commitment to Christ in serving with them, and we call for their commitment to serve and encourage us as well.

We see this concept of church life reflected, among other places, in Paul's use of body imagery when referring to the local church. We see it also in Scripture's "together" and "one another" passages.

Joining a church increases our sense of ownership of the work of the church, of its community, of its budget, and of its goals. We move from being pampered consumers to becoming joyous proprietors. We stop arriving late and complaining that we don't get exactly what we want; instead, we arrive early and try to help others with what they need. We must begin to view membership less as a loose affiliation useful only on occasion and more as a regular responsibility, becoming involved in one another's lives for the purposes of the gospel.

Many Christians today seem to have forgotten church membership—or they've forgotten the church altogether. That's why you find Christian books that talk about growing as a Christian but completely ignore the role of the church.

In Paul's first letter to the Corinthians, the purpose of spiritual gifts is to "build up the church" (1 Cor. 14:12). This is to be one of the main goals of your Christian life. According to Paul, this applies to every Christian.

Incorporation into the church is both a glorious privilege and a practical help. Joining a church will help you to encourage and edify your fellow Christians and to be encouraged and edified by them. It will help both you and others as you struggle with temptation. In my own local church, we covenant together that we will walk together in brotherly love, as becomes the members of a Christian church, exercise an affectionate care and watchfulness over each other, and faithfully admonish and entreat one another as occasion may require.

What about you? Do you love the people of God? Do you just feel well-disposed toward them, or do you actually, actively give to them? Do you use your hands for them? Your money? Your lips?

In the church, discipleship is both an individual project and a corporate activity as we follow Christ and help each other along the way. We can hold each other accountable in times of temptation. We can study God's Word together to prepare us for spiritual warfare. We can sing God's praises together and pray together. We can encourage each other's joy and share each other's burdens. As Jesus told us, "My command is this: Love each other as I have loved you. . . . This is my command: Love each other" (John 15:12, 17). John reinforced that when he wrote, "Dear children, let us not love with words or tongue but with actions and in truth" (1 John 3:18). Link arms with the other Christians around you, to build the church.

5. To Glorify God

Finally, if you are a Christian, you should join a church for the glory of God. Though it may be surprising to us, the way we live can bring glory to God. As Peter wrote to some early Christians, "Live such good lives among the pagans that, though they accuse you of doing wrong, they may see *your* good deeds and glorify God on the day he visits us" (1 Pet. 2:12).

Amazing, isn't it? You can tell that Peter had heard the teaching of his Master. Remember what Jesus taught in the Sermon on the Mount: "Let your light shine before men, that they may see your good deeds and praise your Father in heaven" (Matt. 5:16).

Again, the surprising assumption seems to be that God will get the glory for our good deeds. If that is true of our lives individually, it shouldn't surprise us that it is also true of our lives *together* as Christians. God intends that the way we love each other will identify us as followers of Christ. Recall Jesus's words in John 13:34–35: "A new command I give you: Love one another. As I have loved you, so you must love one another. By this all men will know that you are my disciples, if you love one another."

Our lives together are to mark us out as his and are to bring him praise and glory. Jesus said, "I will build my church" (Matt. 16:18). If Jesus is committed to the church, should we be any less committed to it?

Most Christians who regularly attend a God-centered, Bible-preaching church feel frustration at some point, but we should consider the obligations and opportunities of membership. Our basis as a congregational church family must always be in *being* even more than in doing. If you join a church, you are not included merely for a function you could perform (whether for your sake or the church's), but you are adopted into a family. And the relationships to which you are committing yourself will bring glory to God. This is why, if you are a Christian, you should join a church.

What Does Church Membership Entail?

Fundamentally, church membership entails a life of repentance and belief. God established the church to be the community of those who have been born again. His grace in our life, granting us repentance and faith, is signaled by two things.

1. In Action, Initially by Baptism

As we discussed at the end of chapter 3, the Bible presents baptism as a new Christian's first step; the New Testament assumes that all Christians have been baptized. In Romans 6, for instance, Paul assumes that the Christians to whom he is writing have all been baptized. This universal practice was rooted in the command of Christ recorded in the Great Commission (Matt. 28:18–20) and is written about in the book of Acts and throughout the New Testament. One must wonder why some who say they are Christ's disciples refuse to do something that they know is clearly commanded. As one writer observed,

> The church has not been given authority to make commandments; it is the duty of the church to obey the commandments already made. It is not the prerogative nor the privilege of any church to modify, minimize or in any way obscure . . . any commandment, of Jesus Christ.[8]

To reject baptism or the Lord's Supper or any other clear biblical command is to reject membership among Christ's disciples— among those who follow his commands.

2. In Writing, by Signing a Statement of Faith and Church Covenant

In addition to the biblical commands mentioned above, many Baptist and other evangelical churches express a commitment to God and to each other in writing by signing a "church covenant." This is an agreement members make with each other and with God to live out the Christian life together in a local church.

In my study I have a little booklet that our denomination has kept in print for more than seventy years. Its purpose is to encourage new church members. The first thing in the book is an example of a church covenant. At the bottom of the sample covenant is a place for the person to sign. Such signing of a covenant is not a new practice; it simply fell into disuse in the middle decades of the twentieth century. But earlier in American history, such signing was the general practice. In our church, hanging in a prominent place are the signatures of the founding members of the church, underneath the covenant to which

8 O. C. S. Wallace, *What Baptists Believe: The New Hampshire Confession: An Exposition* (Nashville, TN: The Sunday School Board of the Southern Baptist Convention, 1934), 89.

they subscribed when they joined the church. Consider such signatures, and the seriousness of them. These men and women chose to covenant together in response to God's grace in their lives. Do we do any less today in joining a church?

Special Responsibilities of Membership at Capitol Hill Baptist Church

At Capitol Hill Baptist Church, people attend membership classes before being interviewed for membership. We teach the following five responsibilities of membership.[9]

1. Attend services regularly. In Hebrews 10:25 we read that we should not forsake "the assembling of ourselves together" (KJV). That means we should regularly attend the weekly meetings of the church. At Capitol Hill Baptist, we first gather on Sunday morning and then again on Sunday evening, where we spend more time praying together.

2. Attend communion particularly. In Luke 22:19 Christ commands his disciples to remember and proclaim his death by regularly taking the covenant meal of the Lord's Supper together. It was Capitol Hill's custom a hundred years ago to have Thursday evening "covenant meetings" where members would renew their covenant and check on the status of their relations with each other before taking communion together the following Sunday. And in many churches at that time, to be absent from communion without a clear excuse was sufficient grounds for someone to be excluded from the membership of the church. In our church we don't do that, but I sometimes wonder if we should.

3. Attend members' meetings consistently. As a congregational church, the members' meeting is an important time in our lives together. It is

9 For more on how we apply these nine marks, see Mark Dever and Paul Alexander, *How to Build a Healthy Church: A Practical Guide for Deliberate Leadership* (Wheaton, IL: Crossway, 2021). We also sponsor a long-weekend workshop at our church three times a year called a Weekender. Church leaders interested in attending can go to https://www.9marks.org/events/what-is-a-weekender/ for more information.

the meeting of the church for making decisions as a church, a way to fulfill our Matthew 18 duties.

4. Pray regularly. Paul says we should pray "without ceasing" (1 Thess. 5:17 ESV). If your church has a membership directory, consider using it as a prayer list. We'll discuss this more in chapter 8.

5. Give regularly. Scripture is full of instructions about giving. For example, Solomon taught: "Honor the Lord with your wealth, / with the firstfruits of all your crops" (Prov. 3:9; see Mal. 3:10). Jesus taught his disciples: "Give, and it will be given to you. A good measure, pressed down, shaken together and running over, will be poured into your lap. For with the measure you use, it will be measured to you" (Luke 6:38; see 1 Cor. 16:1b–2). And Paul wrote to the Corinthian Christians that "each man should give what he has decided in his heart to give, not reluctantly or under compulsion, for God loves a cheerful giver" (2 Cor. 9:7).

These five responsibilities are some of what being a member of a church entails.

Are you concerned that such high expectations could put people off or make them feel excluded? I think such expectations actually help. By high expectations, I simply mean that if you're a member of *our* church, we will treat you as if you are converted. We'll assume that you increasingly love God and hate sin, that you are living accordingly, and that you want us to help you do so.

Many churches compromise on this point of high expectations in order to gain a sudden influx of members, but in so doing, they usually doom themselves to losing the gospel, and finally to becoming extinct. Taking unconverted persons into membership in a Christian church will inevitably obscure the gospel. If the gospel is downplayed or confused, the very lifeblood of the church will be cut off, and the church will increasingly lose any distinction from the unbelieving world. And if the salt loses its saltiness, it's good for nothing (Matt. 5:13).

How exclusive, then, should our churches be? Should our churches adjust our times of meeting, the length of our sermons, and the style of our music to the unbelievers we want to reach? How much is our gathering for the sake of those who are not Christians? Do we understand our meetings mainly in terms of evangelism to non-Christians, or do we understand them to be primarily for the building up of the members in Christ?

Church leaders often ask, how *inclusive* should we be? Of course, everyone wants to be inclusive. This is obviously loving. But the question of how apparently *exclusive* we should be perhaps gets to the point more quickly. Do we have to realize that we are out of God's favor before we can be brought in? Is this what we see of evangelism in the earliest churches in the book of Acts?

I do address nonbelievers in my sermons weekly. I have said, for instance, "My non-Christian friend, there is an unavoidable discontinuity between our lives and your life. And we actually serve you best if we're clear about that difference. If you've been enjoying the people, the friendliness, and the helpfulness of the people in our congregation, that's wonderful! I hope that continues. And the good news is that there is even more to all this than you've experienced!"

"Belonging before believing" is a popular idea among church leaders these days. And of course we should be extremely welcoming and friendly with nonbelievers in our churches, even inviting them deeper into our lives. But we must be careful about telling non-Christians the theological lie that they, in the most profound sense, belong. In the most profound sense they don't, and we serve them if we tell them that. We should show unbelievers that there is something more than horizontal community or a vague sense of God's presence in our congregations.

Conclusion

If the church is a building, then we must be bricks in it; if the church is a body, then we are its members; if the church is the household of faith, then we are part of that household. Sheep are in a flock, and branches are on a vine. Biblically, if we are Christians, we must be members of a church. This membership is not simply the record of a statement we once made or of affection toward a familiar place. It must be the reflection of a living commitment, or it is worthless.

Worse than being worthless, it is dangerous. Uninvolved members confuse both real members and non-Christians about what it means to be a Christian. We "active" members do the voluntarily "inactive" members no service when we allow them to remain members of the church. Membership is the church's corporate endorsement of a person's salvation. Yet how can a congregation honestly testify that someone invisible to it is faithfully running the race? If members have left our company and have not gone to any other Bible-believing church, what evidence do we have that they were ever truly a part of us? We do not necessarily know that such uninvolved people are *not* Christians; we may simply be unable to affirm that they are. We don't have to tell them that we know they're going to hell, but we can't tell them that we know for sure that they are going to heaven. Such unattached Christians should unite with a local church.

At Capitol Hill Baptist, by God's grace, we have seen our membership become more meaningful, as all who are members in name have become members in fact. Many members have made a renewed commitment to the life of the church. New members are being instructed in the faith. As we have sought to become the healthy church we were historically, our number in attendance has once again exceeded the number of members. We've also seen many members head out to help other local churches closer to where they live and even start new churches where there are none.

Pray that church membership may come to mean something more than it currently does in your church, so that your church can better know those for whom it is responsible, and can pray for them, encourage them, and challenge them.

We should not allow people to keep their church membership for sentimental reasons. Biblically, such membership is no membership at all. In our church's covenant we pledge: "We will, when we move from this place, as soon as possible, unite with some other church where we can carry out the spirit of this covenant and the principles of God's Word." Such commitment is part of healthy discipleship, particularly in our transient age.

Church membership means being incorporated in practical ways into the body of Christ. It means traveling together as aliens and strangers in this world as we head to our heavenly home. Certainly another mark of a healthy church is a biblical understanding of church membership.

In the next-to-the-last scene in Robert Bolt's play *A Man for All Seasons,* the doomed Sir Thomas More's daughter Meg comes to his cell to convince him to say what he needs to say to free himself. Meg pleads, "Then say the words of the oath and in your heart, think otherwise." She continues to argue with him.

"Well, . . . finally," says More, "it isn't a matter of reason; finally it's a matter of love."[10]

Joining a particular local church is an outward reflection of an inward love—for Christ and for his people. And, as we see so often in this life, the greatest love is rarely merely spontaneous; it is more often planned, premeditated, and characterized by commitment.

We read in Ephesians 5:25 that "Christ loved the church and gave himself up for her." Acts 20:28 reminds us that he bought his church with his own blood. If we are Christ's followers, we too will love the church that he gave himself for.

So, do not merely attend a church (though you should attend), but join a church. Link arms with other Christians. Find a church you can join, and do it so that non-Christians will hear and see the gospel, so that weak Christians will be cared for, so that strong Christians will channel their energies in a good way, so that church leaders will be encouraged and helped, and so that God will be glorified.

Christians in our country used to know all this, but as the nineteenth century wore on, social action replaced church action. Christians shifted their energies away from keeping their own churches pure to

10 Robert Bolt, *A Man for All Seasons* (New York: Random, 1990), 141.

trying to purify their communities.[11] By the time of the 1920s and '30s, evangelicals had learned something of the fickleness of our world through the celebrated Scopes trial and the repeal of Prohibition. The "fundamentalists" withdrew and attempted to preserve the gospel. In all the social involvement of the previous decades, the gospel had not been lost, but the church had very nearly been. The century since then has largely been a time of extreme individualism in American evangelicalism. Now we pray that we are on the verge of a recovery of the church as God's great tool for evangelism, discipleship, missions, and more. Through our love for one another, may God's love for the world again become visible.

Other Resources

- For group study: *Committing to One Another: Church Membership* (2012), by Bobby Jamieson, a seven-week inductive Bible study.
- For deeper reflection: *Church Membership: How the World Knows Who Represents Jesus* (2012), by Jonathan Leeman and *What Is a Healthy Church Member?* (2008), by Thabiti Anyabwile.
- See also Donald S. Whitney, *Spiritual Disciplines for the Christian Life* (1991); Mark Dever's chapter "Regaining Meaningful Church Membership," in *Restoring Integrity in Baptist Churches* (2008); Mark Dever and Jamie Dunlop's *The Compelling Community: Where God's Power Makes a Church Attractive* (2015); Jonathan Leeman, *Understanding the Congregation's Authority* (2016) and *The Rule of Love: How the Local Church Should Reflect God's Love and Authority* (2018); and Mark Dever, *Why Should I Join a Church?* (2020).

11 See further discussion of this shift from purifying the church to purifying society in chapter 5, and also in Gregory A. Wills, *Democratic Religion: Freedom, Authority, and Church Discipline in the Baptist South 1785–1900* (New York: Oxford University Press, 1996).

What's Coming Up

Mark Five: Biblical Church Discipline

Is All Discipline Negative?

What Is Church Discipline?

What Does the Bible Say about Church Discipline?

- Hebrews 12:1–14
- Matthew 18:15–17
- 1 Corinthians 5:1–11
- Galatians 6:1
- 2 Thessalonians 3:6–15
- 1 Timothy 1:20
- 1 Timothy 5:19–20
- Titus 3:9–11

How Have Christians in the Past Handled Church Discipline?

"Our Church Would Never Do This, Would We?"

Why Practice Church Discipline?

What If We Don't Practice Church Discipline?

Mark Five

Biblical Church Discipline

EMILY SULLIVAN OAKEY was born and educated in Albany, New York, where she later became a teacher. As with many other women of the mid-nineteenth century, she spent a good bit of time writing down her thoughts—in journals, articles, and poetry. She published many of her articles and poems in daily newspapers and in magazines. At age twenty-one, perhaps inspired by Jesus's parable of the sower, she wrote a poem about sowing and harvesting. Some twenty-five years later, in 1875, the poem was set to music by Philip Bliss and appeared in print for the first time under the title "What Shall the Harvest Be?"[1] The little group of Christians who formed what would later become Capitol Hill Baptist Church selected that song as the first song to be sung in their meeting together, in February of 1878:

> Sowing the seed by the daylight fair,
> Sowing the seed by the noonday glare,
> Sowing the seed by the fading light,
> Sowing the seed in the solemn night.
> O what shall the harvest be?
> O what shall the harvest be?[2]

1 Theron Brown and Hezekiah Butterworth, *The Story of the Hymns and Tunes* (New York: George H. Doran, 1923), 434.

2 Emily S. Oakley, "What Shall the Harvest Be?," 1850.

Very appropriate words to ring off the bare walls and floorboards of the building they met in. Those thirty people were planning to covenant to form a church: "What would the harvest be?"

In that same church, more than a century later, we are still helping to determine what will be the harvest of the founders' efforts. We do so by what we think and how we live, by whom we plan to see and what we plan to do, by what we feel and what we care about, by what we give ourselves for and what we pray about. What has the harvest been, and what will the harvest be?

This gets to the very heart of our question in this chapter: Are we to live as Christians on our own? Or do we have some obligation to each other? Do our obligations to each other involve merely encouraging each other positively? Or do they include a responsibility to speak honestly to each other of faults, shortcomings, departures from Scripture, or specific sins? Could our responsibilities before God also include sometimes making such matters public?

A discussion of a healthy church must include the topic of church discipline.

Is All Discipline Negative?

Church discipline sounds like a pretty negative topic, I admit. There isn't going to be much about this in "The Positive Bible," is there? When we hear the word *discipline*, we tend to think of correction or of a spanking; we think of our parents when we were little. If we're particularly literate, we have visions of Hester Prynne wearing her scarlet *A* around a nightmarish Puritan New England town of Nathaniel Hawthorne's slanderous and ill-informed imagination.

Without hesitation, we should all admit our need for discipline, for shaping. None of us are perfect, finished projects. We may need to be inspired, nurtured, or healed; we may need to be corrected, challenged, or even broken. Whatever the particular method of cure, let's at least admit the need for discipline. Let's not pretend or presume that we are just as we should be, as if God had finished his work with us.

Once we have come to that admission, however, we should notice that discipline is often positive, or as it is traditionally called, "formative." It is the stake that helps the tree grow in the right direction, the braces on the teeth, the extra set of wheels on the bicycle. It is the repeated instruction to keep your mouth closed when you're eating, or the regular exhortation to be careful about your words. Formative discipline refers to those things that shape people as they grow emotionally, physically, mentally, and spiritually. It's the basic shaping that takes place in our families as well as in our churches. We are taught by books at school, and by sermons and services and classes at church. All of this is part of discipline that is positive, shaping, and formative. Every truth that you have ever heard someone talk about is part of formative discipline. This chapter examines discipline in the broadest sense, not just in its "negative" aspects.

What Is Church Discipline?

When some hear the term *church discipline*, they become defensive and say something like, "Didn't Jesus say 'Judge not, lest you be judged'"? Certainly, in Matthew 7:1, Jesus forbids judging in one sense, and we'll consider that later in the chapter. But note that elsewhere in the Gospel of Matthew, Jesus also clearly calls us to rebuke others for sin, even publicly, if need be (Matt. 18:15–17; see Luke 17:3). Whatever Jesus means by not judging in Matthew 7, he does not mean to rule out the kind of judging he mandates in Matthew 18.

Remember that God himself is Judge, and, in a lesser sense, God intends others to judge as well. He has given the state the responsibility to judge (Rom. 13:1–7). We are told to judge ourselves (1 Cor. 11:28; 2 Cor. 13:5; Heb. 4; 2 Pet. 1:5–10). We are also specifically told to judge one another within the church (though not in the final way that God judges). Jesus's words in Matthew 18, Paul's in 1 Corinthians 5–6, and other passages (which we will consider) clearly show that the church is to exercise judgment within itself.

It's not surprising that the church is instructed to judge. After all, if we cannot say how a Christian *should not* live, how can we say how a Christian *should* live?

Several years ago I was asked to lead a special seminar because our church had been growing numerically and other churches wanted to know how and why that was happening. In preparing for the seminar, I reviewed some of the church growth material produced by our denominational headquarters. One publication said that in order to get our churches growing again, we should "open the front doors and close the back doors." The writer was saying that we need to open the front doors in the sense of trying to make our churches more accessible by helping people to understand what we're doing. Then, the writer said, we need to close the back door, that is, make it more difficult for people to flow through our churches, uncared-for and undiscipled.

These are valid criticisms of many of our churches, no doubt. But as I thought about it, I didn't think either of those were the critical problems we face. What we actually need to do is to close the front door and open the back door! If we want to see our churches grow, we need to make it harder to join, and we need to be better about excluding people. We need to be able to show that there is a distinction between the church and the world—that it means something to be a Christian. If someone who claims to be a Christian refuses to live as a Christian should live, we need to follow what Paul said and, for the glory of God and for that person's own good, we need to exclude him or her from membership in the church.

Biblical discipline should first appear in the way we take in new members. In 1 Corinthians 5, while dealing with a difficult situation in the church at Corinth, Paul made an assumption that we need to consider: "I have written you in my letter not to associate with sexually immoral people—not at all meaning the people of this world who are immoral, or the greedy and swindlers, or idolaters. In that case you would have to leave this world" (1 Cor. 5:9–10).

Notice that Paul has a clear distinction in his mind between the church and the world. Do we as Christians today make the same distinction? Do we assume that the church is different from the world? Not that the church is full of perfect people and the world is full of sinners, but do we assume that there is to be some kind of difference between the lives of those in the church and those in the world? Paul draws a sharp contrast. Membership in a local church is to be reflective (as best we can tell) of true membership in the body of Christ.

So, when we're examining new members, we have to consider whether those who are under consideration are known to be living Christ-honoring lives. Do we understand the seriousness of the commitment we are making to them when they join the church, and have we communicated to them the seriousness of the commitment that they are making to us? If we are more careful about how we recognize and receive new members, we will have less occasion to practice corrective church discipline later.

Book Recommendations on Church Discipline

Since the topic of church discipline hasn't been talked about in many circles for about a hundred years, I suggest the following resources for further study.

The best simple work that I know of is Jonathan Leeman's *Church Discipline: How the Church Protects the Name of Jesus* (2010). For more on the conceptual context of church discipline, see Leeman's *The Rule of Love: How the Local Church Should Reflect God's Love and Authority* (2018).

Paul Alexander and I describe more of how our church deals with discipline in chapter 5 of *How to Build a Healthy Church: A Practical Guide for Deliberate Leadership* (2021).

For historical background, read Gregory A. Wills's, *Democratic Religion: Freedom, Authority, and Church Discipline in the Baptist South, 1785–1900* (1996). Wills studied the practice of church discipline among Baptist churches in the South, particularly in Georgia, in the nineteenth century. The book includes some good stories and shrewd observations.

I also edited *Polity: Biblical Arguments on How to Conduct Church Life* (2000), a compendium of eighteenth- and nineteenth-century works on church discipline and polity, published by 9Marks and available as a PDF at www.9marks.org.

What Does the Bible Say about Church Discipline?

Many Bible passages address discipline; I will examine eight of them.

Hebrews 12:1–14

Hebrews 12 presents discipline as a fundamentally positive thing and reveals that God himself disciplines us:

> Therefore, since we are surrounded by such a great cloud of witnesses, let us throw off everything that hinders and the sin that so easily entangles, and let us run with perseverance the race marked out for us. Let us fix our eyes on Jesus, the author and perfecter of our faith, who for the joy set before him endured the cross, scorning its shame, and sat down at the right hand of the throne of God. Consider him who endured such opposition from sinful men, so that you will not grow weary and lose heart.
>
> In your struggle against sin, you have not yet resisted to the point of shedding your blood. And you have forgotten that word of encouragement that addresses you as sons:
>
> "My son, do not make light of the Lord's discipline,
> and do not lose heart when he rebukes you,

> because the Lord disciplines those he loves,
> and he punishes everyone he accepts as a son."
>
> Endure hardship as discipline; God is treating you as sons. For what son is not disciplined by his father? If you are not disciplined (and everyone undergoes discipline), then you are illegitimate children and not true sons. Moreover, we have all had human fathers who disciplined us and we respected them for it. How much more should we submit to the Father of our spirits and live! Our fathers disciplined us for a little while as they thought best; but God disciplines us for our good, that we may share in his holiness. No discipline seems pleasant at the time, but painful. Later on, however, it produces a harvest of righteousness and peace for those who have been trained by it.
>
> Therefore, strengthen your feeble arms and weak knees. "Make level paths for your feet," so that the lame may not be disabled, but rather healed.
>
> Make every effort to live in peace with all men and to be holy; without holiness no one will see the Lord.

God himself disciplines us and, as we will see, he commands us to do the same for each other. The local congregation has a special responsibility and a special competence in this regard.

Matthew 18:15–17

Matthew 18 is one of the two passages (the other being 1 Cor. 5) most often cited in discussions of church discipline. How do you respond when others sin against you? Do you sound off at them once and then refuse to talk to them anymore? Do you build up resentment in your heart? Here's what the Lord Jesus taught his disciples to do in such situations:

> If your brother sins against you, go and show him his fault, just between the two of you. If he listens to you, you have won your brother over. But if he will not listen, take one or two others along, so that "every matter

> may be established by the testimony of two or three witnesses." If he refuses to listen to them, tell it to the church; and if he refuses to listen even to the church, treat him as you would a pagan or a tax collector.

That, according to Jesus, is how we are to deal with disagreements and difficulties with fellow believers. Are you and others in your church following Christ's instructions here?

1 Corinthians 5:1–11

This is the longest and best-known passage on church discipline. Apparently someone in the Corinthian church was living an immoral lifestyle. Paul says:

> It is actually reported that there is sexual immorality among you, and of a kind that does not occur even among pagans: A man has his father's wife. And you are proud! Shouldn't you rather have been filled with grief and have put out of your fellowship the man who did this? Even though I am not physically present, I am with you in spirit. And I have already passed judgment on the one who did this, just as if I were present. When you are assembled in the name of our Lord Jesus and I am with you in spirit, and the power of our Lord Jesus is present, hand this man over to Satan, so that the sinful nature may be destroyed and his spirit saved on the day of the Lord.
>
> Your boasting is not good. Don't you know that a little yeast works through the whole batch of dough? Get rid of the old yeast that you may be a new batch without yeast—as you really are. For Christ, our Passover lamb, has been sacrificed. Therefore let us keep the Festival, not with the old yeast, the yeast of malice and wickedness, but with bread without yeast, the bread of sincerity and truth.
>
> I have written you in my letter not to associate with sexually immoral people—not at all meaning the people of this world who are immoral, or the greedy and swindlers, or idolaters. In that case you [illegible]ould have to [illegible] world. But now I am writing you that you

> must not associate with anyone who calls himself a brother but is sexually immoral or greedy, an idolater or a slanderer, a drunkard or a swindler. With such a man do not even eat.

Why did Paul say all that? Because he had come to hate the offender? No, but because that man was deeply deceived. He thought he could be a Christian while deliberately disobeying the Lord. Or perhaps he thought—and the church allowed him to think—that there was nothing wrong with his having his father's wife. Paul says that such a person is deluded, and that in order truly to serve such a deluded person and to glorify God, you need to show him the falsity of his profession of faith in light of the way he is living.

Elsewhere in his letters, Paul sheds more light on how such a process of loving confrontation should occur.

Galatians 6:1

This short verse is an important addition to our thinking on church discipline. Here Paul describes how Christians are to restore someone who has been caught in sin.

> Brothers, if someone is caught in a sin, you who are spiritual should restore him gently. But watch yourself, or you also may be tempted.

Paul was concerned not just with what was to be done in such a difficult situation but also with how it was to be done.

2 Thessalonians 3:6–15

It seems some people in the Thessalonian church were being lazy. To make matters worse, they were defending their inactivity, saying that it was God's will. Paul said it was not.

> In the name of the Lord Jesus Christ, we command you, brothers, to keep away from every brother who is idle and does not live according

> to the teaching you received from us. For you yourselves know how you ought to follow our example. We were not idle when we were with you, nor did we eat anyone's food without paying for it. On the contrary, we worked night and day, laboring and toiling so that we would not be a burden to any of you. We did this, not because we do not have the right to such help, but in order to make ourselves a model for you to follow. For even when we were with you, we gave you this rule: "If a man will not work, he shall not eat.
>
> We hear that some among you are idle. They are not busy; they are busybodies. Such people we command and urge in the Lord Jesus Christ to settle down and earn the bread they eat. And as for you, brothers, never tire of doing what is right.
>
> If anyone does not obey our instruction in this letter, take special note of him. Do not associate with him, in order that he may feel ashamed. Yet do not regard him as an enemy, but warn him as a brother.

Not associating with a person is part of the essence of church discipline. While scholars have debated what kind of discipline would result in still treating someone as a brother, it is beyond dispute that this is some action by the church as a whole to correct an individual in sin.

1 Timothy 1:20

Writing to Timothy, pastor of the church in Ephesus, Paul referred to some who had made "shipwreck" of their faith. Look at what he said should be done with such people.

> Among them are Hymenaeus and Alexander, whom I have handed over to Satan to be taught not to blaspheme.

We must not be distracted from our concern for the holiness of the flock. Like Paul and Timothy *and* Alexander and Hymenaeus, if we're to follow Christ, we will need help. And that's what Paul was doing here: helping. The purpose of discipline—even here—is that those who have wandered might repent.

1 Timothy 5:19–20

As he continued his letter to Timothy, Paul wrote specifically about what to do with church leaders who are caught in sin.

> Do not entertain an accusation against an elder unless it is brought by two or three witnesses. Those who sin are to be rebuked publicly, so that the others may take warning.

The honor we show leaders in our local church brings special responsibilities to those same leaders. They must live in such a way so as not to bring scandal to the gospel but honor. Visibility has its benefits and its costs, its opportunities and its dangers.

Titus 3:9–11

Apparently some people in the church where Titus pastored were causing divisions over issues that weren't that important. Paul wrote,

> But avoid foolish controversies and genealogies and arguments and quarrels about the law, because these are unprofitable and useless. Warn a divisive person once, and then warn him a second time. After that, have nothing to do with him. You may be sure that such a man is warped and sinful; he is self-condemned.

Taking all of these passages together, we see that God cares about both our understanding of his truth and our living it out. He cares especially about how we live together as Christians. All kinds of situations mentioned in these passages are, according to the Bible, legitimate areas for our concern—areas in which we as a church should exercise discipline.

One more thing: Did you notice how serious were the consequences Paul mandated in these descriptions of church discipline? "Put out of your fellowship . . . hand this man over to Satan . . . not to associate with. . . . With such a man do not even eat" (1 Cor. 5:2–11); "keep away from" (2 Thess. 3:6); "take special note of him. Do not associate with him, in order that he may feel ashamed" (2 Thess. 3:14–15); "handed over to Satan" (1 Tim. 1:20); "rebuked publicly" (1 Tim. 5:20); "have nothing to do with him" (Titus 3:10).

Is Paul just unusually severe? What did Jesus himself say about the person who refused to listen even to the church? "If he refuses to listen even to the church, treat him as you would a pagan or a tax collector" (Matt. 18:17). This is what the Bible says about church discipline.

How Have Christians in the Past Handled Church Discipline?

In times past, Christians regularly engaged in church discipline. In fact, disciplinary actions were a substantial part of the business at members' meetings of Baptist churches in the eighteenth and nineteenth centuries.

Writing almost eighty years ago, Greek scholar H. E. Dana observed,

> The abuse of discipline is reprehensible and destructive, but not more than the abandonment of discipline. Two generations ago the churches were applying discipline in a vindictive and arbitrary fashion that justly brought it into disrepute; today the pendulum has swung to the other extreme—discipline is almost wholly neglected. It is time for a new generation of pastors to restore this important function of the church to its rightful significance and place in church life.[3]

Greg Wills, professor of church history at Southwestern Baptist Theological Seminary, sheds light on a crucial change between the generations of our great-grandparents and our grandparents: the virtual disappearance of corrective discipline from churches. Wills's book *Democratic Religion* offers a wealth of quotations reminding us that

3 H. E. Dana, *A Manual of Ecclesiology* (Kansas City, KS: Central Seminary Press, 1944), 244.

pastors of the early 1800s clearly considered their most important tasks to be faithfully preaching the Word and faithfully administering godly discipline. In fact, a great part of the historic Baptist commitment to religious liberty was motivated by a desire that churches be free to exercise church discipline without the interference of the state.[4]

Wills shows that in pre-Civil War days, "Southern Baptists excommunicated nearly 2 percent of their membership every year"![5] Incredible as it may seem, their churches grew! In fact, their churches grew at twice the rate of the population growth. So the concern that a move to practice such biblical church discipline might be "anti-evangelistic" seems unfounded, to say the least.

This example also shows us how imperfect church discipline is. Those same churches accepted in membership slaveholders in a way we would find scandalous today. The scalpel is never wiser than the surgeon that wields it.

Jesus intended our lives to back up our words. If our lives don't back up our words, the evangelistic task is injured, as we have witnessed in America. Undisciplined churches have actually made it harder for people to hear the good news of new life in Jesus Christ.

What happened? Why did we stop practicing church discipline? Wills suggests, "This commitment to a holy corporate witness to the world declined as other things gained the attention of the Christians late in the [nineteenth] century and earlier in [the twentieth]." Wills writes:

> In fact, the more the churches concerned themselves with social order, the less they exerted church discipline. From about 1850 to 1920, a period of expanding evangelical solicitude for the reformation of society, church discipline declined steadily. From temperance to Sabbatarian reform, evangelicals persuaded their communities to adopt the moral norms of the church for society at large. As Baptists learned to reform the larger society, they forgot how they had

4 Wills, *Democratic Religion*, 32.

5 Wills, *Democratic Religion*, 22.

> once reformed themselves. Church discipline presupposed a stark dichotomy between the norms of society and the kingdom of God. The more evangelicals purified the society, the less they felt the urgency of a discipline that separated the church from the world.[6]

As Wills explains,

> After the Civil War, . . . observers began to lament that church discipline was foundering, and it was. It declined partly because it became more burdensome in larger churches. Young Baptists refused in increasing numbers to submit to discipline for dancing, and the churches shrank from excluding them. Urban churches, pressed by the need for large buildings and the desire for refined music and preaching, subordinated church discipline to the task of keeping the church solvent. Many Baptists shared a new vision of the church, replacing the pursuit of purity with the quest for efficiency. They lost the resolve to purge their churches of straying members. No one publicly advocated the demise of discipline. No Baptist leader arose to call for an end to congregational censures. No theologians argued that discipline was unsound in principle or practice. . . . It simply faded away, as if Baptists had grown weary of holding one another accountable.[7]

As Baptist churches of the nineteenth century retreated from church discipline, the work of the pastor also changed. It had subtly though certainly become more public. Previously, people thought that the work of a pastor was to see that souls were mended by repeated private conferences with families or individuals. But what occurred more and more were protracted series of meetings and entertainments and impassioned calls to immediate decision, with the pastor called upon occasionally to deal with only the most serious cases of church discipline. The church,

6 Wills, *Democratic Religion*, 10.

7 Wills, *Democratic Religion*, 9.

increasingly, didn't become involved with such problems and, in fact, wasn't even aware of them. There was no longer a community that mutually covenanted together for accountability. Instead, the pastor alone was expected to deal with just a few cases—those that could cause the church the most public embarrassment.

In all of these changes, important boundaries were blurred. The pastor's role was confused. Even more fundamentally, the distinction between the church and the world began to be lost. And this loss was to the great detriment of the churches' evangelistic ministry—and to our own lives as Christians.

All evangelical Christians in the past tended to practice biblical church discipline. In 1561, Reformed Christians expressed their understanding of these matters in the Belgic Confession:

> The marks by which the true Church is known are these: If the pure doctrine of the gospel is preached therein; if she maintains the pure administration of the sacraments as instituted by Christ; if church discipline is exercised in punishing of sin; in short, if all things are managed according to the pure Word of God, all things contrary thereto rejected, and Jesus Christ acknowledged as the only Head of the Church. Hereby the true Church may certainly be known, from which no man has a right to separate himself.[8]

It is clear that, in the past, churches intended to practice biblical discipline.

"Our Church Would Never Do This, Would We?"

Sometimes church members are shocked at the idea of church discipline when they encounter it for the first time, and you hear them say something like, "Our church would never do this, would we?" In fact, that response shows how easy it is to forget what, for centuries, was a common practice among Christians.

8 Philip Schaff, *The Creeds of Christendom: With a History and Critical Notes* (Grand Rapids, MI: Baker, 1983), 419–20.

The local church I pastor in Washington, DC, has from its earliest days recognized the importance of church discipline. When the group of Christians met together that first day and sang that hymn, they incorporated as a church. One of the first things they did that day in February 1878 was to adopt the following rules about the church censuring people either by admonition (warning) or by exclusion, which would happen after they had been warned. Regarding admonishing a member, they said,

> When one member of the church trespasses against another member, if the offence is not of a public character, it is the duty of the offended to seek an opportunity to converse privately with the offender, with a view to the reconcilement of the difficulty, according to the rule laid down in Matthew 18:15.
>
> If the offender refuses to give satisfaction, it shall be the duty of the offended to select one or two members of the church, and with their aid to endeavor to reconcile the offender, according to the rule laid down in Matthew 18:16.
>
> If these efforts fail to secure a satisfactory adjustment of the difficulty, it shall be the duty of the offended to lay the matter before the church, as directed in Matthew 18:17, and if, after the offender shall have been admonished, in a spirit of meekness and forbearance, he or she shall continue obstinate and incorrigible, it shall be the duty of the church to investigate the case, and take such action as may be necessary.
>
> Charges to be preferred against a member shall be in writing, and shall not be presented to the church without the previous knowledge of the Pastor and Deacons, nor until a copy shall have been presented to the offender.

They also discussed what was to happen if the erring member did not repent. The next step was exclusion. They said that exclusion

> . . . is a judicial act of the church, passed upon an offender by the authority of the Lord Jesus Christ, by which he or she is cut off from

> the membership and communion of the church, according to the rule . . . from Matthew 18:17.
>
> No member shall be excluded until he or she shall have been notified to appear before the church, and has had the privilege of answering in person the charges which have been preferred, except in cases of notorious and flagrant immorality, when it shall be the duty of the church to vindicate the honor of its holy calling by proceeding to cut off such an offending member without delay.

What matters were so serious that these founders felt biblically required to respond with such strong measures?

> Members shall be liable to the discipline of the church for the following causes:
>
> For any outward violations of the moral law.
>
> For pursuing any course which may, in the judgment of the church, be disreputable to it as a body.
>
> For absenting themselves habitually without good reasons, from the church at the seasons set apart for public worship.
>
> For holding and advocating doctrines opposed to those set forth in [the statement of faith].
>
> For neglecting or refusing to contribute toward defraying the expenses of the church according to their several abilities.
>
> For treating the acts and doings of the church contemptuously, or pursuing such a course as is calculated to produce discord.
>
> For divulging to persons not interested, what is done in the meetings of the church.
>
> For pursuing any course of conduct unbecoming good citizens and professing Christians.

If you were part of Capitol Hill Baptist Church in 1878, would you have cause to be warned by the church about something? I regularly see the names of our founding members. Recall that their signatures are on the original church covenant that hangs prominently on a wall in our church. Among those first thirty-one signatures, I also find the very names of some of those involved in the first recorded cases of church discipline. I find that two members were excluded (out of about eighty total members of the church) in 1880. Who were they and what happened? We don't know much, but the church clerk seems to refer to this difficult situation in an annual church letter; in his otherwise glowing report for 1879, we have this brief note from Francis McLean, the clerk:

> One thing I must whisper softly: the thrifty growth and the dense foliage do not quite conceal a few apparently dead limbs on the tree. Here lies a responsibility—a care—let us act wisely and well.

It seems that one of those "dead limbs" was actually one of the people who had signed as a founding member of the church. His name was Charles L. Patten. He had served as secretary of the Sunday school. And yet, in the minutes for a meeting of the church on December 17, 1879, we find this brief note:

> Pastor presented applications for letters of dismission from this Church to the First Baptist Church, this city, each dated Oct. 30, 1879, from Sister Alma C. Smith and Bro. Charles L. Patten. Pastor stated these letters had been withheld, in his discretion, and he now presented them for the action of the church. Bro. Williamson moved that Sister Smith be granted letters of dismission. Lost. On motion of Bro. Kingdon, a Committee was chosen, composed of the Pastor, Brethren C. W. Longan, and Ward Morgan, to consider this application of Bro. Patten, and that he be requested to appear before that committee, to state the reasons why he had separated from his wife.

That was in the public meeting of the church. They did not want it thought that Christians leave their wives. About a month later, at a church meeting on January 21, 1880, we read,

> Pastor, on behalf of Committee to investigate case of Bro. Patten, reported that a letter had been written to him, to which he had responded in writing, but that further effort of Committee had failed to meet with any response. The Committee was considered as having reported progress and still retaining the matter in charge.

At the same meeting, a second disciplinary matter was raised in the case of yet another founding member of the congregation:

> Clerk presented the following motion, which was adopted, viz: That a Committee, composed of the Pastor and Deacons, be and is hereby requested to take into consideration such facts in the case of Sister Lucretia E. Douglas, as may explain the reasons, if any, of her nonattendance at the meetings of the church for over a year past, and to recommend at the next Quarterly Meeting what they shall deem to be the wisest and best course in the matter on the part of this church.

Nonattendance, as in the case of Sister Douglas, was considered one of the most sinister of sins, because it usually veiled other sins. When someone began to be in sin, they would usually stop attending.

So, not only *would* Capitol Hill Baptist Church practice church discipline—we can, and we have! And so have many other churches. For most of church history, this has been the regular business of the church.

Why Practice Church Discipline?

1. For the Good of the Person Disciplined. The man in Corinth was lost in his sin, thinking God approved of his having an affair with his father's wife (see 1 Cor. 5:1–5). The people in the churches in Galatia thought it was fine that they were trusting in their own works rather than in Christ alone (see Gal. 6:1–5). Alexander and Hymenaeus thought it was all right for them to blaspheme God (see 1 Tim. 1:20). But none of these people was in good standing with God. Out of our love for such people, we want to see church discipline practiced. We don't want our churches to encourage hypocrites who are hardened, confirmed, and lulled in their sins. We don't want to live that kind of life individually, or as a church.

2. For the Good of Other Christians, as They See the Danger of Sin. Paul told Timothy that if a leader sins, he should be rebuked publicly (1 Tim. 5:20). That doesn't mean that anytime I, as a pastor, do anything wrong, members of my church should stand up in the public service and say, "Hey, Mark, that was wrong." It means that when one commits a serious sin (particularly one that's not repented of), it needs to be brought up in public so that others will take warning by seeing the serious nature of sin.

3. For the Health of the Church as a Whole. Paul pleads with the believers at Corinth, saying that they shouldn't have boasted about having such toleration for sin in the church (1 Cor. 5:6–8). He asked rhetorically, "Don't you know that a little yeast works through the whole batch of dough?" (5:6). Yeast represents the unclean and spreading nature of sin. So, says Paul,

> Get rid of the old yeast that you may be a new batch without yeast—as you really are. For Christ, our Passover lamb, has been sacrificed. Therefore let us keep the Festival [the Passover supper], not with the old yeast, the yeast of malice and wickedness, but with bread without yeast, the bread of sincerity and truth. (1 Cor. 5:7–8)

For the Passover meal, a lamb was slaughtered and unleavened bread was eaten. Paul tells the Corinthians that the lamb (Christ) had been slaughtered, and that they (the Corinthian church) were to be the unleavened bread. They were to have no leaven of sin in them. They, as a whole church, were to be an acceptable sacrifice.

Of course, none of this means that discipline is to be the focal point of the church. Discipline is no more the focal point of the church than medicine is the focal point of life. There may be some times when you are necessarily consumed with discipline, but generally it should be no more than something that allows you to get on with your main task. It is certainly not the main task itself.

4. For the Corporate Witness of the Church. Church discipline is a powerful tool in evangelism. People notice when our lives are different, especially when there's a whole community of people whose lives are different—not people whose lives are perfect, but whose lives are marked by genuinely trying to love God and one another. When churches are seen as conforming to the world, our evangelistic task becomes all the more difficult. We become so like the unbelievers they have no questions they want to ask us. May we so live that people are made constructively curious. (See Matt. 5:16; John 13:34–35; 1 Cor. 5:1; 1 Pet. 2:12.)

5. For the Glory of God, as We Reflect His Holiness. The Scriptures are clear that God created us for his glory (see Eph. 5:25–27; Heb. 12:10–14; 1 Pet. 1:15–16; 2:9–12; 1 John 3:2–3). The most compelling reason to practice church discipline is to glorify God. That's why we're alive! We humans were made to bear God's image, and to carry his character to his creation (Gen. 1:27). So it is no surprise that throughout the Old Testament, as God fashioned a people to bear his image, he instructed them in holiness so that their character might better approximate his own (see Lev. 11:44; 19:2). This was the basis for correction and even exclusion in Old Testament times, as God fashioned a people for himself; and it was the basis for shaping the New Testament church as well (see 2 Cor. 6:14–7:1). Christians are supposed to be conspicuously holy, not for our own reputation but for God's.

We are to be the light of the world, so that when people see our good deeds, they will glorify God (Matt. 5:16). Peter says, "Live such good lives among the pagans that, though they accuse you of doing wrong, they may see your good deeds and glorify God on the day he visits us" (1 Pet. 2:12). This is why God has called us and saved us and set us apart (Col. 1:21–22).

What else should we look like, if we bear Christ's name? Paul wrote to the church at Corinth,

> Do you not know that the wicked will not inherit the kingdom of God? Do not be deceived: Neither the sexually immoral nor idolaters nor adulterers nor male prostitutes nor homosexual offenders nor thieves nor the greedy nor drunkards nor slanderers nor swindlers will inherit the kingdom of God. And that is what some of you were. But you were washed, you were sanctified, you were justified in the name of the Lord Jesus Christ and by the Spirit of our God. (1 Cor. 6:9–11)

From the very beginning, Jesus had instructed his disciples to teach people to obey all that he had taught (Matt. 28:19–20). God will have a holy people to reflect his character. The picture of the church at the end of the book of Revelation is of a glorious bride who reflects the character of Christ himself, while "outside are the dogs, those who practice magic arts, the sexually immoral, the murderers, the idolaters and everyone who loves and practices falsehood" (Rev. 22:15).

Taking 1 Corinthians 5 as a model, churches have long recognized church discipline as one of the boundaries that makes church membership mean something. The assumption is that church members are people who can appropriately take Communion without bringing disgrace on the church, condemnation on themselves, or dishonor to God and his gospel (see 1 Cor. 11).

When we consider such passages, and the qualifications for leaders in the church, we see that Christians more actively bear the responsibility to have a good name than do people in the world. Our secular courts place a strict burden of proof on those who charge others with guilt. We presume innocence until one is proved guilty. But in the church, our responsibility is slightly but importantly different. Our lives are the storefront display of God's character in his world. We cannot finally determine what others think of us, and we know that we are to expect such strong disapproval that we will even be persecuted for righteousness. But so far as it lies within us, we are to live lives that commend the gospel to others. We actively bear a responsibility to live lives that will bring praise and glory to God, not ignominy and shame.

Our biblical theology may explain church discipline. Our teaching and preaching may instruct about it. Our church leaders may encourage it. But it is only the church that may and must finally enforce discipline.

Biblical church discipline is simple obedience to God and a simple confession that we need help. We cannot live the Christian life alone. Our purpose in church discipline is positive for the individual disciplined, for other Christians as they see the real danger of sin, for the health of the church as a whole, and for the corporate witness of the church to those outside. Most of all, our holiness is to reflect the holiness of God. It should mean something to be a member of the church, not for our pride's sake but for God's name's sake. Biblical church discipline is a mark of a healthy church.

What If We Don't Practice Church Discipline?

We have to wonder what it means to be a church if our church won't practice church discipline.[9] Ultimately, this is a question about the nature of our churches.

Greg Wills writes that, to many Christians in the past, "a church without discipline would hardly have counted as a church."[10] John Dagg writes, "When discipline leaves a church, Christ goes with it."[11] If we can't say what something is not, we can't very well say what it is. If we give up the ability to say what a Christian is not, we cannot meaningfully say what a Christian is.

Our lives should back up our professions of faith. We need to love each other. We need to hold each other accountable, because all of us will have times when our flesh wants to go in a way different than what God has revealed in Scripture. And part of the way we love each other is by being honest and establishing relationships with each other and

9 This is not the same thing as a pastor who is committed to recovering the practice of church discipline but who has decided to delay beginning it in order to first teach on the subject. See Appendix 2, "'Don't Do it!' Why You Shouldn't Practice Church Discipline."

10 Wills, *Democratic Religion*, 33.

11 John L. Dagg, *Manual of Church Order* (Harrisonburg, VA: Gano, 1982), 274.

speaking in love to each other. We need to love each other, and we need to love those outside our church whom our witness affects. And we need to love God, who is holy, and who calls us not to bear his name in vain but to be holy as he is holy. That's a tremendous privilege and a great responsibility.

If we want to see our churches healthy, we must actively care for each other, even to the point of confronting. It all gets very practical, doesn't it, when you get right down to it—all this talk about a church, new life, covenant, and committed relationships?

What shall the harvest be?

Sowing the seed by the wayside high,
Sowing the seed on the rocks to die,
Sowing the seed where the thorns will spoil,
Sowing the seed in the fertile soil:

Sowing the seed with an aching heart,
Sowing the seed while the teardrops start,
Sowing in hope till the reapers come
Gladly to gather the harvest home:
O what shall the harvest be?[12]

Other Resources

- For group study: *Guarding One Another: Church Discipline* (2012), by Bobby Jamieson, a six-week inductive Bible study from 9Marks.
- For pastoral application: *Church Discipline: How the Church Protects the Name of Jesus* (2012), by Jonathan Leeman.
- See also Jonathan Leeman, *The Rule of Love: How the Local Church Should Reflect God's Love and Authority* (2018) and Gregory A. Wills, *Democratic Religion: Freedom, Authority, and Church Discipline in the Baptist South, 1785–1900* (1996).

12 Oakley, "What Shall the Harvest Be?"

What's Coming Up

Mark Six: A Biblical Concern for Discipleship and Growth

A Biblical Theology of Growth

A Biblical Practice of Growth

- Expositional Preaching
- Gospel Doctrine
- A Biblical Understanding of Conversion and Evangelism
- A Biblical Understanding of Church Membership
- A Biblical Understanding of Church Discipline
- A Biblical Understanding of Church Leadership
- A Biblical Understanding and Practice of Prayer
- A Biblical Understanding and Practice of Missions

Hopes for Growth

- Pastoral Visitation
- Growth Together as a Church

The Importance of Good Growth

What If We Don't Grow?

Mark Six

A Biblical Concern for Discipleship and Growth

ROB PRAYED TO RECEIVE CHRIST when he was seventeen. He had had a hard few months, and he felt done in. To say that he was at the end of his rope might be too dramatic, but that's basically how he felt. Rob had never been much for church, but he had nothing against it. He wasn't an atheist or anything. He simply had never seen much in it.

Then his friend Shawn invited him to go to a Christian meeting with him, and Rob was feeling so down that he thought, *Maybe this will help.* At the meeting he talked with Shawn and with a nice young lady named Sarah, until almost midnight.

The conversation started out light but became fairly serious when Shawn and then Sarah began to share some things that they had gone through recently. Eventually it just got to Rob. He didn't break down and cry; he just opened up and was more honest with these two people than he usually was even with himself. "My life feels out of control. Everything seems to be going wrong. And the things that aren't going wrong don't seem to matter to me."

And that's when he did it. In five minutes—or less—Sarah and Shawn told him about the wonderful life he could have as a Christian, and the free gift he could have right now of forgiveness from God for everything he had ever done wrong, and eternal life with God in heaven when he died. It seemed like the best thing Rob had been offered in a long time, and it also seemed kind of, well, sweet that these two people would sit there and listen to him and tell him these kinds of things.

When Rob asked how he could "sign up," Shawn and Sarah handed him a little booklet and pointed to a paragraph in bold letters, printed on the back cover. It was a prayer. "Repeat after me," said Shawn, and Rob did. Each time Shawn read a line and paused, Rob repeated the line. He was reading them to God. He was praying. And that was that. Shawn and Sarah told him, excitedly, that he had become a Christian, because God promised that if anyone confessed his sins, God would forgive him. Rob knew that he had done bad things. So he prayed. And there it was. It was over and done with. He was saved.

In the years that followed, Rob lived a pretty upstanding life. By the time he was forty, some people even thought of him as a pillar of the church.

He got involved in a church where the preaching was usually exciting. The sermons were short, to the point, and filled with good stories, memorable anecdotes, and moving illustrations. Rob really loved to listen, especially to the stories.

He would have had to confess, had anyone cornered him, that he didn't really know his Bible very well. Though he taught Sunday school for several years, he couldn't really tell you where most of the books in the Bible were, or why the exodus was important, or what the book of Revelation was about. Rob had his own thoughts about God and shared these with people, but he didn't really get them from the Bible. They were just the things he heard and thought himself.

He imagined the gospel to be a pretty straightforward offer from God—to forgive our sins if we would just own up to them ("Yeah, that one's mine"). He knew that Jesus and the cross were important; he wasn't sure exactly how, but he knew they were important.

If the truth were known, Rob thought of conversion kind of like the decision to buy a new car or some other momentous decision in life.

It was big, and a little scary, but it was just something you had to do. Everyone, he thought, should get around to it sometime, and sooner would be better than later . . . because, you know, you never know . . .

Evangelism, to Rob, was what the church staff did, and what he had done himself maybe a couple of times. He had to do a bit of it back when they had the pastor who was big on knocking on doors, and then once when he went as a chaperone on the youth choir trip and a couple of the boys had some questions about what it meant to be baptized and join the church—so he had talked to them about it.

Actually, Rob himself had never joined the church, but most people probably didn't even realize that. He went through periods of more involvement and periods of less involvement. Sometimes he attended every Sunday for a year and then other times he wouldn't be there for a month, two months, three months; and, honestly, he kind of liked it that way. He was able to pick and choose the things he wanted to get involved with. After all, joining the church had always seemed to him like giving someone a blank check.

And then there were the problems a few years back when his daughter, who was in the church choir, had been taught some things that he thought were just crazy. Why, if they had gone on, his daughter could even have ended up as a foreign missionary or something! So he had forbade her to go to choir, youth group, Bible study, or even church for a while, and he didn't go himself for the better part of a year. He wasn't too worried about it, though, because he believed "once saved, always saved," and he knew that he had been saved because he had prayed that prayer with Sarah and Shawn. He didn't really have anything to worry about.

Besides, at that time they had a pastor with whom he didn't get along very well, and, to be honest, he figured he would wait him out. He had seen pastors come and go. Some of the new things this pastor wanted to do really bothered him. This new pastor wanted to give a lot more money to missions when there was plenty of work to be done on their own building. He talked about the church changing things, like having elders; he even talked about "church discipline" (which to Rob sounded scary, judgmental, and un-Christian). Rob knew that most pastors didn't last long, especially if Rob let it be known that he was avoiding church involvement for a while because of a particular pastor.

Is it surprising that Rob wasn't really growing as a Christian? And, more than that, that it didn't bother him that he wasn't growing as a Christian?

In order to help us consider situations like Rob's, here are five questions:

1. Are such desires for spiritual growth biblical? Or can we as believers be settled, comfortable, and secure like Rob was?
2. If we do want to grow spiritually—as individuals and as a church—how do we do that?
3. What am I trying to do in my own church to help our growth?
4. Is spiritual growth really so important?
5. What if we don't grow?

A healthy church is characterized by having members who are seriously concerned for their spiritual growth. In a healthy church, people want to get better at following Jesus Christ.

A Biblical Theology of Growth

First, is the desire for spiritual growth biblical, or is it merely an example of modern American progress-mania—we worship progress in everything and so we import that value into our understanding of Christianity? Or is a focus on spiritual growth a kind of spiritual self-centeredness where we become Christian-narcissists, overly concerned about our own spiritual virtues?

As we study Scripture, we find that spiritual growth is not merely a concern of forward-looking Americans; it is a concern of the Bible as well.

In the first chapter of the Bible, God commanded the creatures of the land and sea to multiply: "God blessed them and said, 'Be fruitful and increase in number and fill the water in the seas, and let the birds increase on the earth'" (Gen. 1:22). And he gave that command, and more, to Adam and Eve just a few verses later: "God blessed them and said to them, 'Be fruitful and increase in number; fill the earth and subdue it. Rule over the fish of the sea and the birds of the air and over every living creature that moves on the ground'" (1:28).

A few chapters later, after God wiped out the world in judgment with the flood, what was the first thing he commanded the sons of Noah to do? "Then God blessed Noah and his sons, saying to them, 'Be fruitful and increase in number and fill the earth'" (Gen. 9:1).

Later in Genesis, God promised Abraham that the number of his descendants would be great and would increase. When the children of Israel went down into Egypt in captivity, they multiplied and increased in number. That was a sign of God's blessing. God blessed them again when they went into the Promised Land. Even when they were taken into exile in Babylonia, what happened? The Lord instructed them through Jeremiah: "Marry and have sons and daughters; find wives for your sons and give your daughters in marriage, so that they too may have sons and daughters. Increase in number there; do not decrease" (Jer. 29:6).

God does not subscribe to the idea that small is beautiful! Though sometimes less is more, smaller is not necessarily better. I'm not saying that God is from Texas, but that he seems to view abundance as a blessing. One of the ways God encourages righteousness in the Old Testament is by the abundance of blessings he pours out in growth and prosperity. So we read in Psalm 92:12–13:

> The righteous will flourish like a palm tree,
> they will grow like a cedar of Lebanon;
> planted in the house of the LORD,
> they will flourish in the courts of our God.

And in Proverbs, God gives instructions on how we can grow. Basically he tells us to increase strength by increasing wisdom, and to increase wisdom by being with the wise (Prov. 24:5; 13:20).

Of course, we're not to seek the wrong kind of growth. We're not to be too impressed by the increase of physical things such as wealth and possessions. As Psalm 49:16–17 warns:

> Do not be overawed when a man grows rich,
>   when the splendor of his house increases;
> for he will take nothing with him when he dies.

Death garners from us all the possessions we accumulate in this world. So we shouldn't be too impressed by them.

One thing the Bible teaches about growth is that the kingdom of heaven will grow. This was prophesied in the Old Testament, and Jesus promised it as well. We sing that prophecy around Christmastime each year from Isaiah 9:7, in which the Lord promised that the kingdom of his Messiah would grow:

> Of the increase of his government and peace
>   there will be no end.
> He will reign on David's throne
>   and over his kingdom,
> establishing and upholding it
>   with justice and righteousness
>   from that time on and forever.
> The zeal of the Lord Almighty
>   will accomplish this.

The Lord Jesus himself speaks of how his kingdom will grow in fulfillment of this prophecy. He says it will grow from the smallest seed to the largest plant in the garden: "Though it is the smallest of all your seeds, yet when it grows, it is the largest of garden plants and becomes a tree, so that the birds of the air come and perch in its branches" (Matt. 13:32).

The seed, of course, did fall to the ground and die. But though Jesus was crucified and buried, he was raised again, and the kingdom of God that he began to build did exactly what he prophesied it would do. It began to grow. The book of Acts repeats that refrain again and again:

> In those days when the number of disciples was increasing . . . the word of God spread. The number of disciples in Jerusalem increased rapidly, and a large number of priests became obedient to the faith. (Acts 6:1, 7)

> But the word of God continued to increase and spread. (Acts 12:24)

> The word of the Lord spread through the whole region. (Acts 13:49)

> In this way the word of the Lord spread widely and grew in power. (Acts 19:20)

We find numerical growth in the New Testament just as in the Old Testament. But the growth that is discussed and urged and prayed for in the New Testament isn't simply numerical growth. If your church is more crowded with people now than it was a few years ago, does that mean that it is a healthy church? Not necessarily.[1] There is another kind of growth. The New Testament idea of growth involves not just more people, but people who are growing up, maturing, and deepening in the faith. We read in Ephesians 4:15–16: "Instead, speaking the

1 A few years ago, Willow Creek Community Church conducted an interesting self-study that bore this out. See Greg Hawkins and Cally Parkinson, *Reveal* (Barrington, IL: Willow Creek Resources, 2007).

truth in love, we will in all things grow up into him who is the Head, that is, Christ. From him the whole body, joined and held together by every supporting ligament, grows and builds itself up in love, as each part does its work."

How does such growth happen? Ultimately, it happens by God's work. We grow as the body of Christ as God causes growth. According to Colossians 2:19, Christ is "the Head, from whom the whole body, supported and held together by its ligaments and sinews, grows as God causes it to grow."

It is not the preacher who causes a church to grow. God may use a preacher; that's up to God. Paul wrote to the Corinthian Christians about this very point. They were particularly prone to worship eloquent preachers. So Paul reminded them that he "planted the seed, Apollos watered it, but God made it grow. So neither he who plants nor he who waters is anything, but only God, who makes things grow" (1 Cor. 3:6–7).

Paul was a good disciple of Jesus, who himself had taught that the growth of the kingdom of God comes from God and does not ultimately depend on us. In Mark 4 Jesus compares the kingdom of God to a crop that grows while the farmer sleeps; whether the farmer gets up or not, the crop continues to grow. "Night and day, whether [the farmer] sleeps or gets up, the seed sprouts and grows, though he does not know how" (Mark 4:27). Jesus's point isn't that we should be lazy and indolent, but that the growth of the kingdom of God does not finally depend on us. God himself is committed to ensuring the growth of his church.

This is why, when Paul writes to the Thessalonians, he doesn't so much congratulate them on their growth—"Oh, you've grown so well!"—but rather thanks God for it. "We ought always to thank God for you, brothers, and rightly so, because your faith is growing more and more, and the love every one of you has for each other is increasing" (2 Thess. 1:3). Growth doesn't have to produce pride. Growth can cause humility and recognition that it is God who gives growth.

This is why, when Paul wants a congregation to grow, he prays for them. He realizes that growth comes from God. In Paul's first letter to the Thessalonians he prays,

> Now may our God and Father himself and our Lord Jesus clear the way for us to come to you. May the Lord make your love increase and overflow for each other and for everyone else, just as ours does for you. May he strengthen your hearts so that you will be blameless and holy in the presence of our God and Father when our Lord Jesus comes with all his holy ones. (1 Thess. 3:11–13)

In Colossians, Paul again prays that his readers will grow spiritually: "We pray this in order that you may live a life worthy of the Lord and may please him in every way: bearing fruit in every good work, growing in the knowledge of God" (Col. 1:10).

Now, I don't mean to suggest that we have nothing to do with our own spiritual growth. The fact that I've even bothered to write about this means I must believe that we as Christians have something to do with our own spiritual growth. In 2 Peter 3:18, Peter finishes his letter with an exhortation to "grow in the grace and knowledge of our Lord and Savior Jesus Christ." It is an imperative. "Grow!" he says.

We should want to grow spiritually. But how do we do it? In the first chapter of this letter, Peter says, "For if you possess these qualities in increasing measure, they will keep you from being ineffective and unproductive in your knowledge of our Lord Jesus Christ" (2 Pet. 1:8).

What qualities?

> For this very reason, make every effort to add to your faith goodness; and to goodness, knowledge; and to knowledge, self-control; and to self-control, perseverance; and to perseverance, godliness; and to godliness, brotherly kindness; and to brotherly kindness, love. For if you possess these qualities in increasing measure, they will keep

> you from being ineffective and unproductive in your knowledge of our Lord Jesus Christ. (2 Pet. 1:5–8)

We should want to grow. And we grow by cultivating these qualities. Elsewhere Peter emphasizes the importance of knowing God's Word. If you want to grow, he says, do this:

> Like newborn babies, crave pure spiritual milk, so that by it you may grow up in your salvation, now that you have tasted that the Lord is good.
>
> As you come to him, the living Stone—rejected by men but chosen by God and precious to him—you also, like living stones, are being built into a spiritual house to be a holy priesthood, offering spiritual sacrifices acceptable to God through Jesus Christ. (1 Pet. 2:2–5)

Spiritual growth is a solidly biblical concept. It isn't only Americans who are concerned about growth; it isn't just something about our national culture. It is an idea that's in the Bible, and from as far back as creation itself.

A Biblical Practice of Growth

How, then, do we grow as Christians? What kind of church will cultivate such discipleship among its members? In one sense, that's what we're considering throughout this whole book. But how does each of the eight other marks considered in this book affect our growth—individually and corporately—as Christians? I'm convinced that each one of these marks can contribute to our following Christ better. For the spiritual health of the individual Christian, for the good of other Christians, for the health of the church as a whole, for the good of our witness to non-Christians, and for the glory of God, each one of these marks has a contribution to make.

Expositional Preaching

A church in which there is expositional preaching will be a church that encourages Christian growth. God's Word is what we need if we are to grow. The culture around us won't tell us what we most need. We can't even look into our own hearts for such knowledge.

To learn what we most need in our lives, we need to turn to God himself. We need to hear his Word—all of it—preached expositionally, so that we don't just hear selective themes. There are things in the Bible that we want to avoid. None of us is so holy and perfect and well-shaped spiritually that we happily welcome every word in God's book. God save us from being in a church where the Word is preached selectively. We should pray that God will provide his church with preachers who will preach all of his Word.

As we study God's Word, we see his help and his care for his own throughout history. We become aware of the beauty of God's plan. We see the glory of the gospel. We see how God corrects us. Surprisingly, when we hear expositional preaching we become less dependent on the preacher. We're more concerned about the Word of God. So if your pastor is away and someone else is in the pulpit, that's okay. We love our ministers, but more than that we love the Word of God. That's what we want to hear. That's what the church is built on: hearing God's Word speak to us as his Holy Spirit uses it in our hearts. Through his Word, we come to know more of God and of his character.

Be very careful before joining a church that does not stress expositional preaching or before calling a preacher who is not an expositional preacher, who is not committed to preaching all of God's Word, regardless of how uncomfortable parts of it may make us feel.

Gospel Doctrine

We grow as we understand more of the truth about God and about us. We grow as we understand more of his care and his character. We grow as we read the biblical record of his choosing a people and then working with them through very difficult circumstances. We are encouraged by seeing the big picture, the plan, the meaning. We begin to grow in our knowledge of him. We begin to trust him more.

How do we grow in our ability to trust God? We grow in that ability partly through the difficulties God allows us to go through. But experience is only half of it. That's what gives us the opportunity to trust. But why trust him? We trust him because he has shown himself perfectly trustworthy. God's revelation of himself throughout the Word, throughout history, shows him to be worthy of our trust no matter what he might send our way.

As we realize more and more the depth of our need, we are trained to rely on Christ. John Newton, the author of "Amazing Grace," wrote a hymn about trusting Christ and about trying to grow as a Christian:

> I asked the Lord, that I might grow
> In faith, and love, and every grace;
> Might more of His salvation know,
> And seek more earnestly His face.
>
> I hoped that in some favoured hour
> At once He'd answer my request,
> And by His love's constraining power
> Subdue my sins, and give me rest.
>
> Instead of this, He made me feel
> The hidden evils of my heart;
> And let the angry powers of hell
> Assault my soul in every part.[2]

When we begin to have a more biblical understanding of our state as humans, though we're grievously saddened by various results of the fall in our world—such as histories of racial injustice or violent terrorist attacks—we can't say that we're shocked in the way that a non-Christian might be. We understand something of our tremendous capacities as image bearers of God and how terribly, terribly wrong those capacities can go when we don't use them in submission to God.

2 John Newton, "I Asked the Lord," 1779.

As we begin to understand more of our own brokenness, of our own sinful rebellion, we—strange as it may seem—begin to understand more of his love.

Sometimes people make a distinction between "hellfire" preachers and preachers that understand God's love. But that distinction is no more than a caricature. Preachers who talk only about God's love talk about it less and less with every sermon they preach because God's love seems less surprising to them the more they begin to think they've deserved it. There's less and less of a problem that has been dealt with. There's less and less weight that Christ has carried. There's less and less of an extent to which he has gone in his love for us.

When, however, we begin to understand the reality of our sinful rebellion against God, then we begin to understand more of God's love for us in Christ.

A church that is clear on the gospel will help you grow as a Christian. It will help you grow in confidence as you know the love of God. Indeed, you cannot help but grow as you understand more and more what God has done for you in Christ. Do you want to grow as a Christian? Meditate on Charles Wesley's great hymn, "And Can It Be?" Return to being amazed at the gospel. Biblical doctrine is gospel doctrine.

A Biblical Understanding of Conversion and Evangelism

As you realize your own spiritual state and dependence on God for your own Christian life, you don't become indifferent, you become grateful—profoundly and deeply thankful to God that he has had mercy on you and on so many others. Your hope becomes more certain, because you realize your hope isn't based on your own faithfulness but on God's faithfulness. That's a tremendous encouragement to anyone who knows himself to be a sinner. God loves us out of his own nature of love.

As we begin to recognize our own salvation as the fruit of God's work in our lives, we're not even tempted to feel the wrong kind of pride in our own spiritual life, because we understand from the Bible what conversion is. We understand more of what a true Christian is and how we become one—by the grace of God.

The lack of spiritual growth in people who call themselves Christians is often evidence that they have been wrongly evangelized. We lead people who are not Christians to think that they are. One church-growth consultant claimed that "five to ten million baby boomers would be back in the fold within a month if churches adopted three simple changes: 1. Advertise 2. Let people know about product benefits 3. Be nice to new people."[3] That's it? Advertise, put the product benefits up front, and be nice to new people, and five to ten million people will be back in the churches within a month? Perhaps so. But I don't know if we would see them converted.

Don't misunderstand me. It's not as though I want to take down the signs and not advertise. It's not that I don't want to tell people any of the good things about being a Christian and just keep it a secret to myself. It's not that I want us to be mean to new people when they come in. But we have to understand that evangelism is more than all those things. The church is not a booster organization. We're telling people a serious message about their condition before God, and about the tremendous news of the new life God is offering them in Christ. And we're inviting them to enter into that life by dire and desperate means—repentance and faith.

When we begin to understand more of what the Bible teaches about evangelism, we will begin to trust God in helping us to spread the good news. We will feel more like obeying him as we realize that it is not our duty to convert anyone but simply to faithfully tell the news. There is a wonderful freedom in that. I don't have to feel that I have to answer every person's every question. I just have to tell others the truth about Jesus, and love them and pray for them. I'm called simply to be faithful in the message, and that brings a wonderful freedom.

3 Os Guinness, *Dining with the Devil: The Megachurch Movement Flirts with Modernity* (Grand Rapids, MI: Baker, 1993), 38.

More fully understanding God's work in regeneration encourages me to trust God. Understanding the Bible's teaching on conversion and evangelism makes me a better Christian and helps my church become more healthy.

A Biblical Understanding of Church Membership

Living the Christian life means being committed to each other. It entails being part of a community that is centered around Jesus Christ. By dealing with each other, we are forced to deal with areas of our lives that we would otherwise avoid; because of our committed love to each other, we pray and reflect on those areas and repent. Through our commitments and responsibilities as church members, we learn more of what true Christian love is all about. We're encouraged as we see God's work in other people's lives. We're encouraged by seeing the older members being cared for and newer Christians maturing. Even if things in our lives are not going well, we can be encouraged by the work of God in other people's lives. That's how it is supposed to be. That's one of the reasons why God doesn't call us to run this race alone. Being rooted in a church also encourages accountability. It helps us in so many ways to grow as Christians.

A Biblical Understanding of Church Discipline

One of the unintended consequences of a church's neglect of proper discipline is that it gets much harder to produce disciples. In an undisciplined church, examples are unclear and models are confused. "Mr. So-and-So has been a member of the church for forty years, but look what he does." "Well, yes, but he's on all the committees."

Weeds are undesirable. No gardener sets out to grow weeds. They can have bad effects on the plants around them. God's plan for the local church does not encourage us to leave weeds unchecked. He intends, for his own glory, that the church be composed of imperfect people; but he intends that these imperfect people should be people who love him and in whose lives he can work—to make them more holy.

For the good of the one disciplined, for the good of other Christians who see discipline as a warning, for the health of the church as a whole, for the good of our witness to non-Christians, and for the glory of God, we will be helped to grow as we practice church discipline.

A Biblical Understanding of Church Leadership

We'll also be helped as Christians by a biblical understanding of leadership. As God brings people into our lives whom he has called to be spiritual leaders, we gain practical role models and godly vision. God has equipped teachers and Christians we can follow in order to help us grow. He hasn't meant for us to live the Christian life without their aid. We'll consider this more in chapter 7.

A Biblical Understanding and Practice of Prayer

It seems almost too obvious to say that putting into practice what we learn from the Bible about prayer will help us to grow as a Christian, but it's true. Understanding that the God of the universe has not only spoken to us in his Word but that he also wants us to speak back to him in prayer is surprising, humbling, and encouraging.

On top of that, we realize that prayer is a privilege bought for us by the Lord Jesus Christ. Only through him can we confidently know that God will hear our prayers. Prayer causes our love for the Lord to grow and increase. We can see why the Christians in the New Testament turned to prayer so frequently and trustingly.

As the Holy Spirit sanctifies us and our desires become more conformed to his, our prayers change. We find ourselves praying less about our circumstances and more about God's purposes. We find ourselves being bolder in praying big prayers for conversions and for gospel expansion in our city, our nation, and among other peoples around the world. Our desire for God to be glorified increases.

Praying together in our local church shapes and fuels this growth in our own hearts. It reinforces our love of what is best, of what it is that God wants. Rather than wanting to avoid time in prayer with our church family, we begin to feel jealous for it and to desire more of it. We tend to start living our inner life more truly and openly before God and our fellow believers. We lament. We long. We confess. We cry out. We hope. We ask. We question and wonder. We thank God and praise him. All of this flows from a growing understanding of the Bible's teaching on prayer, as we learn more and more how to pray from our church family around us. We realize that our prayers bring God glory. They billboard our dependence upon God to all who hear us pray. And as we rely on God publicly, he is honored and the church is built up. We'll look at this again in chapter 8.

A Biblical Understanding and Practice of Missions

A biblical understanding and practice of missions also helps us to grow in Christ. It reinforces our understanding of the plight of those around us. It keeps the gospel solution front and center in our thinking and in our life together in our local church. It pulls us out of ourselves and helps us look at God's grand purposes and reminds us to look up, at God himself. It helps to reset our expectations and our desires.

Studying God's worldwide gospel plan gets us into God's Word. It puts us in contact with the main storyline of the Bible, from Abraham to the heavenly city. It also deepens our understanding of the importance of some of the things our local church is involved in. It affects our willingness to sacrifice. It makes us more interested in our church's budget. It challenges how we think of our own vacations. It grows our love for people different from us.

Growing in a biblical understanding and practice of missions affects what we pray about. It changes how we think about a new church plant. And it changes how we think about the years we may have in front of us to serve God. We become more interested in the lives and work of others. Our heart for God to be glorified throughout his creation becomes more and more conformed to God's own. That's spiritual growth, isn't it?

As all this is happening in our local church, it's not just happening to us. Other members are having the same experiences. They are freshly seeing God's goodness and grace, perhaps on a scale grander than they had previously considered. The times our church spends in praying for gospel work elsewhere become hallways of memory, reminding us of God's faithful answers in the past and encouraging us to believe in his further answers stretching into the future. And through all of this, our unity deepens and grows. Again, we'll consider more of all of this in chapter 9.

These are some of the ways that our eight other marks of a healthy church contribute to our spiritual growth as Christians.

Hopes for Growth

Before discussing the *importance* of spiritual growth, let me share some of my hopes for my own ministry—for my own life and my own church—in this matter of spiritual growth.

Pastoral Visitation

In my role as a pastor, I hope specifically that, slowly but surely, I'll be able to do regular pastoral visitation in a way that was standard in years gone by.[4] When I first came to Capitol Hill Baptist, I began meeting with current members of the congregation. I or one of the other elders personally interview all potential new members about their understanding of the gospel and about their own testimony of becoming and being a Christian. By doing this, we hope to gain an understanding of these people that goes beyond what can be gained by the brief times we have with each of them—sometimes only at the church door on Sunday morning. Many pastors have pursued this by having a regular visitation schedule, meeting with each member for prayer and asking them about their lives. Questions such as the following, shared with me by another pastor, help us get to know our members:

4 For more on our pastoral practices at Capitol Hill Baptist Church, see Mark Dever and Paul Alexander, *How to Build a Healthy Church: A Practical Guide for Deliberate Leadership* (Wheaton, IL: Crossway, 2021), or come on a Weekender. See https://www.9marks.org/events/what-is-a-weekender/.

- In what particular ways have you grown in your understanding of the Christian life since we last met?
- How have you grown in your practice of the Christian life since we last met?
- In what particular areas do you feel that you need instruction?
- Are you disappointed in your own pursuit of holiness? If so, explain.
- How, specifically, can I pray for you?

This is what I would like to see in the church I serve, and I pray that it will become more typical of your church as well.

Growth Together as a Church

I hope that, more and more, we at Capitol Hill Baptist Church will live out what we have pledged to God and to each other in our church covenant, which reads as follows.

> Having, as we trust, been brought by Divine Grace to repent and believe in the Lord Jesus Christ and to give up ourselves to Him, and having been baptized upon our profession of faith, in the name of the Father and of the Son and of the Holy Spirit, we do now, relying on His gracious aid, solemnly and joyfully renew our covenant with each other.
>
> We will work and pray for the unity of the Spirit in the bond of peace.
>
> We will walk together in brotherly love, as becomes the members of a Christian church; exercise an affectionate care and watchfulness over each other and faithfully admonish and entreat one another as occasion may require.
>
> We will not forsake the assembling of ourselves together, nor neglect to pray for ourselves and others.
>
> We will endeavor to bring up such as may at any time be under our care, in the nurture and admonition of the Lord, and by a pure and loving example to seek the salvation of our family and friends.

We will rejoice at each other's happiness, and endeavor with tenderness and sympathy to bear each other's burdens and sorrows.

We will seek, by Divine aid, to live carefully in the world, denying ungodliness and worldly lusts, and remembering that, as we have been voluntarily buried by baptism and raised again from the symbolic grave, so there is on us a special obligation now to lead a new and holy life.

We will work together for the continuance of a faithful evangelical ministry in this church, as we sustain its worship, ordinances, discipline, and doctrines. We will contribute cheerfully and regularly to the support of the ministry, the expenses of the church, the relief of the poor, and the spread of the gospel through all nations.

We will, when we move from this place, as soon as possible, unite with some other church where we can carry out the spirit of this covenant and the principles of God's Word.

May the grace of the Lord Jesus Christ, and the love of God, and the fellowship of the Holy Spirit be with us all. Amen.

Every time we gather around the Lord's Table and in every members' meeting we convene, the members of the church stand, and we read aloud together this covenant. It expresses the specific commitment we are making to and for each other as a part of our commitment to God.

This covenant also clearly reflects the understanding that growth as a Christian is not just the responsibility of the individual. And it is not only mine as the pastor. Members of the church are to teach each other. That's part of what knits us together as the body of Christ. Our church covenant includes what we as a church pledge to do to help each other grow as Christians. We'll do it imperfectly—there's no doubt about that. Nevertheless, this is my hope: that we in our church (and you in your church) will increasingly work and pray together, walk together, not forsake the assembling of ourselves, endeavor to bring up those that the Lord gives us in his will and ways, rejoice and sorrow with each other, seek to live carefully, work together in ministry, contribute to the expenses, contribute to the needs of the gospel throughout all nations, and know that when we move from this place we'll unite with another church where we can continue to do these things. These are what we pledge to help each other to grow as Christians.

The Importance of Good Growth

Is growth important? Yes, to grow as a Christian is very important. This is how we give testimony to God. When we see a church composed of members growing in Christlikeness, who gets the credit? We've already seen the answer in Scripture: "God made it grow" (1 Cor. 3:6). As Peter writes, "Live such good lives among the pagans that, though they accuse you of doing wrong, they may see your good deeds and glorify God on the day he visits us" (1 Pet. 2:12).

Peter was obviously remembering Jesus's words from the Sermon on the Mount: "Let your light shine before men, that they may see your good deeds . . ." If Jesus had stopped there, it would be natural to fall into the trap of self-admiration, but Jesus continued, ". . . and praise your Father in heaven" (Matt. 5:16). Working to promote Christian discipleship and growth is working to bring glory not to ourselves but to God. This is how God will make himself known in the world.

A healthy church has a pervasive concern with church growth—not simply growing numbers but growing members. A church full of growing Christians is the kind of church growth I want as a pastor. Some today seem to think that one can be a "baby Christian" for a whole lifetime. Growth is seen to be an optional extra for particularly zealous disciples. But be very careful about taking that line of thought. Growth is a sign of life. Growing trees are living trees, and growing animals are living animals. When something stops growing, it dies. Growth may not mean that you negotiate these rapids in half the time you negotiated the last; it may simply mean that you are able to continue in the right direction as a Christian, regardless of the adverse circumstances. Remember, only things that are alive swim upstream; the dead things all float along with the current.

Paul hoped the Corinthians would grow in their Christian faith (2 Cor. 10:15). He hoped the Ephesians would "grow up into him who is the Head, that is, Christ" (Eph. 4:15; see Col. 1:10; 2 Thess. 1:3). It is tempting at times for pastors to reduce their churches to manageable statistics of attendance, baptisms, giving, and membership, where growth is tangible, recordable, demonstrable, and comparable. However, such statistics fall far short of the true growth that Paul describes in these verses, and that God desires. Rather than thinking of growth as a linear graph, recording mounting or declining measurements—totals of services attended, dollars given, books read—perhaps it is better to think of Christian growth as a sort of video game where each day you are given a fresh challenge to live that day as a Christian.

True growth in Christian discipleship is not finally mere excitement, an increase in one's use of religious language, or a growing knowledge of Scripture. It is not even an evident increase in joy or in love or concern for the church. Even increases in zeal and praise to God and confidence of one's own faith are not infallible evidences of true Christian growth. What, then, *is* evidence of true Christian growth? While all these things may be evidences of true Christian growth, the only certain observable sign of such growth is a life of increasing holiness, rooted in Christian self-denial. The church should be marked by a vital concern for this kind of increasing godliness in the lives of its members.

Good influences in a covenanted community of believers can be tools in God's hand for growing his people. As God's people are built up and grow together in holiness and self-giving love, they should improve in their ability to administer discipline and to encourage discipleship. The church has an obligation to be a means of God's growing people in grace. If instead our churches are places where only the pastor's thoughts are taught, where God is questioned more than he is worshiped, where the gospel is diluted and evangelism perverted, where church membership is meaningless, where prayers are brief and missions is neglected, and a worldly cult of personality is allowed to grow up around the pastor, then one can hardly expect to find a community that is either cohesive or edifying. Such a church certainly will not glorify God. So Peter's final benediction to those early Christians he wrote to was a prayer couched in the imperative: "Grow in the grace and knowledge of our Lord and Savior Jesus Christ. To him be glory both now and forever! Amen" (2 Pet. 3:18).

Of the nine marks covered in this book, this is the one I first became concerned about. How many of us have seen large churches with thousands of members who never come, and hundreds of those who do attend seeming not really to care much about God? In any church there will be many very nice people who have lived moral lives; but then there will be some who seem especially to love the Lord, and they will usually stand out from all the rest—they will seem different from the rest of the church. For more than forty years I have been wondering why churches are like this. What has happened in our churches, when people who really live like Christians seem unusual, even compared to other church members? In this book, I have been tracing back the things that I have noticed in this regard, finally getting back to the fount of God's activity among us—his Word.

If we are to grow as individual believers and as churches, we must sit under the Word. We must pray for the Holy Spirit to plant and to weed the gardens of our hearts. This spiritual growth is not optional; it is vital, because spiritual growth indicates life. Things that are truly alive, grow.

What If We Don't Grow?

Finally, what if we don't grow spiritually? What about Rob? Why was Rob apparently not growing in his Christian life? Was Rob perhaps not a Christian at all?

You may think, *Now, that's a little harsh*. Maybe Rob's just one of those "carnal" Christians that Paul talks about somewhere in the Bible.

Yes, in 1 Corinthians Paul refers to "carnal Christians." He writes, "Brothers, I could not address you as spiritual but as worldly ["carnal," KJV]—mere infants in Christ" (1 Cor. 3:1). But who are these people? Are these carnal Christians a "middle category" of people who have Jesus in their lives but not on the throne of their lives? It sounds like a strange idea, doesn't it? On the one hand, you've got Christians who have Christ as Lord, with him on the throne. Then, on the other side, you have non-Christians. But, some argue, there is an interesting middle category, where Christ really is in the person's life but he's not on the throne. These are the "carnal" Christians.

I think a more natural way to read the verse is that Paul is shaming his readers by speaking of these self-confessed Christians as worldly. In calling them "worldly" or "carnal," Paul is intentionally using an oxymoron. An oxymoron is the joining of two contradictory words. In that sense, a carnal Christian would be like hot ice. It's not supposed to make any sense. By writing in these terms, Paul is basically telling his readers, "Get off the fence! You are living differently than you are professing. You cannot do that. Those horses go in opposite directions—so jump on one or the other!"

Many people, by a wrong use of this verse, have been convinced that they are some kind of truly saved person, some kind of real Christian, even though they have not really repented and believed. It's no wonder that the lives of many professing Christians are such messes, when the churches of which they're a part are so confused on such a basic matter.

Consider what it means to be a Christian. It does not mean that you're perfect, but that your heart does intend to seek the Lord. If you are a Christian, it is because God, by his own gracious action in your life, has grown a desire in you to live a life that pleases him more and more. Such growth is a sign of true spiritual life, and another mark of a healthy church.

Other Resources

- For group study: *Growing One Another: Discipleship in the Church* (2012), by Bobby Jamieson, a seven-week inductive Bible study.
- For deeper reflection: *The Life of God in the Soul of the Church: The Root and Fruit of Spiritual Fellowship* (2012), by Thabiti Anyabwile.

- See also Richard Sibbes, *The Bruised Reed* (1631); J. C. Ryle, *Holiness: Its Nature, Hindrances, Difficulties, and Roots* (1877) and *Thoughts for Young Men* (1886); Donald S. Whitney, *Spiritual Disciplines for the Christian Life* (1991); John Piper, *Future Grace* (1995); C. J. Mahaney, *The Cross Centered Life: Keeping the Gospel the Main Thing* (2002) and *Humility: True Greatness* (2005); Colin Marshall and Tony Payne, *The Trellis and the Vine: The Ministry Mind-Shift That Changes Everything* (2009); Mark Dever, *Discipling: How to Help Others Follow Jesus* (2016); Aaron Menikoff, *Character Matters: Shepherding in the Fruit of the Spirit* (2020); Isaac Adams, *Training: How Do I Grow as a Christian?* (2020); and CCEF's online resources at www.ccef.org.

What's Coming Up

Mark Seven: Biblical Church Leadership

The Congregational Context of Church Leadership

The Biblical Qualifications for Church Leadership

The Charismatic Nature of Church Leadership

The Christlikeness of Church Leadership

- Boss
- Out Front
- Supply
- Serve

The Relationship of Church Leadership to God's Nature and Character

Mark Seven

Biblical Church Leadership

"ALL ANIMALS ARE EQUAL, but some animals are more equal than others." With that line in the last chapter of his tale *Animal Farm*, George Orwell delivered his summary critique of Karl Marx and the Soviet Russian government.[1] The story is a well-known one: animals rise up, organize, displace the Joneses (the human owners of the farm), and begin to run the farm for their own benefit—thus the name *Animal Farm*—run by animals, for animals.

Of course, being after the fall, this utopian experiment is bound to fail, and it does. In the end, a new ruling class emerges—the pigs—and by the book's conclusion, they're putting up signs: "All animals are equal, but some animals are more equal than others." Rather than abuse of authority being merely an aspect of a pre-Communist economy as Marx had taught, Orwell saw that the problem was really deeper—the problem is rooted in the nature of human relationships, of reality, of the human heart. Orwell's critique of authority seemed penetrating and biting when it first appeared more than fifty years ago. Today it seems obvious. We've become accustomed to thinking about abuse and power in the same sentence, and about authoritarianism whenever we think about authority.

1 George Orwell, *Animal Farm* (New York: New American Library, 1963), 123.

Whatever the reason, there is a pervasive and inherent suspicion of authority in our society. Perhaps it has to do with the fact that our national government was established in revolt against the claims and demands of the Parliament in London. Perhaps it has to do with the fact that for many Americans, the government that now works to ensure their equal opportunity was the same government that in the past worked to make sure they had none. Perhaps it has to do with a vision of human nobility—the American optimism that believes people are so good that, if left to ourselves, "we, the people" will be the best we can possibly be.

Or perhaps the explanation for our anti-authoritarianism is simpler. Perhaps it has to do with selfishness.

Christianity has always recognized the need for authority in society, in the home, and also in the church, and that last one is our topic for this chapter: biblical church leadership. This topic is particularly important, given the increasingly poor models of authority we seem to have all around us today. In fact, one of the things that made this fourth edition so important in my mind was the recent parade of prominent pastors self-destructing. While their situations have varied, the fact that there have been a great a number of highly publicized, discouraging pastoral disasters is beyond dispute.

Part of the way such a crisis should be addressed is by examining the character of the pastor.[2] Such an approach will be as unpopular as it is untried. Less popular and even less tried would be to consider the New Testament's teaching on the structure of the church. Could it be that we have placed too much stress upon one particular member of the body? Would paying more attention to the New Testament's teaching on structure (church leadership) actually facilitate the godliness of pastors and their relations to the congregation? What does the Bible say about authority and leadership in the church? In answering these question, we'll focus on five aspects of church leadership:

2 See Aaron Menikoff, *Character Matters: Shepherding in the Fruit of the Spirit* (Chicago, IL: Moody, 2020).

1. Its congregational context;
2. Its biblical qualifications;
3. Its charismatic nature;
4. Its Christlikeness;
5. Its relationship to God's nature and character.

The Congregational Context of Church Leadership

The first topic we need to consider when discussing biblical church leadership is the role of the members, the congregation. The Bible's discussion of church leadership always assumes a congregational context. Previous decades and centuries of the church's life have been spent in controversy over exactly whom God has intended to have the final say in what is taught and done in churches. Some have said it is to be the bishops. Others have said it should be one bishop in particular. Still others have said it is to be the ministers or somebody representing them. Still others have said it should be the local pastor or some specially gifted leader whom God raises up.

We can understand the confusion. If you start looking in the New Testament for how we should organize as a church, you won't find a straightforward manual of church government; there is no ideal constitution for a church. But that doesn't mean that the Bible has nothing to say about how we are to organize ourselves. One of the most important passages about church life is Matthew 18:15–17, where Jesus said,

> If your brother sins against you, go and show him his fault, just between the two of you. If he listens to you, you have won your brother over. But if he will not listen, take one or two others along, so that "every matter may be established by the testimony of two or three witnesses." If he refuses to listen to them, tell it to the church; and if he refuses to listen even to the church, treat him as you would a pagan or a tax collector.

Notice to whom one finally appeals in such situations. What court has the final word? It is not a bishop, a pope, or a presbytery; it is not an assembly, a synod, a convention, or a conference. It is not even a pastor, a board of elders, a board of deacons, or a church committee. It is, quite simply, the church—that is, the assembly of those individual believers who are the church.

In Acts 6:2–5 we read of an event in the life of the early church that is important to this discussion. There was a problem, apparently, over the distribution of the church's resources, and this problem was evidently requiring a good bit of the apostles' attention:

> So the Twelve gathered all the disciples together and said, "It would not be right for us to neglect the ministry of the Word of God in order to wait on tables. Brothers, choose seven men from among you who are known to be full of the Spirit and wisdom. We will turn this responsibility over to them and will give our attention to prayer and the ministry of the word."
>
> This proposal pleased the whole group. (Acts 6:2–5)

Luke goes on to name those whom the church chose for this ministry.

One of the complexities of using the New Testament as a guide for how we are to structure our church life is the presence of the apostles in these churches. How much can we later, post-apostolic elders, pastors, and overseers assume the apostles' practice as a guide for our own? Can we define doctrine, delineate error, or recall the words of Christ as these who had been with Jesus throughout his earthly ministry, who were taught by him and instructed by him, and who were specially commissioned by him to be the foundation of his church could? Will the names of those of us who are elders today be inscribed on the foundations of the New Jerusalem, as are the names of the apostles (Rev. 21:14)? The answer to all of these questions is obviously no.

Our problem with the model of the apostles is that, in following it, we present-day church leaders might ascribe too much authority to ourselves, without deserving such authority. Yet here in Acts 6, we see these very apostles handing over responsibility to the congregation; it almost seems that they were recognizing in the church assembly the same kind of ultimate authority, under God, that Jesus recognized in his statement in Matthew 18:15–17.

Finally, to learn more from the New Testament about church life, we turn to the letters of Paul. Here we find a continuation of Christ's teaching and of the practice of the apostles. In Paul's letters we see that the discipline and doctrine of a local church is ultimately held in trust, under God, by the congregation. The discipline and doctrine is finally the responsibility of the congregation under God.

On the question of the responsibility for discipline, for instance, look at how Paul exhorts the *whole congregation* at Corinth in 1 Corinthians 5:4–5: "When you are assembled in the name of our Lord Jesus and I am with you in spirit, and the power of our Lord Jesus is present, hand this man over to Satan, so that the sinful nature may be destroyed and his spirit saved on the day of the Lord." Paul instructs the whole church—not just the leaders—to take action. Indeed, he is upset with the whole church—not just the leaders—that they haven't already taken action and had been tolerating such sin.

In 2 Corinthians 2:6 we see something of how this church responded to Paul's directives. Apparently the man who was in such heinous sin (presumably the same man referred to in 1 Corinthians) had repented. But notice how Paul described the decision the church had made: "The punishment inflicted on him by the majority is sufficient for him" (2 Cor. 2:6). The word in Greek for "majority" seems to presume there would have been some definite number of people and that the greater part of that set number of people would have made the decision. Perhaps you've heard people say there are no church votes recorded in the New Testament. Yet here in this passage, there does seem to be a vote (a "majority") in view. Paul knew that this congregation in Corinth was competent to discipline itself.

Paul believed that individual congregations had the final responsibility even for the teaching they heard. In Galatians, Paul basically says hello, offers a brief prayer for his readers, and then says,

> I am astonished that you are so quickly deserting the one who called you by the grace of Christ and are turning to a different gospel—which is really no gospel at all. Evidently some people are throwing you into confusion and are trying to pervert the gospel of Christ. But even if we or an angel from heaven should preach a gospel other than the one we preached to you, let him be eternally condemned! As we have already said, so now I say again: If anybody is preaching to you a gospel other than what you accepted, let him be eternally condemned! (Gal. 1:6–9)

Throughout this whole letter to the Galatians, Paul tells the church that they are responsible for judging the correctness of the message being presented to them by others. Paul says that the message they have been hearing is not really the gospel. Therefore, they must assume the responsibility of rejecting both that message and those who are delivering it.

It is significant that, in combating this false gospel, Paul didn't simply write to the pastor or the elders, to the presbytery, to the bishop, to the conference, to the convention, or to the seminary. No, Paul wrote to the churches. He wrote to the Christians who comprised the churches and who knew in their own lives the power of the gospel. This is why the congregation's members must be those who are born again. Christ's Spirit is needed to indwell Christ's body. The Spirit guides the church, but only as the church is composed of those in whom the Spirit dwells.

Paul appealed to these Galatian Christians and made it quite clear that not only were they competent to sit in judgment of a message presented as the gospel, but they *were required* to do so. Anytime someone came and presented something else and called it "the gospel," the congregation would have to make a decision. They had an inescapable duty to judge even those who claimed to be apostles.

Paul made this point even more clearly in 2 Timothy, where he counseled Timothy, the pastor of the church in Ephesus, on how to deal with false teachers. As Paul described the coming tide of false teachers in the church, he didn't just mention the teachers themselves. He particularly blamed those who, "to suit their own desires . . . gather around them a great number of teachers to say what their itching ears want to hear" (2 Tim. 4:3). If you are in a church where the gospel is not being preached, I hope you gain from this verse a strong sense of the responsibility you have. Whether in selecting teachers or paying for them, in approving their teaching, or in simply consenting to listen to them repeatedly and happily, the congregation that Paul envisioned here was culpable for the false teaching that they endured and sponsored. They were to be held as guilty as those who actually did the false teaching. Once again we see that final responsibility rested with the congregation itself.

Have you ever listened to a sermon that was so bad you wanted to walk out? I walked out on a sermon once, and I walked out loudly, because I thought what was being said was so terribly destructive of the gospel that it should not be tolerated. I didn't want my bodily presence, sitting there with my mouth shut, to encourage anyone to listen to the speaker. (The speaker was directly contradicting the doctrine of original sin.)

If you sit and listen to trash being presented as the Word of God, you will be held responsible. Indeed, if you sit and listen to *my* teaching, you will bear some responsibility for it.

Every local church in Christendom, from Greek Orthodox to Pentecostal, from Roman Catholic to Baptist, from Episcopalian to Lutheran, from Presbyterian to Methodist, is congregational in nature. They exist only as the people continue to participate in their activities. When the people vote—whether at a congregational meeting or (where that's not allowed) with their funds or their feet—the leaders of the congregation must listen. They don't have to agree, but they must listen. The congregation will have their say. That's a simple fact.

Beyond the simple inevitability of congregationalism, however, the congregation has a wonderful responsibility that should be recognized and encouraged and cultivated. As a congregation, we are responsible to see that we have sound teaching. In our church covenant at Capitol Hill Baptist, we pledge that we will work to make sure that a faithful, evangelical ministry continues in our midst. We have a responsibility to make sure that God is honored among us by having his Word rightly preached, his commands obeyed, and his character reflected in our lives together. This is the responsibility of our church and of every other local church around the world.

Congregations today must make decisions together about discipline and doctrine even as the early disciples did. Does this mean that congregationalism is democracy? Perhaps in some ways, in that the *demos*, the people, make decisions. But there are dissimilarities, too. A church is not just straightforward democracy, for churches recognize our fallen state, our tendency to err, as well as the *in*errancy of God's Word. So the members of a local church are democratic, perhaps, only in the sense that they work together as a congregation to try to understand God's Word.

I certainly do not believe in the inerrancy of congregational votes. Before I became this congregation's pastor, I told them that if I were to be their pastor, we all needed to understand that I would ultimately be working for God, not the people. The congregation could instruct the pastor to do this or that, but the pastor must not mistake such congregational input as, necessarily, divine guidance.

As leaders and congregation, we strive for the unity of the Spirit in the bond of peace; we work together for what we believe would be best for the church. And we work together so long as our understanding of God's Word and his will are sufficiently in line—"in sync" with each other—in order for us to do so.

Is congregationalism democracy? Though congregationalism and democracy have some important similarities and common principles, the simple answer must be no, not entirely. Perhaps the Cambridge Platform of 1648 put it best:

> This Government of the church, is a mixt Government (and so hath been acknowledged long before the term of Independency was heard

> of): In respect of Christ, the head and King of the church, and the Sovereaigne power residing in him, and exercised by him, it is a Monarchy: In respect of the body, or Brotherhood of the church, and power from Christ graunted unto them, it resembles a Democracy: In respect of the Presbytery and power committed to them, it is an Aristocracy (X.3).[3]

Individuals should take an active part in their churches not simply by attending, praying, and giving (though they should do all those things), but by actively getting to know the church family. You should be praying through the list of those other people with whom you have covenanted to serve God. You should listen as other members of the body tell about what God is doing in their lives or about their concerns—and then pray with them. You must realize that part of your obligation and privilege as a member of the church is to get to know other believers and to make yourself known to them. Study God's Word together. Learn to think as a church about God's Word. You should be growing in grace yourself, and in the knowledge of God's Word, in the knowledge of your own heart and of the hearts of your brothers and sisters, and in awareness of the opportunities God is putting in front of your church.

God does not, however, want us to always function as a "committee of the whole." We need to trust that God gives particular people gifts to serve as church leaders. We should therefore desire to see in our church the right balance of authority and trust. It is a serious spiritual deficiency in a church either to have leaders who are untrustworthy or to have members who are incapable of trusting. As individual members, we must be able to thank God for the leaders he puts among us, to recognize those so gifted, and to trust them. In Ephesians 4, Paul speaks of such leaders as God's gifts to his church. We should cultivate a church culture in which such leaders are honored and esteemed.

3 Williston Walker, *The Creeds and Platforms of Congregationalism* (New York: Pilgrim, 1991), 217–18.

The end of Hebrews 13 sounds strange to our modern ears. Pray that God will help us understand it and to apply it well to our own hearts: "Obey your leaders and submit to their authority. They keep watch over you as men who must give an account. Obey them so that their work will be a joy, not a burden, for that would be of no advantage to you" (Heb. 13:17). Think of the pastors you have had in your church. Have you worked in such a way that you have made their leadership of you and their charge of your soul a *joy* to them? Or have you made it a burden?[4]

This passage contains some words we aren't used to hearing today: *obey* and *submit*. Though we don't hear them very often, they are part of God's Word. And they require from us a certain amount of trust.

It is often said that trust must be earned, and I understand what that means. When a new government administration comes in, when we get a new boss at work, or even when a new friendship begins, we want to see by experience how the person or people will weather the difficulties, how they will persevere, and whether they will contribute to the well-being of all concerned. And so, we say, trust is earned. "Show me your competence to lead, and I will give you my trust by following."

But that attitude is at best only half true. Of course, we want to see that leaders in the church, as in any other sphere of life, are capable of holding such responsibilities. Paul himself lays out some qualifications for elders and deacons when he writes to Timothy and Titus.

At the same time, however, the kind of trust that we are called to give to our fellow imperfect humans in this life, be they family or friends, employers or government officials, or even leaders in a church, can never finally be earned. It must be given as a gift—a gift in faith, in trust more of the God who gives than of the leaders he has given (Eph. 4:11–13).[5]

4 For a thorough defense of congregationalism and an explanation of how the congregation's authority can coexist with submission to elders, see Jonathan Leeman's *Don't Fire Your Church Members: The Case for Congregationalism* (Nashville, TN: B&H Academic, 2018).

5 See Jonathan Leeman, *Understanding the Congregation's Authority* (Nashville, TN: B&H, 2016).

That's the congregational context of biblical church leadership.[6] Now we'll consider the leaders themselves.

The Biblical Qualifications for Church Leadership

As a pastor, I pray regularly that God will provide us with good leaders in our own local church. I pray particularly that God will place within our fellowship men whose spiritual gifts and pastoral concern indicate that God has called them to be elders or overseers (the words are used interchangeably in the Bible; see, for example, Acts 20). If it becomes clear that God has so gifted a certain man in the church, and if, after prayer, the church recognizes his gifts, then he should be set apart as an elder.

All churches have had individuals who performed the functions of elders even if they haven't used that word for them. The two most common New Testament names for this office are *episcopos* (overseer) and *presbuteros* (elder). When evangelicals today hear the word *elder*, many immediately think "Presbyterian," yet when Congregationalists first arose back in the sixteenth century, they stressed eldership as well.[7] Elders could be found in Baptist churches in America throughout the eighteenth and into the nineteenth century. W. B. Johnson, the first president of the Southern Baptist Convention, wrote a book on church life in which he strongly advocated the idea of a plurality of elders in the local church.

6 See Mark Dever, *The Church: The Gospel Made Visible* (Nashville, TN: B&H Academic, 2012).

7 Ostensibly, the first Reformer to articulate such "congregationalist" ideals was Jean Morély (1524–1594), a French nobleman who authored a treatise entitled *Traicté de la discipline & police chrestienne* (1562), arguing that the "keys" of electing ministers and excommunication belonged to the church as a whole and depended upon the consent of the congregation. Nevertheless, he insisted that a "council of Elders and Ministers is necessary" for the good order of the church (108). After all, democratic church government without church leadership will be chaos and anarchy, leaving the church subject to the will of "hypocrites and infidels" (110). But when a church is governed by "a great number of pastors and ministers full of knowledge and of the Holy Spirit"—a plurality of elders—it will be "like a furnished city, and like an iron column, and like a brass wall as it withstands the enemies of the truth" (Jean Morély, *Traicté de la discipline & police chrestienne* [Lyon: Ian de Tovrnes, 1562), 110]. Thanks to Caleb Morell for providing this reference and translation.

Somehow that practice fell out of use almost entirely among Baptists (it had never been universal). Whether through inattention to Scripture or the pressures of life on the frontier (where churches were springing up at an amazing rate), the practice of cultivating such congregational leadership stopped among Baptist churches. But discussion of reviving this biblical office continued in Baptist publications. As late as the early twentieth century, Baptist publications were referring to leaders by the title of elder; but as the twentieth century wore on, the idea seemed to vanish, until today it is unusual for a Baptist church to have elders.

There is a growing trend, however, to go back to this biblical office—and for good reason. It was needed in New Testament times, and it is needed now.

The Bible clearly models a plurality of elders in each local church. Though it never suggests a specific number of elders for a particular congregation, the New Testament refers to "elders" in the plural in local churches (e.g., Acts 14:23; 16:4; 20:17; 21:18; Titus 1:5; James 5:14).

Probably the single most useful thing for me in my pastoral ministry has been the recognition of a group of men in our church as elders. Knowing that these are men that the congregation has recognized as gifted and godly has helped me immensely in my pastoral work. We meet and pray and talk over matters and, by so doing, they greatly supplement my wisdom. So my own experience attests to the usefulness of following the New Testament practice of having, where possible, more elders in a local church than simply a lone pastor—and of their being people rooted in the congregation, not simply church staff hired from outside.

This does not mean that I don't have any distinctive role as the pastor, but I am fundamentally an elder, one of the people God has gifted to lead the church together. How do we find such leaders in our church? We pray for wisdom. We study God's Word, especially 1 Timothy and Titus. We see who meets those qualifications. We don't just look for people who are influential in the local community.

In the New Testament, we find hints of the main preacher being distinct from the rest of the elders. A number of references to preaching and preachers would not apply to all the elders in a congregation. For example, in Corinth Paul gave himself exclusively to preaching in a way that non-staff elders in a church could not. Probably the church could support only a limited number of elders full time (see Acts 18:5; 1 Cor. 9:14; 1 Tim. 4:13; 5:17). Preachers seemed to move to an area expressly to preach, whereas elders seemed to be already part of the local community (Rom. 10:14–15; Titus 1:5).

We must remember, however, that the preacher (or pastor) is also fundamentally one of the elders of his congregation. This means that many decisions involving the church yet not requiring the attention of all the members should fall not to the pastor alone but to the elders as a whole. While this is sometimes cumbersome, it has the immense benefits of rounding out the pastor's gifts, making up for some of his deficiencies, supplementing his judgment, and creating congregational support for decisions, leaving leaders less exposed to unjust criticism. It also makes leadership more rooted and permanent and allows for more mature continuity. It encourages the church to take more responsibility for the spiritual growth of its own members and helps make the church less dependent on its employees.

Many modern churches have tended to confuse elders with either the church staff or the deacons. Deacons, too, fill a New Testament office, one rooted in Acts 6. While any absolute distinction between the two offices is difficult, the concerns of the deacons are the practical details of church life: administration, maintenance, and the care of church members with physical needs. In many churches today, deacons have taken some spiritual role, but much has simply been left to the pastor. It would be to the benefit of such churches to again distinguish the role of elder from that of deacon.

Instead of searching for leaders with secular qualifications, we are to search for people of character, reputation, ability to handle the Word, and demonstration of the fruit of the Spirit in their lives. Part of finding good church leaders is finding those whom we can trust and who can trust us as a congregation—who can have enough faith in the congregation's decisions and commitments that they feel that they can work with us and with each other.

That, I think, is why Paul in 1 Timothy 3 emphasizes how the elder deals with his family—because that reveals so much about him and how he would actually work as an elder. It is also interesting to note how many of these qualifications have to do with giving oneself in service for others. Elders are to be other-centered. They are to be irreproachable, particularly in their observable conduct. They are to have an exemplary marriage and family life, to be temperate in all things, "self-controlled, respectable, hospitable, able to teach," not violent or quarrelsome or greedy, not a recent convert, and well respected by those outside the church.

Such must be the case of those who would be shepherds of the church of God. As good shepherds, they are not to fleece the flock in self-interest but to tend and care for each one of the sheep.

One other qualification for pastors or elders is that they be men (1 Tim. 2:12; 3:1–7; Titus 1:6–9). This statement shouldn't be misunderstood. Certainly all Christians are gifted by God for the building up of the body (1 Pet. 4 and 1 Cor. 14). All Christians teach each other by their singing, and in relationships that Paul lays out in Titus 2.

What about the question of gender in church leadership roles? Do we by our practice run the risk of making our doctrine seem arbitrary? That is, do we assiduously guard ordination of elders (because of 1 Tim. 3 and Titus 1), but obscure the divine pedagogy in the consistent symbol that we present by women being the teachers in small groups and Sunday school classes?

Women are highly honored in Scripture. Men and women both are made in the image of God. Furthermore, God has used women singularly in expressing truth about him. Miriam sang (Ex. 15); Hannah prayed (1 Sam. 2); and Mary glorified the Lord (Luke 1:46–51). Deborah was raised up as a judge in Old Testament Israel (Judg. 5) (though that was not a normal appointment for a woman). Elizabeth and Anna both prophesied publicly about the coming of Christ (Luke

1:42–45; 2:38). (It is interesting how many of these instances have to do with childbirth, part of God's special role for women; see 1 Tim. 2:15.) Scripture presents no bar to women teaching men through occasional prayer and prophecy (1 Cor. 12), nor in personal conversation (as with Aquila and Priscilla and Apollos in Acts 18:26).

But the choice of men as public preachers of God's Word is consistent with the role God has assigned men in bearing his image as elders and husbands. Most men are not elders. Many men (like Paul, and even Jesus himself) are not married. But husbands and elders both are to model something of God's own authority, and this is echoed rather than contradicted when the adult teaching ministry of a church is conducted by qualified and gifted men.

In our egalitarian age, we must unashamedly embrace gender as a gift from God, as Genesis 1 and 2 clearly demonstrate. Furthermore, the two genders in their interrelated roles are a signpost and a clue about the larger meaning of life. That's what Paul is saying in Ephesians 5. Indeed, he seems to be saying that God didn't give us the church to teach us about marriage; he gave us marriage to teach us about Christ's love for the church.

Egalitarianism today is often so closely allied with antiauthoritarianism that authority itself is condemned. But Scripture presents authority as coming from God. He alone is the sovereign Lord, and all sovereignty is entrusted by him (see Eph. 3:15). The abuse of something good does not show the thing itself to be bad. Authority itself, as God intends it to be, is good, even life-giving. And proper, biblical submission can also be life-giving. The submission of children to parents, wives to husbands, members to elders, all point to the submission of humans to God. And, ultimately, we have life because in his humanity, the eternal Son incarnate submitted to his heavenly Father's will. It is a lie of Satan to say that submission is inherently demeaning.

It is therefore appropriate that churches limit the role of public teaching to men, symbolizing something of the authority that God has called men normally to bear.[8] And, according to 1 Timothy 2:12, it is especially important that men demonstrate their authority in the church in the public teaching of the Word: "I do not permit a woman to teach or to have authority over a man; she must be silent."

The question of whether only men should be pastors or elders is increasingly becoming a watershed issue, distinguishing between those who accommodate Scripture to culture and those who attempt to shape their lives according to Scripture.

I contrast the error of egalitarianism (the idea that there are no gender distinctions in the biblical offices of the church) with what I, as a Baptist, take to be another error—infant baptism. Infant baptism is not a new idea. If it is, in fact, an error, it's a very old one! It has a long track record. For over five hundred years, many evangelical Christians who have believed the Bible to teach the baptism of infants have continued to be otherwise faithful. In fact, many times their faithfulness has put to shame those of us who may have a better doctrine of baptism!

Egalitarianism is not like that. It is a new idea. It does not have such a long track record. And the record that it has amassed in the last few decades is not encouraging.

Of course, other issues are more central to the gospel than gender. However, few (if any) undermine the authority of Scripture in evangelical churches today as much as egalitarianism. And when the authority of Scripture is undermined, the gospel will not long be acknowledged. Therefore, love for God, the gospel, and future generations demands that we carefully present the Bible's teaching that the leadership of the local church—pastors, elders—be men.

The Charismatic Nature of Church Leadership

Third, we should note the charismatic nature of biblical church leadership. By "charismatic" I do not mean a particular supernatural experi-

8 For further discussion on complementarianism, see *9Marks Journal*, "Complementarianism: A Moment of Reckoning" (December 2019), https://www.9marks.org/journal/complementarianism-a-moment-of-reckoning/.

ence such as speaking in tongues. The Greek word *charisma* (plural *charismata*) simply means a gift of grace—a gift of God's grace. In the Bible, it is clear that God's Spirit gives his church gifts in order to build his people up in the faith. Even our salvation as Christians is referred to as a charisma, a grace gift. The gifts of the Holy Spirit are specific examples of God's grace, whether our very salvation or any of God's other gifts to his children. Paul speaks of the gift of Christ's righteousness (Rom. 5:17) and the gift of eternal life in Christ (Rom. 6:23). The righteousness of Christ is God's charisma to us.

But we also read of more specific examples of God's gifts. Paul speaks of the gifts God gave specifically to his people Israel (Rom. 11:29; see 9:4–5). He also mentions some specific gifts of God to the church:

> We have different gifts, according to the grace given us. If a man's gift is prophesying, let him use it in proportion to his faith. If it is serving, let him serve; if it is teaching, let him teach; if it is encouraging, let him encourage; if it is contributing to the needs of others, let him give generously; if it is leadership, let him govern diligently; if it is showing mercy, let him do it cheerfully. (Rom. 12:6–8)

Notice that all of these gifts are for the benefit of *others.*

In 1 Corinthians Paul refers to teaching, encouraging, giving generously, leadership, and showing mercy as grace gifts. He addresses the Corinthian Christians as those who have been "enriched in every way" and who "do not lack any spiritual gift" (1 Cor. 1:5, 7). When we read through this letter, we find a number of these spiritual gifts mentioned. Paul even calls celibacy and marriage spiritual gifts (1 Cor. 7:7).

In fact, one of the reasons Paul wrote this letter was to instruct these Christians on "spiritual gifts" (1 Cor. 12:1). He goes on in this chapter (beginning at 12:7) to list "extraordinary gifts," as the seventeenth-century Puritan writer John Owen called them. Paul says, "[The Spirit] gives them to each one, just as he determines" (12:11). In 12:27–31

Paul gives another list of spiritual gifts, then concludes by instructing the Corinthians to "eagerly desire the greater gifts."

In 2 Corinthians 1:11 Paul refers to his physical deliverance as a *charisma*, a grace gift. In 1 Timothy 4:14 and 2 Timothy 1:6 he refers to Timothy's calling to the ministry as a gift. As he said to the Ephesians, we have "every spiritual blessing in Christ" (1:3).

All of these gifts have a shared goal. Paul understood spiritual gifts to be given for encouraging each other and building each other up (Rom. 1:11–12). In 1 Corinthians 12:4–7 we see clearly that these gifts are given "for the common good."

First Corinthians 14 provides the most obvious teaching on the purpose of spiritual gifts. Note verse 4, which is often misunderstood: "He who speaks in a tongue edifies himself, but he who prophesies edifies the church." Some think this is a neutral statement, as if Paul were merely commenting that there are two different kinds of good edification: if you want self-edification, you should seek to speak in tongues or pray in tongues; if you want church edification, then you should seek to prophesy. But I don't think that's what Paul means here. In verse 1 he encourages these Christians to desire especially the gift of prophecy. Then in verse 12, he says, "Since you are eager to have spiritual gifts, try to excel in gifts that build up the church." In verse 19 he says, "But in the church I would rather speak five intelligible words to instruct others than ten thousand words in a tongue." Paul says that you have to be able to understand something in order to be edified by it. Intelligibility is necessary for edifying the church! And that, he says, is the goal of spiritual gifts.

Every time *charisma* is used in the New Testament, the context is that of using gifts for building up the body. From Paul's survival of a shipwreck to the list in 1 Corinthians 14, all *charismata* are always for building up the church in some way.

The goal of all of these spiritual gifts, Paul states clearly, is the "strengthening" of the church (1 Cor. 14:26). That's why the Spirit gives these gifts in the church. So in 1 Corinthians 14:4, Paul isn't mentioning two different kinds of edification. He is criticizing any kind of self-serving use of gifts, and he is redefining the goals for these gifts, realigning the Corinthians' purposes with the Spirit's purpose, which is the building up of the church.

Commenting on 1 Corinthians 14:12, John Calvin wrote: "The more anxious a person is to devote himself to upbuilding, the more highly Paul wishes him to be regarded."[9] As Peter writes, "Each one should use whatever gift he has received to serve others, faithfully administering God's grace" (1 Pet. 4:10).

If edification is the goal of the spiritual gifts Christ has given to his church, what does that mean for us and our churches? It means that we are especially to value the gifts that clearly build up the churches. Furthermore, we must realize how important the upbuilding of the church is to be in our lives—not merely organizationally, but building up one another in our love and concern and prayers. We are all called to initiate involvement in each other's lives. As I have mentioned, at Capitol Hill Baptist we covenant together to work and pray for unity, to walk together in love, to exercise care and watchfulness over each other, to faithfully admonish and entreat one another as occasion may require, to assemble together, to pray for each other, to rejoice and to bear with each other, and to pray for God's help in all things.

Imagine two congregations, one with many people speaking in tongues, the other with scores of young people attending the funeral of an older man whom they had come to know as a fellow church member. That second church seems to me to be more "charismatic" in the biblical sense. That second church looks more like what I understand the New Testament to be calling a church to be—a community in which people have learned to love and to care for each other. That's the new society that God is calling us as Christians to be a part of.

Christianity isn't a merely individualistic decision to come to church to see what I can get out of it. "I'll use the preacher as a public lecturer,

9 John Calvin, *Commentary on the Epistles of Paul the Apostle to the Corinthians*, trans. John Pringle (Grand Rapids, MI: Baker, 1981), 20:442–43.

as my own personal spiritual trainer, and insofar as he benefits me, I'll have a better life." That's not Christianity. Christianity in the New Testament has very much to do with our relationships with the people sitting around us in our churches. The care and the concern we take as a covenanted group, our willingness to make a commitment to God fleshed out in our commitments to each other—that defines a healthy church according to the New Testament.

The charismatic nature of the church means God's Holy Spirit is working among us so that we will love and care for each other. It is a grace gift (a *charisma*) for some to get up and lead worship. It is a grace gift for others to read Scripture to those in the hospital. It is a grace gift to take minutes at church meetings. It is a grace gift to teach Greek. It is a grace gift to text or email your pastor and tell him that you're praying for him. Those things, according to the New Testament, are charismatic gifts. Paul never intended to give an exhaustive list of *charismata* in the seventeen gifts listed. Whenever the church is working by the power of the Spirit for the upbuilding of the body, the Spirit's gifts are present. Any understanding we have of biblical church leadership must be seen in that context.

As a church, leadership is exercised in a covenanted congregational context that is specially equipped by God. That is the charismatic nature of biblical church leadership.

The Christlikeness of Church Leadership

Of course, Christ himself is "the head of the body, the church" (Col. 1:18; see Eph. 1:22–23). He alone is the cornerstone and the capstone (1 Pet. 2:6–7). Jesus Christ is ultimately the leader of the church universal, and every particular local congregation.

It's no surprise then, that inside local congregations, the leaders are to reflect the character of Christ, something of his roles and responsibilities. I've developed a mnemonic device to help remember four aspects of Christ's leadership. I call it BOSS; it can be illustrated by four triangles pointed in different directions. BOSS represents four roles that Jesus filled as a leader and that he calls today's church leaders to fill.

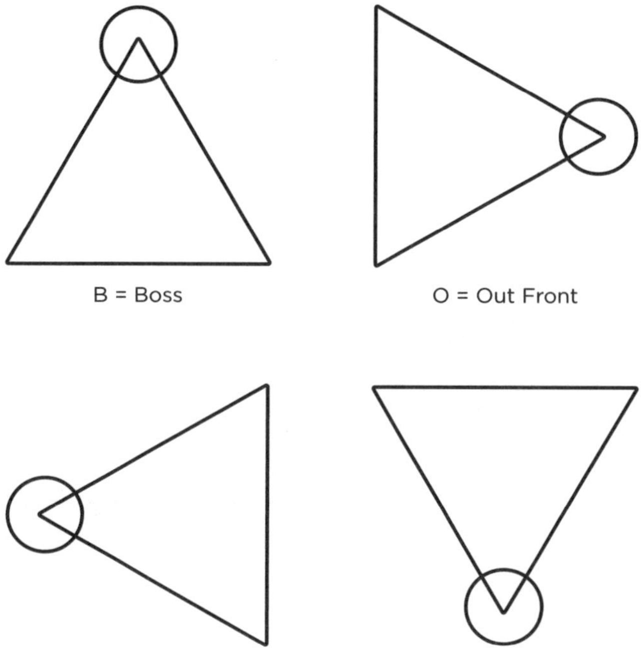

B = Boss

O = Out Front

S = Supply

S = Serve

While these aspects of leadership may apply to many walks of life, I discuss them in the context of being a Christian and exercising leadership in a congregational context.

Boss

Christ himself commanded many things. For instance, he commanded us to instruct others (Matt. 28:20). Paul, too, commanded. He told Christians to tell others what to do. He instructed elders to decide what should be taught, though to do this with gentleness and with patience and endurance (2 Tim. 2:24–25; 4:2). Elders must teach carefully, because God will hold us responsible for how faithful we have been to his Word (see James 3:1). Clearly, church leaders—like any leaders—must sometimes command, making decisions and taking responsibility for them.

Some today are uncomfortable with this. But Jesus clearly instructed his followers (and that includes us) to do the same—to teach, to give instructions, to be willing to exercise authority when he calls us to do so. This kind of leadership should not be avoided. Though such authority may be abused, authority itself is a good thing, and we can help to recover a godly respect for authority by exercising it carefully.

Out Front

The triangle marked "Out Front" points to the right, with the rightmost tip circled. This represents another part of leadership—being out front, taking the initiative, and setting the example. Much of leadership is example-setting and initiative-taking. In John Keegan's classic work, *The Mask of Command*, Alexander the Great is presented as great basically because he personally and fearlessly led his troops into the most dangerous parts of the battle.[10] Probably the most feared general in all of World War II followed Alexander's example. The German tank commander Rommel, the "Desert Fox," was often out in front of his troops, which was unusual for generals in World War II. When a battle involving his forces began, the word went out, "Rommel in the lead!" That message galvanized the troops to follow him.

Another part of biblical leadership is that of setting an example. Jesus said in John 13:34, "As I have loved you, so you must love one another." Paul wrote, "Your attitude should be the same as that of Christ Jesus" (Phil. 2:5). Peter exhorted some early Christians to remember that "Christ suffered for you, leaving you an example, that you should follow in his steps" (1 Pet. 2:21). To the Corinthian Christians, Paul wrote, "Follow my example, as I follow the example of Christ" (1 Cor. 11:1). And Paul specifically told the Thessalonian believers that he labored to make himself a model that they could follow (2 Thess. 3:7–9). He deliberately worked to live a model life—not a perfect life, but still an

10 John Keegan, *The Mask of Command* (New York: Viking, 1987).

exemplary one. Paul offered his own life as the example, leading out in front to show how it is to be done.

And this is what leaders in the church today are to do. As part of our leadership, we're to be examples (see John 13:15; Phil. 3:17; 1 Tim. 4:12; Titus 2:7; James 5:10).

Supply

The triangle marked "Supply" points to the left, with the left-most tip circled. This triangle reminds us that another part of leadership is supply.

Consider an army with a vital supply line stretching out to the frontline troops. Good leadership strategically works to give shape and focus and freedom to the work that others are called to do. Leaders direct the traffic of the church, cutting up ministry into bite-sized bits that others will be able to do.

If we are called to be suppliers, we go back behind the lines and give people the tools they need to go out themselves. Having prepared his disciples, Jesus sent them out (Luke 9–10). They failed in Luke 9, but Jesus sent them out again in Luke 10, and they succeeded. Jesus, in this example, was back behind the lines, supplying and equipping others.

Of course we can't go with the people we send out, as Jesus can by his Spirit. Our situation is more like Paul's when, in his last letter, he instructed Timothy to teach those who can teach others (2 Tim. 2:2). Paul understood that he could greatly multiply his ministry as he supplied the resources for others to do their own ministries.

Serve

The triangle "Serve" is pointing down, with the lowest tip circled. This represents the role of service. This is the second S in BOSS, and is perhaps the most distinctly Christian kind of leadership. We see it in Christ most fully as he gave himself for us on the cross, dying for us so that we might live to him. Moving descriptions of this self-sacrificial service are found in each of the Gospels, with further reflections throughout the New Testament. Philippians 2 and 1 Peter 2 are particularly clear and moving.

This is the example of leadership that Christ has left us. And this is especially the case if we are called to be leaders in a congregation. Peter writes,

> To the elders among you, I appeal as a fellow elder, a witness of Christ's sufferings and one who also will share in the glory to be revealed: Be shepherds of God's flock that is under your care, serving as overseers—not because you must, but because you are willing, as God wants you to be; not greedy for money, but eager to serve; not lording it over those entrusted to you, but being examples to the flock. And when the Chief Shepherd appears, you will receive the crown of glory that will never fade away. (1 Pet. 5:1–4)

All four of these different aspects of leadership—the boss commanding, the out-front example, the supplying of what's needed, and the serving—will be part of biblical church leadership.

The Relationship of Church Leadership to God's Nature and Character

As we conclude our look at church leadership, we should consider how the exercise of such leadership relates to God's nature and character.

Leadership is not finally just a matter of church politics. One time while I was in Cambridge, a friend I was dining with expressed anger at a recent decision of the city council to sell off some land beside a school near his house. As he talked, I recalled how typical this was of my friend. He was always expressing anger about this or that thing that some authority had done. So I asked him a simple, direct, unqualified question: "Do you think authority is bad?" I thought he would give me a carefully crafted answer, shaded with subtle meanings. But I was shocked by his unnuanced, simple, direct, unqualified answer: "Yes. Authority is bad."

Recognizing the fallen nature of human authority and the fact that authority can be abused is a good and healthy thing. Of course, power apart from God's purposes is always demonic. But a suspicion of all authority is also very bad. It often reveals more of the person questioning than of the authority being questioned. To live as God meant us to live, we must be able to trust him, and we must be able to trust those made in his image. Abuse of such authority is a particularly terrible evil because it so exactly slanders God.

This is not to say that godliness is gullibility, but it is to say that the capacity to trust is a crucial component of reflecting the image of God and of operating within the relationships of life in which that image is played out and expressed.

As Paul prays for the Christians in Ephesus, he tells them that he prayed to "the Father, from whom his whole family in heaven and on earth derives its name" (Eph. 3:14–15). Paul's point is not simply that God is the Father of his church family, the church universal (though that's certainly true), but that God is the Creator who has made us in his image, and that even the very social structures of authority that we have in our families derive from him and from his authority. So authority and leadership are not matters of indifference to us as Christians; they are matters of great concern, because they are part of the image of God that we are to reflect in our lives.

A world without authority would be like desires with no restraints, a car with no controls, an intersection with no traffic lights, a game with no rules, a home with no parents. It might go on for a little while, but before long it would seem pointless, then cruel and unutterably tragic.

In their book *Authority: The Most Misunderstood Idea in America*, Eugene Kennedy and Sara Charles argue that "the stabilizing character of healthy authority is what has been missing. Its return is what will make us more confident and less anxious in managing our lives."[11] They

11 Eugene Kennedy and Sara Charles, *Authority: The Most Misunderstood Idea in America* (New York: Free Press, 1997), 2.

suggest that "healthy authority matches the needs and goals of serious intimate relationships, because its concern is not to overcome others but to fuel the growth of people who feel safe with each other."[12] According to these authors, in movies such as *Pleasantville*,

> Greater sexual freedom, in and of itself, is viewed as the fruit of a noble rebellion against inhuman and repressive forces. Such a thing is validated in popular culture as an end in itself. Unqualified sexual liberation, that is, sex detached from human relationships, becomes a central tenet of the popular wisdom.[13]

And yet to take that intimacy outside of the structure of commitment, authority, submission, and covenant love is to uproot some of the most important lessons we can learn as creatures made in God's image—how we are to relate both to each other and to God.

I remember once preaching through 1 and 2 Samuel, and finding David's last words in 2 Samuel 23. I was struck by these words, and wondered why I hadn't noticed them more before: "When one rules over men in righteousness, when he rules in the fear of God, he is like the light of morning at sunrise on a cloudless morning, like the brightness after rain that brings the grass from the earth" (2 Sam. 23:3–4). What a beautiful description of healthy authority and its fruit!

I think I noticed David's words more at that time because I was a man exercising growing authority, both in my family and in my church. This made the truth of them more obvious to me, and more important and precious.

The family is supposed to be our training ground in loving authority. It is a "ramping-up" place that God has given us to learn love, respect, honor, obedience, and trust, in order to prepare us for relating to others and ultimately to God himself.

12 Kennedy and Charles, *Authority*, 35.

13 Kennedy and Charles, *Authority*, 30.

When we exercise authority in a good and proper way— through the law, around the family table, in our jobs, on the football field, in our homes, and especially in the church—we help to display God's image to his creation.

Our conduct in the church in regard to this matter of leadership is to be such that the gospel is not brought into disrepute but rather is held up to be the glorious light of hope and truth in the world. Our lives together are to be as pure as can be, so that God's heart of love for the world will shine clearly through us.

This is a tremendous call that God gives us, to recognize and respect godly authority in the church. This is a sign of a healthy church and of healthy Christians. This is our call. This is our privilege. And there is a world that needs to see people made in the image of God living out that image in this way. Let's pray that we can do that together in our churches—for our churches' health and for God's glory.

Other Resources

- For group study: *Leading One Another: Church Leadership* (2012), by Bobby Jamieson, a six-week inductive Bible study from 9Marks.
- For pastoral application: *Finding Faithful Elders and Deacons* (2012), by Thabiti Anyabwile.
- See also: Charles Bridges, *The Christian Ministry* (1830); Mark Dever, *The Church: The Gospel Made Visible* (2012) and *Understanding Church Leadership* (2016); Jeremy Rinne, *Church Elders: How to Shepherd God's People Like Jesus* (2013); Phil A. Newton and Matt Schmucker, *Elders in the Life of the Church: Rediscovering the Biblical Model for Church Leadership* (2014); Jonathan Leeman, *Understanding the Congregation's Authority* (2016) and *One Assembly: Rethinking the Multisite and Multiservice Church Models* (2020); Aaron Menikoff, *Character Matters: Shepherding in the Fruit of the Spirit* (2020); Mark Dever and Paul Alexander, *How to Build a Healthy Church: A Practical Guide for Deliberate Leadership* (2021).

What's Coming Up

Mark Eight: A Biblical Understanding and Practice of Prayer

Mark Eight

A Biblical Understanding and Practice of Prayer

> Everyone thinks that advertising is full of lies, but it's not what you think. The facts presented in advertising are almost always accurate, not because advertising people are sticklers but because their ads are very closely regulated. If you make a false claim in a commercial on network television, the Federal Trade Commission will catch it. Someone always blows the whistle. The real lie in advertising—some would call it the "art" of advertising—is harder to detect. What's false in advertising lies in the presentation of situations, values, beliefs, and cultural norms that form a backdrop for the selling message. Advertising—including movies, TV, and music videos—presents to us a world that is not our world but rather a collection of images and ideas created for the purpose of selling. These images paint a picture of the ideal family life, the perfect home.

That was the late advertising pioneer and executive, Jay Chait, writing a number of years ago in *Forbes*.[1] Is it true that advertising doesn't lie, it just misinforms?

1 Jay Chait, "Illusions Are Forever, *Forbes ASAP*, October 2, 2000, 139.

These days it seems marketing, advertising, and publicity are not only for diamonds and movies but for churches too. With a background as a journalist, a former member of Capitol Hill Baptist published a book titled *Successful Church Publicity* almost eighty years ago.[2] In it he instructed pastors how to best publicize their church and its work. His advice seems plain, however, compared to the culture we live in today. Churches have learned marketing principles and more.

Even church names are designed to be vague, nonthreatening, and inclusive. Gone are denominational distinctives like Methodist or Presbyterian, which might make some people feel excluded. Popular in names are words like *community* or *fellowship* or, better yet, words that sound mysterious and enticingly suggestive like *the branch*, *mosaic*, *nexus*, or *imago*. Main Street Baptist Church—that is, the Baptist church that meets on Main Street—sounds rather bland.

One church's website describes its building as having "stunning beauty." Another church calls itself a church of "compassion, conviction, and connection." And still another promises those who come "an intimate encounter with Christ." The "church" just a block east of ours has a sign out front saying "Best in DC," quoting a review written by a secular magazine, without ever making it clear that they are a fairly recent cult which, among other things, denies the Trinity and says that Mary is divine.

What is the role of self-promotion, even among biblical churches? I'm not trying to be Negative Norman. I have no objection to calling the news we have to give *good*! But I can't help but think of Proverbs 27:2: "Let another praise you, and not your own mouth; / a stranger, and not your own lips." As a church, should we promote ourselves with our own advertisements? How does a church faithfully publicize its activities without trying to wrongly distinguish and elevate its excitingness or success or effectiveness over against other churches that

2 Carl F. H. Henry, *Successful Church Publicity* (Grand Rapids, MI: Zondervan, 1943).

claim to promote the same good news? How can our church make sure that our efforts and credit go to praising someone better than ourselves, someone truly worth directing attention to and worthy of our praise?

That brings us to our topic in this chapter. Here we want to think about a biblical understanding and practice of prayer as one thing that marks out a healthy church—and not mainly prayer in the life of the individual Christian but what we do when we gather as a church.

Book Recommendations on Prayer

R. C. Sproul's *The Prayer of the Lord* (2009) is a wonderful, short book that covers the Lord's Prayer and discusses prayer in general.

D. A. Carson's *Praying with Paul* (2015) examines Paul's prayers throughout the New Testament. When you study them, you will see that he prays primarily for churches.

I also recommend Paul Tautges's *Teach Them to Pray: Cultivating God-Dependency in Your Church* (2010).

John Onwuchekwa's *Prayer: How Praying Together Shapes the Church* (2018) is short and easy to read. He addresses prayer in the lives of individuals (which is what books on prayer are about) as well as prayers in the life of the congregation as we prayer together.

If you would like to think more about prayer, you can go to the CHBC website and listen to a couple of my sermons on this topic. Go to our resources section and search for "prayer." The first two sermons that pop up may be helpful to you.

I also recommend listening to David Platt's "The Role of Desperate Prayer in Relenting Wrath" (2014), available at the Together for the Gospel website (t4g.org).

In this chapter, we will do three things. First, we will define prayer. Second, we'll consider how prayer works. Third, we'll examine how prayer should function in the life of the local church.

What Is Prayer?

Although many definitions of prayer could be given, I will simply say that prayer is talking to God. This "talking" can be in song or in writing. It can be unspoken thought and, according to Romans 8, it might even at times be something difficult to put into words. But typically in the Bible, prayer is talking. It is David in the Psalms and Jonah in the fish. It is the way Jesus instructed us to love our enemies—we should talk to God on their behalf and for their good (Matt. 5:44). We should pray for them, as Jesus did from the cross (Luke 23:34). It's what the disciples were doing when God poured out his Spirit at Pentecost—they were together talking to God (see Acts 1:14). God treasures the expressions of his saints. He views their prayers as incense (Rev. 5:8; 8:3–4).

Prayer is not some mysterious energy of the universe. According to the Bible, praying is not tapping into an impersonal force that is there, like the wind, to be harnessed by whoever puts up the sail of a "faith-filled" prayer. Prayer is not a kind of cosmic ATM, or shallow meditation, or just talking to yourself. Prayer is talking to God. And it works because the God of the Bible is real, and he really listens! Jesus taught his disciples to pray for our daily bread; consider how often God has answered *that* prayer in your life!

Prayer can be done anywhere, anytime, by anyone. Just to be clear, however, according to the Bible God hears both *all* prayers and only *some* prayers. He hears all prayers in that he knows what we will say before we even say it. But he has obligated himself to hear—*in the sense of obliging himself to answer*—only the prayers of those he has adopted as his children by faith in Christ. God delights to answer the prayers of those who are not his spiritual enemies, but who are his dearly bought children.

Because the God of the Bible is the true and living God, he speaks. He is not like man-made idols that may have carved noses but cannot smell, carved eyes but cannot see, carved ears but cannot hear, carved mouths but cannot speak. God is real. His existence does not depend on the arguments we may have with friends to try to make them believe. Everyone on the planet could stop believing in God, and he would continue to exist. And our most fundamental worship of God is to listen to his Word. We are to read and study God's Word, to believe God, and to obey him.

Because God has made us in his very own image, he calls us not only to hear him but to speak back to him. In the very form of our prayer—forming ideas and words that we then speak back to him—we imitate and reflect him. We display his own speaking nature. We engage with him in a relationship. He speaks by his Spirit in his Word. We listen and talk back to him in our prayers. This is far from being merely a "sort of" relationship, in a made-up, religious sense. Our relationship with our Creator is the truest, deepest relationship to which all of our other relationships are meant to point and lead. And prayer is a vital part of that relationship.

Does Prayer Work?

The sovereign God uses the means of our prayers to accomplish his purposes. We ask him to do what only he can do.

The Bible is filled with accounts of God hearing and answering the prayers of his people. We read again and again in Psalm 107 that "they cried to the LORD in their trouble, / and he delivered them from their distress" (Ps. 107:6, 13, 19, 28). When Hannah was childless, she prayed. When Jonah was in the fish, he prayed. When the early Christians were facing persecution in Acts, they prayed. Moses, Gideon, Samuel, Solomon, Elijah, Cornelius, Paul—they all prayed. Supremely, Jesus Christ prayed. They all prayed when they wanted to communicate with God. They were not simply performing empty religious rituals. They wanted God to do something!

But how long do you keep praying about the same things? Jesus taught his followers that we should never give up in prayer. I assume he taught this precisely because he knew we would be tempted to do so! You may be thinking, "I've tried this. Prayer simply doesn't work. I've prayed for things, and I've trusted God before. And it didn't work." To you I would ask, Did the church at Jerusalem pray just once? Or for fifteen minutes? Or for half an hour? Was Jonah in the whale one hour, or one day? How long do you think Hannah prayed for a child? Days? Months? Years?

Don't misunderstand me. We don't always get what we ask for in our prayers and even those times we do, we never "earn" the answers to our prayers through length of time or repetition. Nevertheless, God does instruct us time and time again to be persistent in our prayers (see Luke 18 for a story Jesus tells about that). So if you have prayed. And prayed. And prayed—God's Word holds out hope.

You may be Jonah on that third day. Keep praying.

You may be that church praying for the twelfth, but final, hour.

You may be Hannah, offering up her last prayer for a child to God.

We have a God who delights in hearing our hearts. It is through praying that we experience much of our relationship with God.

For some of us the ship has sailed, the time has passed, the loved one has died, the day of opportunity is gone. We may no longer hope that God will change history, but we continue to wait in hope because we know his character, and we know what he has done for us in Christ. We trust that he is good, and that one day we will understand more fully why he has done what he has done. Though we didn't see the answer to a specific prayer, we trust that the larger prayer of our life toward God will be fully answered in a way that is most satisfying to us.

So are you convinced, Christian? Or do you think that prayer is optional and not really necessary? Friend, prayer is as necessary as talking to your husband or wife, to your parents, or your children, if you want to have a relationship with them. Keep praying. Prayer without perseverance is prayer in vain. When you understand prayer, you will know God better and trust him more.

Prayers God Doesn't Hear

Sometimes God regularly answers prayer, sometimes he refuses to answer prayer, and sometimes he won't even hear them. In the Old and

New Testaments, God sometimes refuses to hear prayers. In Ezekiel 20, the elders of Israel come to inquire of the Lord, but the Lord refuses to listen. In a sense, the elders pray to pray. They ask, "Can we pray to you?" and God says, "No." Why? "They rebelled against me and were not willing to listen to me" (Ezek. 20:8). After recounting a series of their rejections of God, Ezekiel says, "When you present your gifts and offer up your children in fire,"—this was the false worship they were involved in, thinking they could simply turn to God in prayer in the midst of idolatry—"you defile yourselves with all your idols to this day. And shall I be inquired of by you, O house of Israel? As I live, declares the Lord God, I will not be inquired of by you" (Ezek. 20:31).

But as Christians, we can be sure of our wise heavenly Father's loving hearing of our prayers. Remember Paul's prayer in 2 Corinthians 12: "Three times I pleaded with the Lord about this, that it should leave me. But he said to me, 'My grace is sufficient for you, for my power is made perfect in weakness'" (2 Cor. 12:8–9). Why was Paul's prayer not answered? Why didn't his prayer "work"? Was it because of sin in Paul's life? Was he being disobedient, as the elders of Israel were? Of course Paul was imperfect. He was not sinless, and he was well aware of that. Paul was a sinner saved by grace. But his life was not characterized by the kind of unrepentant state of sin, which God hates. Paul was a Christian. To suggest that he must have been harboring some hidden sin for which this was punishment is to be no better than Job's "comforters."

So ask yourself, did Paul's prayer work? The thorn was not removed. The torment did not end. But Paul came to know the living God better. The world came to know the living God better. Did the Israelite elders' prayer in Ezekiel 20 work? They didn't get to inquire of the Lord, but God did make himself known. In both cases men came to God with a request. In both cases God refused their request. Through both prayers, God was made known. To the elders of Israel, this was not the answer they were looking for. But to Paul, what he desired more than anything else, even more than the removal of his thorn, was that God would be made known.

God tells Paul, "My grace is sufficient for you, for *my power is made perfect in weakness*." In other words, Paul and those he ministered to would know God better by Paul's weakness. And that's what Paul most deeply wanted. That was the prayer of Paul's life.

The great Puritan Joseph Hall once said, "Good prayers never came weeping home. I am sure I shall receive, either what I ask or what I should ask."[3] Paul received here better than what he had asked. "Therefore," Paul writes, "I will boast all the more gladly about my weaknesses, so that the power of Christ may rest upon me. For the sake of Christ, then, I am content with weaknesses, insults, hardships, persecutions, and calamities. For when I am weak, then I am strong" (2 Cor. 12:9–10). Paul boasted of his weakness. He delighted in his trials because he had committed his suffering to the Lord in prayer and God had willed not to take it away . . . yet.

The same sovereign God who allowed Job to be tried so incredibly; the same sovereign God who called Abraham to be willing to sacrifice his long-sought son; the same sovereign God who gave his one and only Son for those who hated him: this is the God who called Paul to bear with his thorn, to endure its torments *for a season*.

Reflecting personally, this is the God who has heard our prayers for the conversion of our loved ones, the growth of our churches, the spread of the gospel through recovered and new churches locally and beyond. God has determined to make himself known through such answers, and even through his refusals to answer prayers. As with evangelism, the preaching of the gospel, or even the writing of this book, God has determined not only the ends but also the means. God has predestined before the foundation of the world to work through our prayers. Through prayer God gave the somewhat faithless Jonah life and repentance. He gave Peter freedom from jail. And he gave Hannah a child. God would have Jonah alive. God would have Peter free. And God would give Hannah a child. But not without their prayers.

3 Joseph Hall, *Devotional Works*, vol. 6, *The Works of Joseph Hall*, ed. Josiah Pratt (London: C. Whittingham, 1808), 13.

That confidence in God leads a local church to give much time to prayer in our life together.

How to Pray Together as a Local Church

First-time visitors to our congregation often comment on how much time we spend praying together and sitting silently as others lead in prayer.

In many ways, this practice of prayer should not surprise us. From the first Christians on, praying together is a pattern in the New Testament. The first Christians met to pray (Acts 1:14, 24; 2:42). One of the results of God's pouring out his Spirit on his people at Pentecost was that people met to pray. The circumstances of the prayers in the New Testament vary—offered inside or outside, at various hours of the day and night, sometimes with singing, sometimes with fasting, sometimes kneeling, sometimes with eyes or hands uplifted or laying hands on someone. This great variety seems to illustrate the biblical command to pray without ceasing, through a variety of circumstances (1 Thess. 5:17). I believe this great variety applies to the practice of prayer in the local church. People can be legalistic about particular ways to pray, as if prayer can take only one form. But many of the differences in how churches pray are not problematic, but are simply wonderful reflections of the unique aspects of different congregations' individual characters.

We can, however, make some statements about prayer that apply to *every* church. For the rest of this chapter, I make a number of those statements.

Our public prayer life together as a church should grow out of our individual prayer lives. God's instruction in 1 Thessalonians 5:17 to pray without ceasing should encourage us to set aside some time daily to pray. All the basic aspects of prayer should be in our personal prayer time—praising God for who he is, thanking him for what he has done, confessing who we are and what we've done, and making requests for ourselves and for others. Sometimes people remember this with the acronym ACTS—Adoration, Confession, Thanksgiving, Supplication.

You can integrate *what you pray about* and *who you pray for* when you're in the privacy of your home with the prayer life of the whole congregation. Consider studying in your personal times the passage of Scripture that is going to be preached on the following Lord's Day. Let your requests to God for Elizabeth and Bob and Joe and the other members of your church be shaped by the passage of Scripture. This can also help you pray for others that you don't know well, and it works to prepare your heart for the message to come from that part of God's Word.

Consider praying through your church's membership directory. At CHBC, we have a directory that lists all the members. Special sections in the back list former interns and staff so our members know where they are now. There is a section for all the children of members of the church. And one for our supported workers. Because our directory has about sixty pages, it can easily be prayed through monthly by praying through two pages a day. That's what I've done myself and encourage others to do. If we love one another, as we're commanded to do (John 13:35; 1 Thess. 3:12; 2 Thess. 1:3), and have covenanted to do as members, surely that will include praying for each other (James 5:16).

Some of our practices in prayer will vary over time. Just as circumstances varied in the New Testament, they vary in churches today. For example, thirty years ago our church was much smaller and many of our members were older; that had implications for how often we could meet to pray and what time of day we could meet. One newer prayer meeting is hosted by some of the members of the church for the conversion of international students; they meet on Sunday afternoons. Our churchwide prayer meeting used to meet on Wednesday nights, but now we meet on Sunday nights. At times in the life of our church, we've had special meetings for extra prayer, like when we chose our first set of elders. After our nation was attacked in 2001, we hosted a special public meeting. The enduring fact is that we give ourselves in biblical prayers to God for his work here and around the world; there is great liberty in exactly how we do that as a local church.

Some specific words can be especially helpful in leading a church well in prayer. For example, using the plural *we* in the prayers we offer aloud around each other is exampled for us when Jesus taught us to pray "*our* Father." When you or I lead in prayer publicly, we need to remember that we're not just having our own personal devotionals out in public with others listening in; rather, we have the opportunity to lead a whole group of people into the presence of our heavenly Father. In such a position, we would rarely use the word *I*. We would almost always refer to "we" and "our" precisely because we intend to speak to God not simply for matters that concern us as individuals, but for matters that concern the church as a whole. So we pray for *our* joy, not my joy; for *our* work, not my work. We find matters of common concern and interest, and together we go to God in prayer, with one person leading by voicing concerns on behalf of the entire congregation.

Now if *we* is the "hand," as it were, of the one leading in prayer, we the congregation verbally "take the leader's hand" when we say "Amen" at the conclusion of the prayer. *Amen* is Hebrew for "this is true" or "I agree." This is where we get to verbally own, to all those who can hear us, that this prayer is not simply the prayer of the one who verbalized it, but that it is our prayer too. We say "Amen" to it, we agree with what has been prayed, and we publicly accept and affirm this as representing us to God.

In the churches I once visited in China, the declaration of "Amen!" at the conclusion of prayers sounded like claps of thunder. One brother would pray for quite a while, leading you to wonder whether people were really paying attention. But then at the conclusion of the prayer, everyone would clearly and emphatically "own" the prayer as soon as it was concluded with a loud, "Amen." No one could be in any doubt about the unity that such praying represented. That unity is what we're supposed to convey and experience in the local church as we pray together in a way that shows that *we know* that we are praying together. The offer of the plural and the acceptance of the prayer by a clear "Amen" help our church to pray together better.

Different kinds of public prayers help us as a local church. Some churches may have long, spontaneous prayers by a pastor or another member. Others may have various short, planned prayers, as in some church's written liturgies. At CHBC, our longer public prayers tend to be planned and written out, whereas our shorter public prayers tend to be spontaneous. Both kinds of prayers serve our life together well.

Our longer, planned prayers in our Sunday morning services are opportunities to give careful, sustained, reverent, worshipful, hopeful attention to the attributes of God, to his goodness to us, to our sins or our needs, or to gospel work elsewhere. In the prayers in the Old Testament Prophets, the audience of the prayers often switches back and forth from God to the people hearing (or reading) the prayer, and back again. In public prayer, that is understandable. We have to realize that part of what we're doing when we open our mouth in public is teaching others, otherwise leaders wouldn't need a microphone and the congregation wouldn't need to listen.

Some people are surprised at the thought of preparing a prayer ahead of time. They have learned to associate spontaneity with sincerity and preparation with formalism and even hypocrisy. While these are certainly dangers, they aren't inevitable. Preparation does not necessitate insincerity.

Robert Baillie recounts one of the days of prayer that he attended during the Westminster Assembly. "Dr. Twisse having commenced the service with a short prayer, 'Mr. [Stephen] Marshall prayed large two hours, most divinely confessing the sins of the members of the Assembly, in a wonderful, pathetick [meaning "moving"], and prudent way. After, Mr. Arrowsmith preached an hour, then a psalm; after which, Mr. Vines prayed nearly two hours, Mr. Palmer preached an hour, and Mr. Seaman prayed nearly two hours, then a psalm. Mr. Henderson then spoke of the evils of the time, and how they were to be remedied, and Dr. Twisse closed the service with a short prayer and blessing."[4]

4 *Robert Ballie's Letters*, 2:18–19, cited by James Reid, *Memoirs of the Westminster Divines* (Edinburgh: Banner of Truth, 1982) vol. 2, 77–78.

These pastors would prepare for their prayers as much as they would prepare for their sermons.

Pastors or members giving attention and thought to what they will pray about beforehand in no way indicates insincerity in prayer! The care we take in preparing to lead in prayer helps us do this well. It usually takes me about forty-five minutes to prepare the pastoral prayer or one of the other longer prayers in our morning service.

But spontaneous prayers can have much to offer too. They are flexible. We can respond to something we've just learned. We can pray about more different separate events or situations or people. At CHBC our shorter prayers of intercession on Sunday evenings aren't prepared, because the people I ask to lead them aren't given any advance notice. People who might be reluctant to lead in public from the front are much more willing to lead in brief prayers from their seats. Letting someone know that I'm calling on him before I or someone else shares the request allows that person to note down names and particulars, and then, when the time comes, to lead us in brief, direct prayers of petition to God. The variety of people sharing and praying, the variety of matters prayed about, and the brevity of the prayers help us to cover a wide variety in a comparatively short time. So different kinds of prayers—long and short, planned and spontaneous—help us as a local church.

One of our longer prayers on Sunday morning is directed specifically toward praising God. Jesus taught his followers to begin their prayer, "Hallowed be your name." In Psalm 145 David specifically extols and commends God, reflecting on his grace and mercy and goodness. It is good for us to hear prayers of praise, inspired and uninspired. There is so much good to say about God! And it is wonderful to say it back to him. Consider this past week. Did you give much time to thinking about God? Did you recognize and praise him as the one and only self-existing God? No one made him. No one could, because he was before everyone else. He alone is everywhere. He has all power and authority. He is the almighty God! He is the Lord Most High! He is the sovereign Lord, the Ancient of Days, avenging and awesome, blessed and compassionate, gracious and eternal, faithful and holy, Creator and forgiver. He is the God of comfort and glory, of heaven and earth, of justice and love, of peace and truth.

Not only do we praise God, the Father of our Lord Jesus Christ, for his character, but we *thank* him both for his character in himself and for what he has done for us: supremely, he has saved us! This is what the choirs in heaven are doing in Revelation, day and night: "Worthy are you, our Lord and God, / to receive glory and honor and power, / for you created all things, / and by your will they existed and were created" (Rev. 4:11). The point of so many prayers in the Bible is simply to praise God. Acts 4:24–30 is an example.

> And when they heard it, they lifted their voices together to God and said, "Sovereign Lord, who made the heaven and the earth and the sea and everything in them, who through the mouth of our father David, your servant, said by the Holy Spirit,
>
> "'Why did the Gentiles rage,
> and the peoples plot in vain?
> The kings of the earth set themselves,
> and the rulers were gathered together,
> against the Lord and against his Anointed'—
>
> for truly in this city there were gathered together against your holy servant Jesus, whom you anointed, both Herod and Pontius Pilate, along with the Gentiles and the peoples of Israel, to do whatever your hand and your plan had predestined to take place. And now, Lord, look upon their threats and grant to your servants to continue to speak your word with all boldness, while you stretch out your hand to heal, and signs and wonders are performed through the name of your holy servant Jesus."

Although the point of the prayer might appear to be the request in verses 29–30, most of the prayer states the truth about this God they are beseeching. Acts 4:24–28 is all praise and thanks, acknowledging God in his good and sovereign actions. We remember that these particular praying believers were scared. Peter had just been arrested. They may have been afraid to meet together. Yet rather than spending most of their time interceding, they spent it praising and thanking God.

As a church, we should spend time thanking God regularly for all that he has done in saving us. He has become a faithful husband to the unfaithful, he adopted us when we had impoverished ourselves, and he has given us his very self as our inheritance. We can thank him for the judgment that he has rendered and that Christ has taken for us. We can thank him for keeping us and ruling us. We can thank him for his assurance that the good work he has begun in us he will complete. We can thank him for his kindnesses to us in his sovereignty, for the hope-giving prospect of heaven, for the comfort we can take in his sovereignty over all kings on earth and all nations. We can thank him for the gift of his Word and the light he gives us through it. We can thank him, as the psalmist does in Psalm 119, for his law. We can thank him for engaging with us, for leading us, and for loving us.

Let's stare at God—Father, Son, and Holy Spirit—and in prayer thank him for his loving-kindness, his unchangeableness, his righteousness, his patience with us, and his complete reliability that allows us to readily turn to him in prayer. Let's spend so much time praying in our public services that some people grow bored talking to the God that they only pretend to know. Let's praise him as the living, good, never-changing God that he is. And let's give time in our service to doing this in prayer.

One of our longer prayers on Sunday morning is directed to leading us in confessing our sins to God. "Forgive us our debts," the Lord taught us to pray. We're commanded to confess our sins in James 5:16 and 1 John 1:9. David does this in Psalm 32:5. Sometimes people wonder if confessing our sins is something we do only once, when we begin our Christian life. In one sense, this is right. Certainly we don't have to notice and confess every sin we commit in order to be saved by faith in Christ. If that were the case, no one would be saved. We don't have that level of self-knowledge. When we are born again, we are brought from spiritual death to life, adopted as God's children, and united to Christ by faith. We are accepted in the beloved. That is a once-for-all privilege of ours, and praise God that it is! But in the same way that repentance and faith are not only one-time events but an ongoing part of the Christian life, even so it is necessary for Christians to confess their sins to God in prayer. The Greek word for *confess* basically means "to say the same thing as." When we confess our sins, we are publicly taking God's side in all our disputes with him. We are admitting that he is right and that we've been wrong. By doing this, we continue to remind ourselves of our need for Christ.

When we have a public prayer of confession, we make it clear to all present that we do not think we are the "good people" meeting today, or that we can save ourselves by our own virtue. We highlight the gospel. We make it clear that we are the kind of people who need to be saved.

By confessing our sins seriously and publicly, we continue to exult in God's mercy. Sometimes people think that doing this is morbid negativity. "Why get so down on yourselves?" they say. "Just take a little Joel Osteen pill!" "Talk about happy, positive things!" But this attitude is far from the truth and true gospel joy. True joy is not the result of ignoring sin but of embracing the truth of the gospel in spite of it.

Notice the joy of a congregation as they sing the third verse of "It Is Well." "My sin, not in part, but the whole, is nailed to the cross and I bear it no more, praise the Lord, praise the Lord, O my soul!"[5] Whenever our church sings these words, it feels like the roof is about to come off our old meeting house! Redeemed hearts know the joy of Christian's burden falling off and rolling into the tomb. We know the joy of having been forgiven. Confessing our sins publicly is hardly an exercise in spiritual negativity and self-condemnation. It is an opportunity to remind ourselves of God's mercy and to marvel afresh at

5 Horatio G. Spafford, "It Is Well with My Soul," 1873.

his grace, as we explore the depth of our own sins and consider the extent of his forgiveness and mercy. This is why it's a good thing that our public prayers include confessing our sins.

It is good to dedicate one of our prayers to asking God to help others and to help us as a church. This is what is sometimes called the pastoral prayer. "Your kingdom come. . . . Give us this day our daily bread," the Lord taught us to pray. During the pastoral prayer at CHBC, we ask God to help us, and while the particulars vary from week to week, the basic categories are usually represented. We don't want to be like the church John Stott once described. "I remember some years ago visiting a church incognito. I sat in the back row. . . . When we came to the pastoral prayer, it was led by a lay brother, because the pastor was on holiday. So he prayed that the pastor might have a good holiday. Well, that's fine. Pastors should have good holidays. Second, he prayed for a lady member of the church who was about to give birth to a child that she might have a safe delivery, which is fine. Third, he prayed for another lady who was sick, and then it was over. That's all there was. It took twenty seconds. I said to myself, it's a village church with a village God. They have no interest in the world outside. There was no thinking about the poor, the oppressed, the refugees, the places of violence, world evangelization. . . ."[6]

In the pastoral prayer I begin by praying for those present who are in particular need or who sense their need (the two aren't always the same). We will pray about matters brought up in the text about to be expounded. We pray together for those in positions of authority, as Paul instructed Timothy, "First of all, then, I urge that supplications, prayers, intercessions, and thanksgivings be made for all people, for kings and all who are in high positions, that we may lead a peaceful and quiet life, godly and dignified in every way. This is good, and it is pleasing in the sight of God our Savior" (1 Tim. 2:1–3). This may sometimes mean praying for the president, for other government leaders, or for those in

6 Bill Turpie, ed., *Ten Great Preachers* (Grand Rapids, MI: Baker, 2000), 117.

positions of responsibility and influence in our culture. I then usually pray for our own congregation, including categories of members and some members by name.

I pray for other local churches, because we are more concerned that the spiritually famished eat the true gospel than that they're fed it at our restaurant. We want people to hear and believe the good news. And we thank God for the other churches he's raised up to do that. In fact, one of the great answers to our prayers at CHBC is God's kindness poured out in the raising up of many new churches, as well as the recovery of older sister congregations who now are faithful and prospering. I lead us in praying for those who have gone out from us to preach the gospel, for our persecuted brothers and sisters, for gospel work in places around the world, for Christians here in America, and then for our own congregation. In all of this, we ask for God's help, and we show publicly that we need him. At CHBC this prayer is always done by one of our elders, usually by the pastor who is about to preach.

Prayer should characterize not only our public services but also elder meetings, staff meetings, and our interpersonal interactions. It should not be unusual in our churches to hear that people are praying for you, or to even see two or three members praying together after a service, or perhaps arranging to meet during the week to pray. In our elders meetings and staff meetings, we usually have times of prayer for our congregation as a whole and for individual members. When questions come up, we pray. When we begin and end times together, we pray. We want prayer to characterize our life together.

Have a regularly scheduled time of prayer each week, and expect members to attend. One of our former pastors (who left to lead another congregation) wondered if the many good things that happened at our church over the years were the result of so many members regularly gathering to pray. He exhorted us to not neglect our times of public prayer as a church.

We try to make this expectation clear in our times together, in our conversations, in our membership classes, and in our membership interviews. While we are happy for visitors to attend any of our public services, we *expect* members to be present on Sunday mornings for our main public worship service as we disciple each other in the Word and prayer, and as we join together in corporate quiet time at the beginning of each week God gives us. And we also expect our members to come back together for our Sunday evening prayer service to hear some of what God is doing in our members' lives or in the lives of others whom we know and love and support, and to pray for each other.

Someone may object, "Isn't this an extrabiblical expectation?" My reply is, "Kind of." In Hebrews 10:24–25 we read, "And let us consider how to stir up one another to love and good works, not neglecting to meet together, as is the habit of some, but encouraging one another, and all the more as you see the Day drawing near." In our congregation, we've decided that it builds us up to meet twice on the Lord's Day, and since we have the freedom to do that, we are choosing to do that. After all, we have so much to pray about!

On a Sunday evening at CHBC, the pastor who leads in prayer organizes the items we will be praying about. We tend to say no to a lot, just for the sake of time. Some things can be shared with family or friends or a small group. We may have another pastor in the area come and share about how his congregation is doing. We try to limit our time to items that we think are particularly edifying and appropriate for the church as a whole. So we always pray for the regular preaching of God's Word here, and for upcoming elders meetings. We never want to take God's blessings for granted. We pray for sister congregations that we've planted or had a special investment in. We pray for our witness of unity in diversity, that our community will act to demonstrate and display the gospel. We pray for our evangelism and for conversions, and for those who've been baptized in the morning service. We pray about relationships in our church, about transparency, humility, and godliness. We pray that a servant attitude would mark our membership. We pray for our teenagers, for a culture of discipling in our church, for our giving, and for various mercy ministries we're involved in. We love hearing from and praying for our supported workers when they are in our area. We pray for special evangelistic events coming up. We have so much to pray about!

These are some of the things we pray about together every Sunday night, as we catechize each other in the Christian life through prayer. After all, if people miss Sunday morning, they can always listen to the sermon later online. But if they miss Sunday evening, they will have missed out on the family time for the week.

Of course, no individual Christian has to join this particular congregation. There are plenty of other churches in our area that Bible-believing Christians can unite themselves to in order to obey God's Word. But we understand that we have the freedom to decide as a group that such an expectation benefits all of us, and so we do. Our habits of prayer are edifying for our church's life together, for the members of it—even for those who are providentially hindered from coming—and certainly for my own soul. Many Sunday evenings seem marked by a special sense of God's presence in the singing of his praises, in testimonies of God's grace that are shared, in news of a need or in God's provision of the answer, in hearing the congregation pray, in the Word, and in the deep joy of that final song as we end the Lord's day together on the precipice of another week of life. The expectation of the member's regular attendance at the prayer meeting of the church on the Lord's Day greatly contributes to the health of our local church.

Let's review these nine simple statements about the role of prayer in the life together of a local church:

1. Our public prayer life together as a church should grow out of our individual prayer lives.
2. Some of our practices in prayer will vary over time.

3. Some specific words can be especially helpful in leading a church well in prayer.
4. Different kinds of public prayers help us as a local church.
5. One of our longer prayers on Sunday morning is directed specifically toward praising God.
6. One of our longer prayers on Sunday morning is directed to leading us in confessing our sins to God.
7. It is good to dedicate one of our prayers to asking God to help others and to help us as a church.
8. Prayer should characterize not only our public services but also our elders meetings, staff meetings, and our interpersonal interactions.
9. Have a regularly scheduled time of prayer each week, and expect members to attend.

Conclusion

Old Testament scholar Alec Motyer said that to abandon prayer is to embrace atheism.[7] But, practically speaking, isn't that what too many churches have done today? How much time is spent in prayer in the average evangelical church service today? Do we consider how we are weakening ourselves and our witness when we do that? If we're not gathered around God, why are we gathering at all?

One friend has called prayer "reality attacks." Spending time together in prayer to God reminded the Christians in Acts 4 that the sovereign was not the government who could harass Peter and John, but rather the God who was above *all* governments! The more Christianity is openly despised by the world around us, the more we will need the "reality attacks" of prayer to remind us of what will be the reality on the last day.

Moses Hall's courage was fueled by prayer. Hall was an African-Jamaican pastor in Jamaica in the early 1800s. Some African Christians who were enslaved in Jamaica were gathering regularly to pray, even

7 Alec Motyer, *Psalms of the Day: A New Devotional Translation* (Fern, Ross-shire, UK: Christian Focus, 2016), 246.

though such prayer meetings were outlawed by their masters. This is an account of one occasion.

> Determined to put an end to slave meetings [in Jamaica], some slave owners broke up a prayer meeting being led by a slave named David, one of [Moses] Hall's assistants. They seized David, murdered him, cut off his head, and placed it on a pole in the center of the village as a warning to the other slaves.
>
> Eerily like crucifying Jesus as a public warning.
>
> They dragged Moses Hall up to the grisly object.
>
> "Now, Moses Hall, whose head is that?" the leader of the murderers asked.
>
> "David's," Moses replied.
>
> "Do you know why he is up here?"
>
> "For praying, Sir," said Moses.
>
> "No more of your prayer meetings," he said. "If we catch you at it, we shall serve you as we have served David."
>
> As the crowd watched, Moses knelt beside the pole and said, "Let us pray." The other black [Christians] gathered around and knelt with him as he prayed for the salvation of [David's] murderers.[8]

When we pray, we call on the God of the universe to help us glorify him. And we remind ourselves of who it is that we should really fear and regard and reverence and love.

Do you understand a little more of how God may use the time we spend praying together as a church? Of course, much of the way God uses prayer will be in undramatic ways. Over the years, more than one member has communicated thanks for how our church has taught them to pray. Perhaps they're trying to teach their children, and they remember back to what they have heard on a Sunday night. Or maybe they're asked to pray at a public event, and they remember back to how

8 Mark Sidwell, *Free Indeed: Heroes of Black Christian History* (Greenville, SC: BJU Press, 2001), 29.

they've heard us lead in prayer on Sunday morning. Perhaps they've been in a dry period spiritually, and they simply have been longing for the kind of guided spiritual quiet time that our Sunday morning services are for them, like physical therapy for your soul, when you've been wounded or hurt or exhausted spiritually.

I relish such testimonies. A church that is known for its prayer life is not indulging in self-promotion but in God-promotion. We realize that every time we pray, we are advertising our own inadequacy. We need somebody else. Moses Hall wasn't trumpeting his own courage—he was openly displaying his utter reliance on God, who was entirely up to the task! When we spend time together in prayer, we put to death wrong legalistic or moralistic ideas of Christianity. In advertising our neediness, we separate the gospel from the kind of "positive confession" false teaching that is all too prevalent today. We lift up the God who has faithfully pursued us in amazing love in Christ. We show that God is our hope. As our prayer advertises our dependence upon God and the fact that God is dependable, our prayers become praise. And such prayer should and will mark a healthy church.

Other Resources

- Arthur G. Bennett, *Valley of Vision* (1975); R. C. Sproul, *The Prayer of the Lord* (2009); Paul Tautges, *Teach Them to Pray: Cultivating God-Dependency in Your Church* (2010); D. A. Carson, *Praying with Paul: A Call to Spiritual Reformation* (2014); Donald S. Whitney, *Praying the Bible* (2015); John Onwuchekwa, *Prayer: How Praying Together Shapes the Church* (2018) and *What If I Don't Desire to Pray?* (2020).

What's Coming Up

Mark Nine: A Biblical Understanding and Practice of Missions

What Should Churches Believe about Missions?

What Should Churches Do in Missions?

1. Learn about God's Word and God's World
2. Pray for the Spread of the Gospel in Other Places
3. Plan to Make Your Church Increasingly Useful to the Spread of the Gospel
4. Pay to Support Those Who Go Out for the Sake of the Name Who Can't or Shouldn't Support Themselves
5. Send Pastors and Others to Help Establish Churches in Gospel-Needy Places Far Away
6. Care for Those You Send
7. Wait for a Faithful Witness to Be Well Established, and Help Those Sent Out to Endure

Mark Nine

A Biblical Understanding and Practice of Missions

IS BIGGER AND FASTER always better than smaller and slower?

There once was a delicious drink with powerful positive side effects. When this drink was introduced to a new country, everyone who drank it loved it! Not only was the drink good, but it was *good for* them, too. When some business consultants ran across this new drink, they saw marvelous possibilities. "Don't you want more people to drink this marvelous beverage?" they asked the man who held the franchise of the drink. "Wouldn't you like more people to be helped by it?" "Yes," the man said. "Then just leave it to us," they said.

Within a few weeks, bottles of the drink began appearing in vast numbers in cities throughout the country. Rumors about the drink's great taste and beneficial effects had already been circulating, and a national ad campaign had launched. But as the bottles were snapped up, opened, and drunk, people were underwhelmed. It was a good drink. But it wasn't really what they had heard from their friends or seen advertised on billboards. It was just another drink, like many others on the shelves of their stores.

When the original franchise owner heard people's response, he couldn't believe it. His product had never failed before. What was going on? He went to a store, opened one of his drinks, and took a sip. Then he understood. In order to sell the drink more quickly and on this great a scale, someone had changed the formula to something that could be produced more quickly and cheaply. It was no longer the drink that he had first sold to the few people who loved it and were helped by it. But now his opportunity to introduce the drink to the nation was lost! His problem wasn't the same one he started out with—no one knew of the drink. Now, he had the far worse problem—everyone knew about it! Or at least they *thought* they did! But what they didn't know, and what would be much more difficult to convince them of, was that what they knew about was a fake. Had the man's opportunity been forever lost? Would whatever he did now just cynically be viewed as a desperate attempt at rebranding?

Thank God Christianity isn't just a good-tasting drink with beneficial side effects. But there is no doubt that our commission to take the good news of Jesus Christ around the world has been made more challenging by those who, in the name of making it bigger and faster, have actually substituted a watered-down product for the real one. Though this product has grown quickly, it's not entirely clear what exactly it is. Is it positive thinking or good vibes? Is it a cultural religious heritage? How often have "Christian" churches and "Christian" missions really just involved lost people telling lost people how to have religion, rather than forgiven, born-again people telling lost people how God can save them through Jesus Christ?

We may be tempted to say our church's missions work is exciting and important, but what's *really* exciting and important is our God and what he's done for us in Jesus Christ. Sometimes churches feel the need to exaggerate the excitement of their particular work. But what is truly amazing about it is the whole work itself, not our particular role in it. What we get to do is not evangelize the world in this generation. We get to tell the truth about Jesus Christ to everyone he gives us the opportunity to.

A true biblical understanding of missions is amazing; its practice translates into the ordinariness of learning a language, risking rejection, sharing the gospel, or learning a bus schedule in a new place. I'm convinced that one of the marks of a healthy church is a biblical *understanding* and *practice* of missions. Those are the two matters we want to consider in this chapter. I pray that as you read this, God will help you to understand what he intends for his churches and that your particular church will be helped.

What Should Churches Believe about Missions?

Missions is not a word we find in the Bible, but it is a biblical idea. Missions is taking the gospel across boundaries—especially the boundary of language. While evangelism is telling the gospel, sometimes to people who don't know it, *missions* is evangelism in a place and among a whole people where it's largely unknown. This mission is nothing less than "to transform the nature of humanity."[1] To transform in what way? To bring us into a reconciled relationship with God, our good Creator and Judge.

This is the basic storyline of the whole Bible. In the beginning, the scope of the Bible is cosmic. It is worldwide. God creates a world that he calls good, mankind falls, and God promises redemption. Then the story seems to restart on a very small scale. God calls one man from modern-day Iraq, Abram. In Genesis 12 God tells him that through him all the families of the earth would be blessed. So the trajectory is set for the Old Testament—God would bless Israel, the nation descended from Abram, as a precursor and as a means to bless the whole world. God's role in the world is shown in his decisive defeat of the mighty Egyptian Empire as he frees his people Israel from slavery.

And yet, as the Lord said through the prophet Isaiah to his special servant in Isaiah 49:6,

> It is too light a thing that you should be my servant
>   to raise up the tribes of Jacob

1 Rosaria Butterfield, *Openness Unhindered* (Pittsburgh, PA: Crown & Covenant, 2015), 18.

> and to bring back the preserved of Israel;
> I will make you as a light for the nations,
> that my salvation may reach the end of the earth."

So the servant comes: Jesus Christ is crucified and rises again. And the Son of God teaches his disciples, "All authority in heaven and on earth has been given to me. Go therefore and make disciples of all nations, baptizing them in the name of the Father and of the Son and of the Holy Spirit, teaching them to observe all that I have commanded you. And behold, I am with you always, to the end of the age" (Matt. 28:18–20). Jesus was saying, "As much as it takes and as long as it takes, I am with you to the end!" We see the disciples scattering in the book of Acts and the gospel going throughout the Mediterranean world and beyond, fulfilling Jesus's command. And we see its final fulfillment in the book of Revelation, which is filled with scenes like this:

> After this I looked, and behold, a great multitude that no one could number, from every nation, from all tribes and peoples and languages, standing before the throne and before the Lamb, clothed in white robes with palm branches in their hands, and crying out with a loud voice, "Salvation belongs to our God who sits on the throne, and to the Lamb!" (Rev. 7:9–10)

The basic story of the Bible was never merely ethnic and local or national and parochial—it was always as wide as the creation and the Creator's claims.

This is not the invention of some later missiologist. This is the basic idea of the Bible. Therefore, we must be especially clear about the gospel, the good news, that is at the heart of it all. This good news about Jesus Christ is so important that Paul calls for the damnation of any who would change the basic message of the gospel (see Gal. 1:8). This message is the means by which God will reconcile the world to himself, and so bring redemption to all who will trust in Christ.

The gospel of Jesus Christ is the only means of our being converted from spiritual death to spiritual life, from being condemned to being saved. This is how the apostle Paul understood his whole ministry. Paul recounted the risen Christ's words to him at his conversion on the road to Damascus:

> I have appeared to you for this purpose, to appoint you as a servant and witness to the things in which you have seen me and to those in which I will appear to you, delivering you from your people and from the Gentiles—to whom I am sending you to open their eyes, so that they may turn from darkness to light and from the power of Satan to God, that they may receive forgiveness of sins and a place among those who are sanctified by faith in me. (Acts 26:16–18)

This good news is what has led to our own conversions! And it is what we share with others in our evangelism.

This is the heart of everything we do. The nature of truly believing includes repenting of our sins, so there is in true Christianity a quality of self-denial. It's not the added optional extra mature thing to do—"if you feel really guilty, you can start living radically." No, you're not a Christian if you don't take up your cross. Repentance and faith are part of that basic gospel message as we pursue holiness, and as we love God and others. And it is in this combination of self-sacrifice and love of God and others that we find the seed of missions in our churches. If that seed of understanding the gospel is missing, then all the missions programs in the world won't do anything for us. Missions begins with our understanding of the gospel and conversion.

You could say that missions begins at home, with a concern for the conversion of your family. Teach, befriend, evangelize, and disciple your children. Have a concern for your friends; friends share the gospel with friends. What does it mean for you to be prepared to share the gospel at work with someone this week?

Establishing an evangelistic Bible study at your workplace may not be all that different from evangelizing in Singapore or Moscow. Evangelism requires the same basic components, no matter what the context may be. So don't wait to start evangelizing. Why not find a Muslim friend in your neighborhood and offer to read through the Koran with him if he'll read through the Bible with you? As you share the good news with real people, you prepare yourself to do that in any place God may call you.

As we grow in understanding the Bible's big picture, discipling Christians naturally becomes more important to us. So at CHBC, we work for a culture of evangelism and discipling. This culture is the foundation of a culture of missions. Do not underestimate how you handicap missions in a church by making evangelism seem optional in the Christian life. Baked into our basic discipling of each other in Scripture and holiness should be a concern for evangelism and missions. How we as individuals spend our money is part of our church missions program. How we spend our time is too. Are you modeling that well? Are you being obedient in sharing the gospel? Are you modeling praying and giving, particularly for the gospel to go out to all the nations? That's how we participate in the big story of the Bible.

In coming to Christ, God moves us from being self-focused to God-focused. That causes us to notice others as spiritual beings, to think of the future of our children and youth, to reach out in evangelism to others who don't know the Lord yet, and then, ultimately, to go into the whole world, teaching those who have never heard the good news. So missions isn't something occasional and optional; it is an essential extension of what God has always been about in this world, to bring glory to himself through us. Healthy churches are marked by a biblical understanding and practice of missions. But if these gospel seeds are in place in our churches, what will that look like in practice?

What Should Churches Do in Missions?

Let's consider seven ways your local church can pursue a biblical practice of missions.

1. Learn about God's Word and God's World

We begin with the Word and the big picture we've been considering. At CHBC, this is something that the pastors deliberately teach the congregation. Our Sunday morning "core seminars," which include one class specifically on missions, help members share the gospel. We host a missions reading group on Sunday afternoons. And in every sermon, we want to learn what God would teach us in his Word about his world.

The main way a church becomes a missionary-sending church is by the preaching of God's Word. Our expositions of Scripture should show that Scripture clearly points to the cross of Christ as the center of human history; they should encompass the whole world, as the aim of Christ's work. Each Sunday we try to show the gospel in its glorious offer and summons to non-Christians, and in its life-encompassing scope and extent to Christians. Pray that your church would apply the Word well in its preaching.

The Presbyterian church I attended in college had regular bulletin inserts that informed us about the church around the world so that we could better pray. I encourage you to get resources that tell you about different countries in order to help you knowledgeably pray.

Have you considered using social media for prayer? Your Twitter feed can inform your daily prayer list. For example, you could follow some Twitter accounts of friends who work with college students, or domestic and international news sources. Learn to pray about everything from unemployment to terrorism, from the president to the most recent 9Marks conference in Spanish. You can't pray for a place, let alone develop a heart for it, if you don't even know about it! Thank God for your church's outward focus, and pray that as you study God's Word and grow spiritually, your outward focus will only increase.

2. Pray for the Spread of the Gospel in Other Places

We want the gospel to be central not just in our sermons but also in our prayers. As we saw in the last chapter, we cannot consider what it means be a missions-sending church without thinking specifically about prayer. At CHBC, our missions work is intertwined with our prayer life—in our individual prayers, in the Sunday morning pastoral prayer, and in our Sunday evening prayer meeting.

First, members praying through the membership directory is the basic way we love each other, beyond attending regularly and giving regularly. And it's basic to our work in missions. Pray through your church's membership directory. Pray that your fellow members would have wisdom to know how God would use each one of us in assembling that international chorus we find in the book of Revelation. Make your church membership directory a tool for missions. Our membership directory has a special section in the back to encourage prayer for pastors who've gone out from our congregation, missionaries we support financially, and those who've served us on staff or who have been interns.

In our Sunday morning pastoral prayer, we try to model how to think about this world and what's happening in it from a gospel-centered perspective. (This helps conversations about such topics become more naturally evangelistic.) We pray for other churches, God's work in pastors sent out from our church, persecuted Christians, and the spread of gospel-preaching churches around the world. We pray especially for the spread of the gospel in unreached areas.

Our congregation also makes the effort to end every Lord's Day together in order to hear updates and to pray. Our Sunday evening prayer meeting would naturally become inwardly focused if I did not push hard to make it otherwise. How do I do that? By carefully guarding what we spend time hearing and praying about. Nearly every Sunday I make at least one member of our church mad at me by saying no to a request to pray for the health of a family member. I do pray for these items personally, and we encourage our members to use their small groups for personal prayer requests. But our Sunday evening prayer time would become a hospital list if all nine hundred members shared personal requests. Instead, we work hard to keep those

Sunday evening prayer times focused on the expansion of the gospel. Sometimes we'll hear about an evangelistic Bible study at work, or our college ministry's work at Howard University, or a supported worker laboring overseas. Whether it's Merob sharing about Ethiopia or Rob sharing about Sudan or Johab sharing about Brazil, I love the way we begin each week bathing the spread of the gospel in prayer. If our members are involved in upcoming evangelistic opportunities, I invite them to share about it, so we can pray about it as a church. Church members, do not deprive your pastors of at least having the option to inform others about your efforts. Some churches ask if there are any evangelism stories—spontaneously—to share. I love the assumption that evangelism is always happening.

If this doesn't sound like your local congregation, pray that God would make your church a missions-sending church. If this is your congregation, thank God and pray that he would give you the joyful privilege of participating in his great worldwide work even more.

3. Plan to Make Your Church Increasingly Useful to the Spread of the Gospel

We want to care for other churches. A biblical understanding of the church as an assembly is helpful in this.[2] When you make the mistake of thinking that having one church means having one *preacher* rather than one *assembly*, you unwittingly inject a self-focused competitiveness into your relationship with sister congregations. Some churches that meet in multiple places or times work against this, but I can tell you from personal experience that gathering all together as we have done for almost 150 years on our particular corner is not only biblically faithful to what it means to be a church—to regularly assemble together—but it is also a powerful encouragement to having a greater outward focus as a church. When some churches get too full, they simply start another service or another site. But unless we want to build a bigger building,

2 See Jonathan Leeman, *One Assembly: Rethinking the Multisite and Multiservice Church Models* (Wheaton, IL: Crossway, 2020).

or do nothing, we have no choice but to try to help other churches in our area, and even work to start new ones.

As we try to help other churches by supplying preaching or by encouraging fellowship between pastors, we also have tried in a concentrated way to help local congregations that were down to ten or fifteen people revitalize. And by God's grace, we have seen this happen. This is relevant to us as we consider missions, because this kind of working with other churches teaches us to look at Christianity in the local area, not just in our church. And that's the same skill we need as we work to see the gospel spread to the nations.

What would it take for the gospel to spread in your area? Think about who you work with and live with and eat with. What are you doing to reach them? Would any of them appreciate an invitation to come to church with you and then come to your house for dinner? Do you help with evangelistic work on college campuses? College students, do you realize the unique international friendships you are being offered during your student days? Could you consider teaching English as a second language and sharing the gospel with those you come to know? Could you join a ministry to international college students, perhaps hosting exchange students, and work to share the gospel with those who are here from overseas? Make friends with people from other countries, invite them to church, and take them out to lunch after the service to talk about it. What international communities could your church get to know and love? Turkish? Afghan? Chinese?

Are other international communities nearby that you could engage with the gospel? Could you reach gospel-less places nearby? Could you volunteer at a local pregnancy center? Is there gospel work to be done in the jails? Some of our CHBC members live at a homeless shelter, and others are involved serving there. Is that the kind of thing you should perhaps be helping with? Are there refugees in the area that you could be working with, and helping other Christians to connect with as well?

Part of the way we *plan* to make our church useful in missions may surprise you—it's by what we *don't* do. It is by having very few programs that require our members' attendance. We demand a lot of our members on Sundays, and then we leave them alone the rest of the week. We want our members to have time during the week to serve others, to build relationships with non-Christians, and to help out in their community. Some churches, with the best of intentions, have so many programs that they make godliness seem like coming to the church building for a program rather than getting to know and love their neighbors or coworkers or family members. So even in the things that we *don't* do as a church, we are allowing time for more real ministry to occur.

What about your church? Pray that your church would be useful, like Paul assumed the church at Rome would be. Consider Romans 15:24: "I hope to see you in passing as I go to Spain, and to be helped on my journey there by you, once I have enjoyed your company for a while." Paul assumed that the local church in Rome (where he had never been) would be a hub for missions activity. That kind of usefulness in missions is what we can be praying for and planning for in our churches.

4. Pay to Support Those Who Go Out for the Sake of the Name Who Can't or Shouldn't Support Themselves

The phrase "for the sake of the name" comes from one of John's epistles:

> Beloved, it is a faithful thing you do in all your efforts for these brothers, strangers as they are, who testified to your love before the church. You will do well to send them on their journey in a manner worthy of God. For they have gone out for the sake of the name, accepting nothing from the Gentiles. Therefore we ought to support people like these, that we may be fellow workers for the truth. (3 John 5–8)

Just as the Philippians supported Paul so that he could labor among the Corinthians, it is our privilege, duty, and honor to get to support those involved in missions today. This is one reason why our giving and our church budget are so important. The elders of CHBC have an informal agreement that 15 percent of our total budget will be given to international missions. It's similar to how we as individuals give the first portion of our money to the Lord's work, and how, even in the structure of our calendar week, the first day is set aside to the Lord. In that same way, we mean to give the first 15 percent of our giving to gospel work where it's especially needed overseas. Just as you can use your church membership directory to pray for missions, you can do the same thing with your church budget. Do you pray for those workers your church is supporting? Always try to pray for what you pay for. Never send money without prayers.

Other money our church gives helps other world missions causes. Our support for 9Marks helps them train pastors and send materials around the world. Even some of our staff's salaries are really used to help other churches, as they give their time to doing so. We want to give with discernment, with generosity, and with joy. Let's think about each of those for just a minute.

Obviously, we have to give with discernment. Whom will we support to take the gospel overseas? In our church we focus on whether people are going to take the gospel to the unreached peoples, largely to be found in the 10/40 window. Is the particular work they want to do going to result in people hearing the gospel and churches being planted? Will they do the work well? Do we know them well? Have they been raised up here? Are they active in the church? We want to use the congregation's money with discernment.

We also want to give with generosity, so people can prepare well, go, stay, and minister there. Just as churches should be generous in providing for their pastors, if you are going to entrust someone to bring the gospel overseas, you should certainly pay them well enough to do that. This is Paul's point when he exhorts Titus to make sure that two Christian workers who are sent out "lack nothing." God has been so kind to us; we want to be open-handed with what he's entrusted to us. Our practice at CHBC is to focus our support on a few workers and to support them heavily. If we become one of a hundred churches giving five hundred dollars a year to a family, we don't really feel fully connected to them and their work, and we leave them effectively unaccountable. So we tend to support a few, and to support them well.

Finally, we should give with joy! God loves a cheerful giver (2 Cor. 9:7). And why shouldn't we be full of joy in our giving? What do we have that we have not received? Everything we have, we have received. We are temporary stewards, at best, so we want to send our gifts on ahead with *joy*.

5. Send Pastors and Others to Help Establish Churches in Gospel-Needy Places Far Away

We want all our members to understand that we're all entrusted with the gospel *here*, and that understanding brings us one step closer to some of us becoming missionaries *over there*. All of our members have verbally shared the gospel in their membership interview. And if they were baptized here, they publicly shared their testimony before they were baptized. This helps to prepare us to share the gospel with others. We want all of our members to know that they should pray and give and evangelize and consider going.

Sometimes members of evangelical churches feel a little guilty, knowing that *some people* need to go overseas for the cause of world missions. And then every once in a while, praise God, a young couple appears who actually want to go! So the church sacrifices the young couple to the "missions gods" and prays for them to be appeased. Meanwhile, everyone quietly breathes a huge sigh of relief, thanking God that it didn't have to be them, while at the same time patting themselves on the back, thinking, "We are a missionary-sending church!"

Of course there's nothing wrong with sending missionaries. But what is even better is building a culture in your church where all members eagerly consider—whether they end up staying or going—how they can orient their life around the Great Commission.

If you are beginning to think seriously about going overseas yourself, you might want to try an experiment. After the church service this coming Sunday, introduce yourself to someone you don't know. See if you can be of any help to that person spiritually. Or speak to another member about how he or she is doing. Our love for one another is a fundamental part of our witness (John 13:34–35). Practice that skill, and pray for your speech to be helpful to others.

We know that each person we send out is like a pebble thrown in a pond, with ripples radiating out. But we want to pick the right pebbles, and we want to throw them in the most needed parts of the pond.

We *don't* encourage lone-ranger kinds of missionaries. Don't make life-altering decisions alone. Be in conversation with your pastors and other members who know you well. Seek counsel.

The biblical pattern is to evangelize the world through planting churches. In the Old Testament, God takes the whole people of Israel. In Revelation we read that the redeemed consists of a whole people. In between, we find Jesus telling his disciples that the whole world will know that they are his disciples by their love for one another. The witness of the local church together is how Christ is revealed to the world. So when Jesus gives the Great Commission in Matthew 28:18–20, what do the disciples do? Just look at the book of Acts. They spend their whole lives evangelizing and planting churches. That is the normal pattern for how Christianity spreads. Jesus thought it up. It is not usually fast. It's not usually headline grabbing. And yet that is how we get to Revelation 7, where "a great multitude that no one could number, from every nation, from all tribes and peoples and languages [stands] before the throne and before the Lamb, clothed in white robes, with palm branches in their hands, and crying out with a loud voice, "Salvation belongs to our God who sits on the throne, and to the Lamb!" (Rev. 7:9–10). That's how every Christian church has come into existence since the resurrection of Jesus Christ.

Since the Great Commission is accomplished through planting churches, *training pastors is central to missions.* Consider Acts 15:36 and Titus 1:5:

> And after some days Paul said to Barnabas, "Let us return and visit the brothers in every city where we proclaimed the word of the Lord, and see how they are." (Acts 15:36)

> This is why I left you in Crete, so that you might put what remained into order, and appoint elders in every town as I directed you. (Titus 1:5)

Planting churches means raising up pastors who will lead these new church plants, whether here in the United States or abroad. That is why pastoral training is central to missions.

Whom do we send? *We send people overseas who are already actively sharing the gospel here.* Some have been members of our church for years. Others have come for a short season to be trained in the internship or by time on staff.

By God's grace, we can see the ripple effects of some of the pebbles we've thrown out. Listed below are a few of those pebbles and the ripples coming out from them that God has allowed us to be a part of. Two things I want to note. First, we can be tempted to want the results of our missionary activity to be big and to happen quickly. But the ripples we see can appear to happen very slowly. Second, our participation in missions is nothing extraordinary. This is how Christianity normally spreads.

So, learn and pray. Plan and pay. Send pastors and church planters. And then care for those you send.

6. Care for Those You Send

We can care well for our supported workers only if we know how they are doing. While we can communicate with them virtually, we also try to arrange for workers to take sabbaticals with us so our members can get to know them. When they visit, we hear testimonies from them. When they are not around, we take time during our evening service to have members share updates about how we can pray for our supported workers and how we can help them. We also try to visit each of our supported workers in their place of service at least once every few years.

Another way we care for those we send out is through our Sunday school curriculum.[3] Our children learn about the workers we support in their classes. Every week a portion of our children's ministry focuses on that week's VIPP (Very Important Person of Prayer). In our Great Commission Club on Sunday nights they learn more about missionary history and the needs of the world around us.

We also send some of our members on short-term trips to support workers who are in a region for the long term. We only do trips that the workers there ask for.[4] So we do a lot of babysitting for long-term missionaries during their conferences. We also organize trips built around distributing Scripture. In a normal year, I take a short trip overseas at least twice. I meet with pastors, and I speak at conferences in different parts of the world.

Sometimes we encourage members to move with their secular jobs to a certain place where they can support a ministry that could use the support of wisdom, encouragement, prayer, and perhaps financial support from another tithing member. In all these ways, we try to care for those we send, encouraging them in practical ways.

7. Wait for a Faithful Witness to Be Well Established, and Help Those Sent Out to Endure

Spreading the gospel around the world is not like you might have seen in the movies. If you ever hear about the rapid spread of the gospel, assume the person intends to tell the truth, but that he or she is probably misinformed. It's not that the gospel never spreads rapidly. It's just that it rarely does. Real rapid rarely happens. God ordinarily uses the ordinary. As Michael Horton has said, "Everyone wants to change the

3 See our Sunday school resources developed by Connie Dever at The Praise Factory, https://praisefactory.org./

4 See J. Mack Stiles and Leeann Stiles, *Mack & Leeann's Guide to Short-Term Missions* (Downers Grove, IL: InterVarsity Press, 2000).

world, nobody wants to do the dishes."[5] Living the Christian life overseas has its challenges, but it is not fundamentally different in its nature than living the Christian life here. As in parenting or in the workplace, so in missions. Good work takes time. Thus children are formed in families and Christians in churches over decades, not over a weekend.

We want our workers to be faithful to the gospel and not to feel the pressure to produce numbers. Much fruit comes only after years of laboring. Praise God for the great missions effort that is going on now among evangelical churches in America. But pray that God would protect us from the idolization of the rapid, because it will hinder the spread of the gospel as surely as the social gospel did a century ago.[6] False converts will be named converts. Christianity will be confused with what is not Christianity. And the gospel will be obscured.[7]

Instead, we want to support *real* work. We want all of our members to be expectantly waiting on God to work and patiently supporting those who go. The love and prayers of long-term supporters of missionaries help those who have gone to wait patiently for visible results in God's timing.

So what should churches do to be faithful in missions? Learn and pray, plan and pay. Send pastors and care for them. And wait.

Conclusion

I want to conclude by sharing a portion of an email I received from someone who visited our church on a recent Sunday.

> Thank you for texting me on Saturday, encouraging me to come back for the morning service. The message you brought was exactly what I needed to hear.

5 Michael Horton, *Ordinary: Sustainable Faith in a Radical, Restless World* (Grand Rapids, MI: Zondervan: 2014), 19–20.

6 See the forthcoming book by Matt Rhodes on this topic, *No Shortcut to Success: A Manifesto for Modern Missions* (Wheaton, IL: Crossway, 2022).

7 See Mark Dever "Endurance Needed: Strength for a Slow Reformation and the Dangerous Allure of Speed" (sermon, Together for the Gospel, Louisville, KY, 2016), http://t4g.org/resources/mark-dever/asl-endurance-needed-strength-slow-reformation-dangerous-allure-speed/.

> In my prayers last night, I laid myself at God's feet and truly repented of my sin, and gave myself wholly to him. I felt the burden of my sin being lifted off of me, and it was the most amazing thing I have ever felt. I have laid my trust fully on God, and he has heard my prayers and opened up my heart to receive his Spirit. The joy I feel now is like nothing I have ever experienced, and I cannot stop thanking and praising God for his wonderful and generous mercy.
>
> I just ask that you could continue to pray that God could continue to reveal his glory and power to me and that he can continue to guide my footsteps to walk in the light with the Holy Spirit.

We want to bring God glory in many ways, and this is surely one of the greatest and most important, because this is where it all starts and where we all began. God is glorified by such conversions! And such conversions will never be experienced by many around the world today because the gospel message isn't known among them. Let that sink in. "How are they to believe in him of whom they have never heard?" (Rom. 10:14).

Remember what missions is? Missions is taking the gospel across boundaries—especially the boundary of language. If evangelism is telling the gospel, sometimes to people who don't know it, missions is evangelism, telling the gospel, in a place and among a whole people where it's largely unknown.

No one is saved apart from hearing the gospel of Jesus Christ (see Rom. 10:17), and that normally happens through the ministry of the Word. That's why the imprisoned Paul wrote this encouraging note to a pastor in modern-day Turkey: "Until I come, devote yourself to the public reading of Scripture, to exhortation, to teaching. . . . Keep a close watch on yourself and on the teaching. Persist in this, for by so doing you will save both yourself and your hearers" (1 Tim. 4:13, 16).

In one sense all the marks of a healthy church lead here. I once asked a worker in a closed country how we could better support him. He said, "Keep working on making [your] church healthy, and work to make more churches like it, because if you don't, there won't be anyone left to send out missionaries like us!" That's ultimately how we love God and love others, isn't it?

So membership in a healthy local church—the normal reflection of our being identified with Christ by faith—is the first step in sending missionaries to plant healthy local churches.

If you want to see twenty-first-century churches sending out preachers of the same gospel as they did in the past century, then you must give attention to expositional preaching, gospel doctrine, conversion and evangelism, church membership, church discipline, discipleship and growth, church leadership, prayer, and missions. This will help churches to remain faithful until Christ returns.

And what will fuel us with such endurance and patient, hopeful laboring while waiting? Some would point us to grand plans, like the man in India who told me he could evangelize the entire country in his lifetime if he were simply given enough money. But I believe that such plans to "Christianize" this nation may do more harm than good, spreading more confusion than clarity about the gospel. Some would point us to the greatness of the need and quote numbers of those who are lost. Surely no heart of love can coolly consider fellow sinners perishing under God's good judgment, and not desire to share the gospel with them. But here, too, I fear that the needs so exceed what any one person—even any one church—can do. Such statistics should be used sparingly, more for prayers and for personal reflection and decisions than simply to spur people to decisions.

What motivation is left to us? Love to neighbor, which flows from our love to God. Most fundamentally, God's great love shown to us is our motivation. I find that as the years go on, my understanding of God's grace and mercy becomes more wonderful to me. As I've seen and done more that begs for forgiveness, and as my witness to God's track record of goodness gets longer and more remarkable, my amazement at him increases. Surely our motivation to patiently labor is in being most fully consumed with God and his great love for us in Christ.

I think that is how we best hear Christ's call to take up our cross and to give him our all.

In C. S. Lewis's *Prince Caspian*, Lucy Pevensie finally sees Aslan again after a long absence.

> "Dear Aslan," sobbed Lucy. "At last."
>
> The great beast rolled over on his side so that Lucy fell, half sitting and half lying between his front paws. He bent forward and just touched her nose with his tongue. His warm breath came all round her. She gazed up into the large, wise face.
>
> "Welcome, child," he said.
>
> "Aslan," said Lucy, "you're bigger."
>
> "That is because you are older, little one," answered he.
>
> "Not because you are?"
>
> "I am not. But every year you grow, you will find me bigger."[8]

The more we know God, the more he correctly consumes our vision, our hearts, and our whole lives. The God of all the world wants all of us and all of who we are. A sound local church shows our devotion to him by our complete devotion to his work.

Other Resources

- Robert E. Coleman, *The Master Plan of Evangelism* (1964); John Piper, *Let the Nations Be Glad! The Supremacy of God in Missions* (1993); Iain H. Murray, *Revival and Revivalism* (1994); Michael Reeves, *The Unquenchable Flame: Discovering the Heart of the Reformation* (2009); Andy Johnson, *Missions: How the Local Church Goes Global* (2015); Jim Osman, *Truth or Territory: A Biblical Approach to Spiritual Warfare* (2015); and Matt Rhodes, *No Shortcut to Success: Why 21st Century Missions Doesn't Need a Revolution* (2021).

8 C. S. Lewis, *Prince Caspian* (New York: Harper Collins, 1951), 148.

- For missionary autobiographies and biographies see *John G. Paton: An Autobiography* (1889); S. Pearce Carey, *William Carey* (1923); Courtney Anderson, *To the Golden Shore: The Life of Adoniram Judson* (1956); William Blair, *The Korean Pentecost and the Sufferings Which Followed* (1977); Mark Sidwell, *Free Indeed: Heroes of Black Christian History* (1995); Peter Masters, *Missionary Triumph Over Slavery: William Knibb, and Jamaican Emancipation* (2006).

Appendix 1

Tips for Leading the Church in a Healthy Direction

The Healthy Direction

When we can rightly assume that most of those within a church are regenerated and that they are committed to the church, then the New Testament image of the church as a body and as a family can become a living, vital reality.

In his goodness, God has called us to live out the Christian life together. In being part of a church I have grown as a Christian because of God's work through my brothers and sisters. I think that's normal. I don't think that's meant to be unusual. God intends to work on us by his Spirit through each other. Relationships imply commitment in the world; surely they imply no less in the church.

In the third commandment (Ex. 20:7; Deut. 5:11), God warned his people not to take his name in vain. By this he does not mean just avoiding profanity. More than that, he is saying, "Don't take my name upon yourself, don't claim to be my follower, if you're not going to live like one of mine." That, no less than profanity, would be taking God's name in vain.

That command is for us as a church as well. Many churches today mistake selfish gain for spiritual growth. We mistake mere excitement for true worship. We treasure worldly acceptance rather than living in a way that will incur worldly opposition (see 2 Tim. 3:12). Regardless of their statistical profiles, too many churches today seem unconcerned about the very biblical marks that should distinguish a vital, growing church.

The health of the church should be the concern of all Christians, because it does involve the spiritual life of everyone who is a Christian and a member of a church, especially of those called to be leaders in the church. Our churches are to display the glorious gospel of God to his creation in an amazing variety by all the different personalities he puts in the church and the ways he allows them to relate together and to show his glory. That's what we're called to; we're called to display God and his character in a glorious way to his creation (Eph. 3:10). We are to bring him glory by our lives together.

Tips for Leading

I had thought of writing a book for pastors called *How to Get Fired . . . And Fast!* I could sum up the basic idea of this unwritten book in one sentence of Pauline proportions: A pastor could go into a church members' meeting questioning the salvation of some of the church members, refusing to baptize children, advocating a priority of congregational singing over performed music, asking to remove the Christian and national flags and to stop any kind of altar calls, replacing committees (even the nominating committee) with elders, ignoring the secular rotation of Mother's Day, Father's Day, Labor Day, Halloween, Veterans Day, New Year's Day, Martin Luther King Jr.'s birthday, Valentine's Day, Memorial Day, the local high school graduation, and the Fourth of July, begin practicing church discipline, removing women from elder-like positions in the church, and stating that he had theological opposition to multiple services on Sunday morning. Such a pastor might not get much farther than his next members' meeting. While I could write such a book, I think that first I should take a more constructive approach. I fear that some may read this book and immediately go into their churches impatient for radical change. But with a little wisdom, patience, prayer, careful instruction, and love, we might be surprised how far we can get with our churches. The story of the persistent tortoise and the hurrying hare becomes a parable for pastors.

Here are four characteristics that you as a pastor should cultivate to help implement the changes you feel are needed in your church.

1. Be Truthful

Ask God to keep you faithful to his written Word. Never underestimate the power of teaching truth. Pray that you will have integrity within yourself, in your own thinking. Pray that you will be honest with all—in responding to questions, but even more actively, in working to help people get to know you.

2. Be Trustful

Rely on God rather than on your own gifts and abilities. Spend time in prayer privately, with others, and with the congregation. Be patient. Recall Paul's words to Timothy in 2 Timothy 4:2: "Preach the Word; be prepared in season and out of season; correct, rebuke and encourage—with great patience and careful instruction."

Give your ambitions to the Lord. Be willing to trust him with your life; be willing to pray that God may leave you in your present place of ministry for the rest of your life. Longevity was factored in by God in bringing children to adulthood; such longevity has also characterized many fruitful ministries. The Puritan pastor William Gouge often said that the height of his ambition was to go from Blackfriars (his church) to heaven. Gouge was pastor of that same church from June 1608 until his death on December 12, 1653. He was pastor of the same church for forty-six years. Pray that God will increase your faith and help you see that his concern for his church is even greater than your own.

3. Be Positive

Pray that you neither be nor be perceived to be fundamentally a critic. Set forth a positive agenda. Clarify God's vision for his church, and your particular plans, in terms of both long-term goals and more immediate goals. Pray that God will help you to build solid personal relationships. Pray particularly that God will help you to develop more leaders within the church (2 Tim. 2:2). Pray that God will make you a personal example of and a chief advocate for evangelism and missions. Pray that God will increase your zeal—and your church's zeal—for his glory.

4. Be Particular

Contextualize God's concern for his church. Use the good resources of your church's own history. Learn from older members about the history of your church. Be an ecclesiastical dendrologist (a person who studies trees). At Lincoln Cathedral, one tour guide told me that dendrologists had taken core samples from the forty-six-foot oak beams that have held up the cathedral's roof for centuries and figured out when the tree was planted and when it was harvested. The ones he showed us had been more than 150 years old when harvested, many having been planted in the 900s and harvested in the 1100s.

Become the chief student of your church's history. By doing this you show respect, and you learn.

May you become the agent for recovering what has been the best in your church's past and the agent for leading your church into the great things God has for it in the future, as your church displays the character of God to his creation. This burden of display is our awesome responsibility and our tremendous privilege. May God make your church a healthy church, and may he pour out his Spirit on churches across our land and around the world to do the same, for his own glory. And may God bless you in the attempt.

Appendix 2

"Don't Do It!" Why You Shouldn't Practice Church Discipline

"DON'T DO IT." That's the first thing I tell pastors when they discover church discipline is in the Bible. I say, "Don't do it, at least not yet." Why this advice?

Let's think about what happens in the process of discovery. When pastors first hear of church discipline, they often think the idea is ridiculous. It sounds unloving, counterevangelistic, weird, controlling, legalistic, and judgmental. It certainly seems unworkable. They even wonder if it's illegal.

They Open Their Bibles

Perhaps when no one is looking, these pastors look back at their Bibles. They come across passages like 2 Thessalonians 3:6, or Galatians 6:1, or the classic text on discipline, 1 Corinthians 5. They consider the Old Testament background of excommunication, and they recall that God has always purposed for his people to be a picture of his own holiness (Deut. 17:7; Lev. 19:2; Isa. 52:11; 1 Pet. 1:16).Then, they turn to Jesus's own teaching, and discover that, in the same chapter in which Jesus condemns judgmentalism (see Matt. 7:1), he also warns the disciples to be on their guard against false prophets and against those who claim to follow him but do not obey his Word (Matt. 7:15–20; 21–23). Finally, they get to Matthew 18, where Jesus instructs his followers to exclude the unrepentant sinner in certain situations (v. 17). Maybe churches *should* practice discipline?

What finally sends these otherwise nice, normal, well-adjusted, previously popular pastors over the edge is their discovery that some churches do, in fact, practice church discipline. Not strange, maladjusted churches, but happy, growing, large, grace-oriented churches like Grace Community in Sun Valley, California, or Tenth Presbyterian in Philadelphia, or First Baptist in Durham, North Carolina, or the Village Church near Dallas.

Now these pastors are in trouble. They realize they need to be obedient. They feel compelled by the biblical picture of a holy, loving, united church, a church that reflects the one, holy, loving God. They understand their failure to practice discipline hurts their church and its witness to the world.

It's at this point that a sullen resolve often seems to set in. "I will lead this congregation to be biblical at this point if it's the last thing I do!" And, too often, it is.

Like a Bolt Out of a Clear Blue Sky

Into the peaceful, well-meaning life of an innocent, Bible-believing congregation, the lightning bolt of church discipline strikes! It may be in a sermon. It may be in a conversation between the pastor and a deacon. It may be in a hastily arranged motion at a members' meeting. But somewhere it hits, usually accompanied by great earnestness and a torrent of scriptural citations. Then, the sincere action is taken. The response comes. Misunderstanding and hurt feelings result. Counter charges are made. Sin is attacked and defended. Names are called. Acrimony abounds! The symphony of the local congregation transposes into a cacophony of arguments and accusations. People cry out, "Where will this stop?" and "So do you think *you're* perfect?"

What's the pastor to do? My advice would be, "Don't get yourself into this situation in the first place. Once you've discovered that corrective church discipline is biblical, hold off on practicing it for a while." (Church discipline is both corrective and formative, the latter referring to the church's work of teaching or forming Christians.)

Now at this point maybe you're thinking, "Mark, are you telling us to disobey the Bible?"

In fact, I'm not. I'm trying to help you do what Jesus instructed his disciples to do (see Luke 14:25–33): count the cost before you begin. Make sure your congregation sufficiently understands and accepts this biblical teaching. Your goal is not immediate compliance followed by an explosion, but rather a congregation being reformed by the Word of God. You want them going in the right direction. And that requires patient shepherding.

How to Shepherd Your Church toward Discipline

First, *encourage humility*. Help people to see that they may be mistaken about their own spiritual state. Consider the example of the man in 1 Corinthians 5 as well as Paul's exhortation to the Corinthian Christians more broadly in 2 Corinthians 13:5. Paul charges us to examine ourselves to see if we're in the faith. Do your church members recognize that they are to help one another do that?

Second, *make sure that your congregation has a biblical understanding of church membership*. People don't understand discipline because they don't understand membership. Membership is a congregational relationship. It is not created, sustained, or ended merely by the act of an individual; an individual cannot join a church unilaterally without the congregation's consent. Likewise, an individual cannot continue in membership, or leave the membership of a particular congregation, without the congregation's explicit or implicit approval (except by death). That's a mouthful, but what I'm basically saying is that it is a church's business to decide who its members are. And members cannot simply leave when they're in unrepentant sin.[1]

1 For a fuller discussion of this matter, see Jonathan Leeman, "The Preemptive Resignation—A Get Out of Jail Free Card?," *9Marks Journal* (November/December 2009), https://www.9marks.org/article/preemptive-resignation-get-out-jail-free-card/.

Such a vision of membership, however, must first be positively presented. Understand what the Bible teaches about church membership. Make sure that you've familiarized yourself with several crucial points and passages that you can remind members of when they ask. Look for opportunities in your sermons to teach on the distinction between the church and the world, and how that distinction is important for the nature and mission of the church. Help your congregation to assemble such a picture of God's plan for his church that the outlines of discipline begin to become conspicuous by their absence from your church's practice. Remember that the members must understand membership and discipline because they're the ones who must carry it out.

Third, *pray that God would help you to model ministry* to other Christians in your church by your public teaching and your private work with families and individuals. Work toward creating a culture of discipleship and accountability in your church, where Christians understand that a basic part of their following Jesus is helping others to follow Jesus (both through evangelism and discipling other Christians). Help them to understand the special responsibilities they have toward other members of their particular congregation. Teach them that the Christian life is personal, but not private.

Fourth, *prepare your congregation's written constitution and covenant.* Consult Ken Sande's article on the 9Marks website for some general legal advice.[2] Begin teaching premembership classes in which matters touching membership and discipline are explicitly taught.

Fifth, and finally, in your pulpit ministry, *never tire of teaching what a Christian is.* Regularly define the gospel and conversion. Explicitly teach that a church is intended to be composed of repenting sinners who are trusting in Christ alone, and who give credible professions of that trust. Pray that you would be centered on the gospel. Resolve that, with God's help, you will slowly but steadily lead your congregation to

2 Ken Sande, "Informed Consent: Biblical and Legal Protection for Church Discipline," *9Marks Journal* (February 2010), https://www.9marks.org/article/informed-consent-biblical-and-legal-protection-church-discipline/.

change. Pray that, rather than being a church where it's strange to ask people how they're doing spiritually, you would become a church where it would begin to seem strange if someone *didn't* ask about your life.

You Know You're Ready When . . .

You know your congregation is ready to practice church discipline when:

- Your leaders understand it, agree with it, and perceive its importance. (Mature leadership shared among several elders is the leadership model most consistent with Scripture and very helpful for leading a church through potentially volatile discussions.)
- Your congregation is united in understanding that such discipline is biblical.
- Your membership consists largely of people who regularly hear your sermons.
- A particularly clear case comes along in which your members would fairly unitedly perceive that excommunication is the correct action. (For example, excommunication for adultery is more likely to yield agreement among your members than excommunication for nonattendance.)

So, my pastor friend, though you may have once thought that the idea of church discipline was ridiculous, I pray that God will help you to lead your congregation to see that it is a loving, provocative, attractive, distinct, respectful, gracious act of obedience and mercy, and that it helps to build a church that brings glory to God. But remember, when you first become convinced of the biblical case for church discipline, your first step in an established congregation is probably to begin by *not* practicing discipline, so that someday you can.

Appendix 3

The Original 9 Marks Letter

This is the letter I wrote to the elders of a church I had planted and pastored years earlier in Massachusetts, which was now searching for a pastor. It is in this letter that I first laid out "nine marks of a healthy church."

Dear brothers and sisters, 30 October 1991

I have for some time been thinking and praying about writing a letter to you. I will address this letter to the elders, since biblically you are the ones who are responsible for the spiritual well-being of the flock; but I have no qualms about it being shared more generally.

I am delighted at the stability and growth God has graciously given you as a church over the last five years. That has in no small part, I feel, been given through a faithful and committed eldership, and particularly through Zane's commitment to sound, biblical preaching. As you approach this difficult time of transition, I have a few thoughts about what you should look for in a pastor. Note, adherence to the nine items I intend to outline here will not insure that the person is a good pastor, but I feel that the lack of any of them would be an inadequacy which would slowly but cumulatively affect the church in a negative way. So, I would take all of these to be essential, but not in and of themselves sufficient. For instance, you could have someone who held to all of these interrelated points, and yet was simply not gifted or called to be a pastor. Indeed, I trust such is the case with the vast majority of members at New Meadows currently. On the other hand, let a man be never so gifted in personal relationships and communications, even a strong adherent to the authority of Scripture and to the practice of personal prayer, and yet miss any one or two of the matters below, and, given time, I'm convinced that New Meadows would become the leaking bucket that too many churches are today—holding no more living water than the world around them. I point these out after much thought and prayer, because, unfortunately, they are rarely prized among those who profess themselves called to be pastors and shepherds today. So, to summarize, I am not here giving you an exhaustive checklist of what I think you should look for in a pastor. There are many more issues which will play into that choice. I am, however, giving you a list of qualifications that are both needed and sadly, rare, which I pray to God you will trust him to have for you in the pastor he intends.

The first quality I would tell you to make sure is present in anyone you would ever consider calling to the eldership, but particularly to the pastorate, is a commitment to *expositional preaching*. This presumes a belief in the authority of Scripture, but it says something more. I'm convinced that a commitment to expositional preaching is a commitment to hearing God's Word. If you have someone who happily accepts the authority of God's Word, yet who in practice (whether intending to or not) does not preach expositionally, he will never preach more than he already knows. When one takes a piece of Scripture and simply exhorts the congregation on a topic that is important, but doesn't really preach the point of that passage, one is limited to hearing in Scripture only what one already knew upon coming to the text. It is in being committed to preaching Scripture in context, expositionally, having as the point of the message the point of the passage, that we hear from God those things which we do not already intend to hear when we set out. And, from the initial call to repentance to the latest thing the Spirit has convicted you about, our whole salvation consists in hearing

God in ways that we, before we heard him, would never have guessed. To charge someone with the responsibility of the spiritual oversight of the flock who does not in practice show a commitment to hearing and to teaching God's Word, is to at least put a drag on, and at most put a cap on, the growth of the church at the level of the pastor. The church will slowly be conformed to his mind, rather than to God's mind.

The second quality I would hope you to require in anyone whom you would call to the eldership would be that he be sound in his full theological system—and that means being what has come to be called *reformed.* To misunderstand doctrines as fundamental as *election* (Does our salvation issue ultimately from God or us?); *human nature* (Are people basically bad or good? Do they merely need encouragement and enhanced self-esteem, or do they need forgiveness and new life?); *the nature of Christ's work on the cross* (Did he make possible an option for us? Or was he our substitute?); *the nature of conversion* (more on that particularly below); *and the certainty we can have of God's continuing care based fundamentally on his character rather than ours,* is no simple matter of lunchroom humor at the seminary, but rather is of real importance for faithfulness to Scripture and for real pastoral issues which constantly arise. For any Christian, but particularly for an elder, to resist the fundamental idea of God's sovereignty over all of life while practicing Christianity is really to play with pious paganism. It is to baptize a heart which is in some ways still unbelieving, and to set up as an example a person who may well be deeply unwilling to trust God. In a day when our culture demands us to turn evangelism into advertising and explains the Spirit's work as marketing, in which God in churches is so often made over in the image of man, I would be especially careful to find a man who had a biblical and experiential grasp of the sovereignty of God.

The third quality that any elder who is to be active in leading the church should have is a *biblical understanding of the gospel.* J. I. Packer lays out beautifully the relation of the last point to this one in his introduction to John Owen's *The Death of Death in the Death of Christ.* If you haven't read that recently, reread it now while you're in the process of praying and looking for a new pastor. A heart for the gospel means having a heart for the truth—God's presentation of himself, of our need, of Christ's provision, and of our responsibility. To present the gospel as simply an additive to give non-Christians something they naturally want anyway (joy, peace, happiness, fulfillment, self-esteem, love) is partially true, but only partially true. And, as Packer says, "A half-truth masquerading as the whole truth makes it a complete untruth." Fundamentally, we need forgiveness, we need spiritual life. To present the gospel less radically than this is to ask for false conversions and increasingly meaningless church membership, both of which will make the evangelization of the world around us all the more difficult.

The fourth quality that any elder should be required to have is a *biblical understanding of conversion.* If conversion is basically presented as something we do, rather than something God does, then we misunderstand it. Although conversion certainly includes our making a *sincere commitment, a self-conscious decision*, it is more than that. Scripture is clear in teaching that we are not all journeying to God, some having found the way, others still looking. Instead, it presents us as needing to have our hearts replaced, our minds transformed, our spirits given life. None of this we can do. We can *make* a commitment, but we must *be* saved. The change each human needs, regardless of how we appear externally, is so radical, so near the root of us, that only God can do it. We need God to convert us. I'm reminded of Spurgeon's story of how as he was walking in London, a drunk came up to him, leaned on the lamppost near him and said, "Hey, Mr. Spurgeon, I'm one of your converts." Spurgeon's response was, "Well, you must be one of mine—you're certainly not one of the Lord's!"[1] American churches, Southern Baptist churches, are full of people who have made sincere

1 C. H. Spurgeon, *The Soul Winner* (Grand Rapids, MI: Eerdmans, 1963), 37. Thanks to Mike Gilbart-Smith, who pointed out that I here mistakenly described this as happening to Spurgeon, when, in fact, Spurgeon recounted it as having happened to Rowland Hill. Now I've become the father of an apocryphal story about Spurgeon—very frustrating to a would-be historian!

commitments at one point in their lives, but who evidently have not experienced the radical change which the Bible presents as conversion. The result, according to one recent study, is a divorce rate that is 50 percent above the national average. The cause, at least in part, must be the unbiblical preaching about conversion by thousands of Southern Baptist pastors. Again, if you've not held to the first three things mentioned above, it's hardly surprising that this one would go wrong as well. [Please don't misunderstand me as insisting on an emotionally heated conversion experience at a particular point. I'm insisting on the theological truth underlying conversion, not a particular experience of it. You know the tree by its fruit.]

The fifth quality that anyone you ever entrust with the spiritual responsibility of teaching (of which all elders are to be capable, 2 Tim. 2:2) should have is a *biblical understanding of evangelism*. If your mind has been shaped by the Bible on God and the gospel, on human need and conversion, then a right understanding of evangelism will naturally follow. Biblically, evangelism is presenting the good news freely and trusting God to bring conversions. Any way in which we try to force births will be as effective as Ezekiel trying to stitch the dry bones together. And the result will be similar. Again, if conversion is understood as merely a sincere commitment at any given point, then we simply need to get everyone to that point any way possible. Biblically though, while we're to care, to plead, to persuade, our first duty is to be faithful to the obligation we have from God, which is to present the good news he's given us. He will bring conversion from that. If there is a sizable discrepancy between the membership of a pastor's church and the attendance, I would naturally wonder about what they understood conversion to be and what kind of evangelism they had practiced in order to create such a large number of people uninvolved in the life of the church, yet certain of their own salvation, with the blessing of the church. I could give you bibliographies on each of these points, but I won't, assuming you already know the books I would suggest. In a series of evangelistic addresses I did this past February in the university here, I concluded that the three things which I must convey to people about the decision they must make about the gospel (God, man, Christ, response), is that the decision is costly (and therefore must be carefully considered), *and* urgent (and therefore must be made), *and* worth it (and therefore should be made). That's the balance I should strive for in my evangelism.

Sixth, following from what I just said, I would require a *biblical understanding of church membership*. Sadly, if it were the case, my guess is that most Southern Baptist pastors would be more proud of the six thousand members their church had than they would be ashamed that only eight hundred attended. Written numbers can be idols as easily—perhaps more easily—than carved figures. But it is God who will assess our work, and he will weigh it, I think, rather than count. If the church is a building, then we must be bricks in it; if the church is a body, then we are its members; if we are the household of faith, it presumes we are part of that household. Sheep are in a flock, and branches on a vine. Forget the particular cultural ephemera for a moment—white cards with names on them, lists on a computer—biblically, if we are Christians, we must be members of a church. We must not forsake the assembling together of ourselves (Heb. 10:25). It is not simply a record of a statement we must make; it is a reflection of a living, vital commitment.

Seventh, and perhaps most initially difficult in your situation, I would require that the person understand and be convinced of the New Testament practice of having a *plurality of elders* (see Acts 14:23, Paul's regular practice of referring to a number of elders in any one local church). I am completely convinced of this as the New Testament practice, and as particularly needful in churches then and now without an apostolic presence. That does not mean that the pastor has no distinct role (look up in a concordance references to "preaching" and "preachers"), but that he is also and fundamentally part of the eldership. This means that decisions involving the church, yet which do not come to the attention of the whole church, should not so much fall to the pastor alone as to the elders as a whole. While this is cumbersome at points (as I'm sure you know only too well), it has immense benefits in rounding out the pastor's gifts, in giving him good support in the church, and in too many other ways to mention now. Anyway, this would have to be made quite clear when calling a pastor. If he is a typical Southern Baptist, he will assume that the elders are either deacons or that they are there simply to help him do what he wants to do. He may well not have a good appreciation for the fact that you are inviting him *fundamentally* to be one of the elders, and, among you, the pastor, the primary teaching elder. I'm convinced that if most pastors understood this idea, they would leap at the idea, given the weight it removes from their shoulders. And, I'm also worried that many of those who wouldn't, wouldn't do so because of unbiblical understandings of their own role, or, worse, unsanctified self-centeredness.

The eighth issue I would want to have clearly understood and affirmed by any new elder in the church is the issue of *church discipline*. This is one of the things which gives meaning to being a member of the church, which has been universally practiced by the church, and yet which has almost entirely faded out of Southern Baptist church life in the last three generations. Jesus's words in Matthew 18 and Paul's in 1 Corinthians 5:4–13 (along with other passages) clearly show that the church is to exercise judgment within itself, and that this is for redemptive, not revengeful purposes. If we cannot say what a Christian does not live like, we cannot very well say what she or he does live like. One of my concerns with churches' discipleship programs is that they are, again, like pouring water into a leaking bucket. While this issue is fraught with problems in pastoral application, the whole Christian life is, and that should never be used as an excuse to leave either unpracticed. It should mean something to be a member of the church, not for our pride's sake, but for God's name's sake.

Finally, the ninth issue which I would require an elder to understand is the role of the church in promoting *Christian discipleship and growth*. As I mentioned above, when the church does not exercise discipline, one of the unintended consequences is the increased difficulty in that church growing disciples. Examples are unclear, models are confused. The church has an obligation to be a means of God's growing people in grace. Yet if they are places in which only the pastor's thoughts are taught, in which God is more questioned than worshiped, in which the gospel is diluted and evangelism perverted, in which church membership is made meaningless and a worldly cult of personality is allowed to grow up around the pastor, then one can hardly expect to find such a group being either cohesive or edifying to each other, let alone glorifying to God. When we can honestly assume that those within the church are regenerated, and that those who are regenerated are committed to the church, then the corporate New Testament images of the church can become not merely good sermons, but thrilling lives together. Relationships imply commitment in the world; surely we wouldn't think it would be any less the case in the church?

Well, friends, I could go on for much longer. You've been patient to read this far. I don't mean to suggest that you don't already know all of the above and are not committed to it yourself, but I do care deeply for New Meadows. I feel some sense of obligation in my heart and in prayer. I thought it right to express that on paper. I do not have a vote in the eldership or in the church (nor should I!) but I wanted to write this with the hopes that it might be helpful in some of your discussions, prayers, and evaluations. Know that more importantly than sending this letter, I'll be daily joining with you in prayer for the church, especially during this crucial time,

as your brother in Christ, Mark

General Index

Scripture Index

IX 9Marks

Building Healthy Churches

9Marks exists to equip church leaders with a biblical vision and practical resources for displaying God's glory to the nations through healthy churches.

To that end, we want to see churches characterized by these nine marks of health:

1. Expositional Preaching
2. Gospel Doctrine
3. A Biblical Understanding of Conversion and Evangelism
4. Biblical Church Membership
5. Biblical Church Discipline
6. A Biblical Concern for Discipleship and Growth
7. Biblical Church Leadership
8. A Biblical Understanding of the Practice of Prayer
9. A Biblical Understanding and Practice of Missions